I'LL SEE YOU AGAIN

I'LL SEE YOU AGAIN

Jackie Hance
with Janice Kaplan

Gallery Books

New York   London   Toronto   Sydney   New Delhi

G

Gallery Books
A Division of Simon & Schuster, Inc.
1230 Avenue of the Americas
New York, NY 10020

First Gallery Books hardcover edition April 2013

For information about special discounts for bulk purchases,
please contact Simon & Schuster Special Sales at 1-866-506-1949
or business@simonandschuster.com.

The Simon & Schuster Speakers Bureau can bring authors to your live event.
For more information or to book an event contact the Simon & Schuster Speakers
Bureau at 1-866-248-3049 or visit our website at www.simonspeakers.com.

Manufactured in the United States of America

10 9 8 7 6 5 4 3 2 1

Library of Congress Cataloging-in-Publication Data is available.

ISBN 978-1-4516-7477-4
ISBN 978-1-4516-7478-1 (ebook)

To the community

of loving friends and family

who have helped us find light

in the darkness

I'LL SEE YOU AGAIN

PROLOGUE

July 26, 2009

Warren drives frantically toward the police barracks in Tarrytown, New York, tightly clutching the wheel of his Acura. His three little fair-haired daughters should be heading home right now in a two-tone red Windstar, driven by his sister, Diane, but something has happened. He's gone to the spot on the road where he told his sister to wait, but saw no sign of any of them. Not Diane or her two children. Not his three girls.

Cars don't disappear. Children don't vanish from the earth.

The police barracks looms ahead. Warren rushes in, and his father, who has come with him, follows behind. Warren starts to blurt out his story, but the troopers are already aware of the situation.

"Somebody else gave us the information," one tells him. "Maybe your wife."

The police claim they have done a twenty-five-mile-radius search, and there's no sign of the missing car. Later, Warren will wonder how they could have missed it.

Children don't vanish from the earth.

After his last call with her, when she sounded so ill, Diane stopped answering her cell phone. Now Warren suggests that the police try to track it. Cell phones have GPS, and pinging a signal always works in the movies. If they locate the phone, maybe they can find her. In the background, Warren hears one of the officers take a 911 call from his friend Brad, who has also called to report the situation. Missing car. Missing children. Huge worry.

The police, less concerned, gently urge Warren to leave.

"There's a diner about a mile down the street," one of the cops says. "If your sister wasn't feeling well on the road, maybe that's where she went, to get something to eat."

Warren and his father drive to the diner, but the Windstar isn't in the parking lot. As they drive around aimlessly for a few minutes, a sense of futility engulfs them, and Warren turns back to the police station. This time, the moment Warren pulls up, a trooper rushes out and opens the door of a police vehicle.

"Get in the car," he calls out to Warren. "I've got to take you to the hospital."

Warren feels the blood drain from his head. "This is bad," he says to his father.

They get to the hospital, and Warren rushes in, yelling for his girls—his daughters, his life. Nobody has told him anything.

"Where are my children?" he asks.

A trooper who is waiting there takes him to a side room. He tells Warren the news.

Warren slams his fist, making a hole in the wall. Then another. He would punch a hole in the universe if he could, stop time, make it turn back. The trooper begins to sob, devastated. He shows Warren a picture of his own baby and Warren claps him on the back as the trooper cries in sympathy and fear and frustration.

A strange composure descends on Warren. He wants to talk to somebody about organ donation, to see how he can help even as his own life is disintegrating. But there is confusion everywhere, and the troopers are gone.

He asks for a room with a phone where he can be alone.

His first call is home.

Warren's father's version of a BlackBerry is a scrap of paper in his wallet with phone numbers of all the aunts and uncles and cousins. He hands it to Warren, who calls every one. He wants to be the one to tell them.

An hour or so later, three of his close friends come into the hospital. Brad and Rob flank Warren and lead him outside, where their friend Doug is in a car to whisk him home. As his father stays behind to wait for Diane's husband, Warren's community of friends is already coming together to protect him.

A hundred yards away, reporters are beginning to arrive at the hospital with microphones and cameras. It's a big story. Someone must have something to say. But nobody notices the grieving father as he leaves the hospital.

Part One

2009

One

Summers are supposed to be relaxing, so how did this one become so hectic? I thought as I started packing up Emma, Alyson, and Katie for a weekend trip with their aunt Diane, uncle Danny, and two little cousins.

The girls had more activities than ever, and I seemed to spend all day driving them one place or another. The camping trip this weekend would be a peaceful break for everyone, even though I didn't like the thought of Emma, Alyson, and Katie—eight, seven, and five years old—going away without me. We were almost never apart. But they had been looking forward to joining their aunt and uncle at the upstate campground—and I would have two whole days with no car pools to drive.

I pulled the girls' duffel bags out of the closet and lined them up in the bedroom.

The pink duffel said *Emma* in blue lettering. The blue one had *Alyson* inscribed in pink. And the smallest purple bag had a pink *Katie* on it. Very cute. Just like my girls: each bag was distinctive, and the three together created a lovely harmony.

I took shorts, T-shirts, and bathing suits from the dresser drawers and piled them on the beds so that the girls could make their own selections. Though they were young, each of my daughters already had a sense of style and definite ideas about what to wear, so it wouldn't do just to make the decisions for them.

A few minutes later, Emma, Alyson, and Katie crowded into the room, chatting and giggling, and started to pack. The sounds of three little girls make a special kind of music, and the walls of our house always resounded with the girls' laughter and the sweet clamor of happy voices. I wasn't looking forward to the quiet that would descend when they left.

"We need bathing suits!" said Emma. "Don't forget bathing suits, Mommy!"

"They're on the bed," I said, pointing. Emma and Alyson were already good swimmers, and Katie had been learning this summer at camp. I myself rarely stepped into an ocean or a pool, but I was glad my daughters had more courage. I didn't have to worry about them in the water.

"You're getting to be such a good swimmer," I said to Katie. "You're going to have so much fun at the lake."

"Would you swim with us if you came?" Katie asked.

"I don't like lakes," I admitted. "They're all icky on the bottom."

"Oh, Mommy, you're silly!" said Alyson.

"We'll wear water shoes so the lake won't feel icky," said Emma, being practical.

Alyson turned her bright smile at me. "Do you think the crab would have gotten you if you had water shoes?"

I laughed. The Mommy-bitten-by-a-crab story was part of family lore. When I was exactly Alyson's age, I had gone into the ocean one day near my childhood home in New Jersey. I felt a sharp ping on my toes and ran screaming from the water. When I got to the beach, I saw that the nails on both of my big toes were gone.

I concluded that a crab had bitten them off.

And they never grew back right.

Hence, my fear of water.

Now Emma looked at me skeptically as I retold the story. She was old enough—and smart enough—to ask a lot of questions.

"How could one crab bite off both your toenails?" she asked.

"I don't know, but it happened," I said.

"Mommy, there are no crabs in lakes, so you'd be okay," Alyson promised.

We got busy filling duffels with all the clothes three little girls could possibly wear in two days. I looked around the room to make sure they hadn't forgotten anything important.

"Don't forget your bear," I told Katie, whose favorite stuffed animal was the Build-a-Bear that we had made together at the local mall. "And everybody bring your journals so you can write about the weekend," I added. I wanted them to be able to tell me about every detail when they came back.

While the girls put the finishing touches to their camping bags, I dashed down to the kitchen to pack bags of food for them to take. I'd bought marshmallows and other ingredients to make s'mores, which seemed necessary for a camping weekend. Plus Honey Nut Cheerios, their favorite cereal, and peanut butter for Emma, who liked nothing better than low-fat smooth Skippy. She couldn't be tricked into trying another brand (or even full-fat) because she immediately knew the difference. Not knowing what type of peanut butter Diane would pack, I figured better safe than sorry.

I suddenly felt a hole in the pit of my stomach. Call me sentimental, but I was going to miss my girls terribly over the weekend. Of course, I hoped they'd have fun, but I already couldn't wait to get them back so we could continue with our hectic summer.

With the girls going off, I should have been looking forward to a weekend alone with my husband. But the girls were my full-time job and our mutual joy. Weekends were usually dedicated to the girls' sports and play rehearsals and parties. We did everything as a family, and the girls filled our every minute. Given two days with my husband without children, I didn't feel excited, I felt anxious.

They'll be back on Sunday, I reminded myself. *Stop worrying.*

Warren's sister, Diane Schuler, had organized the trip. She planned to drive to the campgrounds with our daughters, as well as her two small children, Bryan and Erin. Her husband, Danny, would head there earlier to set up everything for their arrival. He and Diane had bought a camper a few years before, and they loved bringing it to the Hunter Lake Campground in the Catskills during the summers, using it as a base for activities.

The girls had gone on a similar camping trip with their aunt Diane and uncle Danny the previous year and considered it a perfect summer treat.

"Should Mommy come with you next time?" I had asked them after they came home from the last trip.

"No!" Emma and Alyson insisted. "This is our special trip!"

Only Katie had hesitated. "Do you and Daddy go camping?" she asked.

"Not really," I admitted. "That's why you have aunts and uncles—to do the things that parents don't."

The girls' uncle Danny loved to hunt and fish and hike. Since Warren is more a football and baseball type, he didn't mind letting Danny oversee an outdoor weekend for the girls. Warren had gone camping on family vacations when he was growing up, since at the time, it was all his family could afford.

"The reason I work is so I never have to go camping again!" he joked to me once.

Given my aversion to bugs and swimming outdoors, I heartily supported the sentiment. But we wanted the girls to have every experience possible, and if Diane and Danny could give them a taste of the outdoors, we were all for it. The girls had spent all week talking excitedly about how they would get to go fishing, swimming, and rowboating, so I lived vicariously through their excitement, relieved I didn't have to actually partake.

The camping trip, though, would be one of the rare times that the girls and I were separated. We had fun being together, so whether cooking dinner or baking cupcakes, dashing through the grocery store or buying new clothes, they hung close, my constant companions. I would miss them, but they'd be together with adults who loved them, in a place they'd been before. What could happen?

Thinking about my three girls at a campsite for two days, I had the same mundane concerns any mom would have. Did the girls need extra-strength bug spray? Would they be able to sleep in a strange place? How would they handle slimy creatures at the bottom of the lake? (Obviously my worry, not theirs.) I reminded myself that going to the Catskills with loving family members wasn't exactly a trek on the wild side.

In fact, the only hitch at all had occurred the night before when Diane called to say her and Warren's father wouldn't be joining them. Mr. Hance had been on the trip last year when Emma, Alyson, and Katie ventured to Hunter Lake for the first time with their cousins and aunt and uncle. Five children, however well behaved, can wander in many directions, and I felt better having three adults instead of two there to help supervise.

"I'll get someone else to join us," Diane said, mentioning various members of the extended family whom she might ask. I agreed, but tonight she called back after the girls were asleep to say that everyone she contacted was busy. She would drive the kids herself.

I felt an irrational tremor of anxiety.

"Diane doesn't have another adult in the car," I told Warren after we hung up. "Maybe the girls shouldn't go."

"Why? You drive five kids all the time," he said.

He was right. Carpooling remained a fact of life in our town, and Diane's children or the girls' friends would often pile into our minivan. I'd shuttle a pack of children to soccer practice or gymnastics class or a birthday party without a second thought. An upstate trip somehow seemed different to me, but Diane reminded me that the campground wasn't that far away, just an hour or so in traffic. Relax. All would be fine.

Diane had always been trustworthy.

While they waited to leave for their trip on Friday, the girls practiced gymnastics on the front lawn. Emma and Alyson did graceful cartwheels and Katie tried a few somersaults. Looking at my three daughters playing happily together gave me a warm glow. My girls were more than just siblings. They were best friends.

Though she arrived a few minutes late, Diane seemed happy and ready for the weekend when she drove up to our house with her two kids in tow. Since my car had a third row of seats, we moved kids and equipment from her Jeep to my red Ford Windstar. Katie needed a booster seat, so we strapped that in tightly. Always well-organized, Diane had juice boxes ready at each seat and DVD players in each row to keep the children entertained.

"Everyone go the bathroom now," Diane called out cheerfully. "We're not stopping until we get there!"

Emma took the seat next to her two-year-old cousin, Erin. Tall and slim, Emma looked and acted older than eight, and her outgoing, mature attitude made her an ideal in-car babysitter. Talented in both sports and school, she had a bit of my perfectionism about her. She liked to smooth her hair into a perfect ponytail in the morning ("No bumps!" she always insisted), and her clothes were always carefully chosen each morning. She had a flair for the dramatic, and when she starred in the school play that year as Cinder-elly, I had a feeling she might have found her future career.

In the car, Emma made sure her sisters had their own iPods so there wouldn't be any arguments about what music to listen to.

"Everyone have their pillows?" Emma asked, looking around. She was ever the good big sister and older cousin, making sure everyone was comfy for the ride.

Seven-year-old Alyson buckled her seat belt with her usual air of delight. Easygoing and happy, she had been born smiling and never stopped. Her first-grade teacher once said to me that Alyson was the kindest girl in the class—and the most popular. Even the boys wanted to be her friends because she could run, jump, and climb the monkey bars as hard and fast as anyone. Alyson could make everyone—including her mother—feel a bit brighter with her ready smile and generous nature. She exuded sunshine, and today was no different.

As the baby in the family, five-year-old Katie sometimes got clingy, but this trip didn't unsettle her at all. After a big hug—she was a specialist in giving hugs—she got in the car, ready for the much-anticipated adventure. Katie was all about the love, offering kisses freely and asking for them often. Her big sisters always said that I spoiled her, but what third child isn't treated just a little differently? With Emma and Alyson so close in age, they always had each other. And Mommy and Katie stayed home together, going about their day while the big sisters attended school.

Warren pulled up to the house just as Diane started to drive away. He had already said his good-byes to the girls in the morning before he went to work, assuming they'd be gone before he arrived home. But because Diane had been late, he had another chance.

"I get to say good-bye to my girls again!" he said. He rushed over to give each of them another hug and kiss and make sure everyone was safely buckled in. We both waved as they left.

As I watched the car disappear down the street, I began to cry.

"What's wrong?" Warren asked.

I shook my head, unable to explain. I wanted to be with them.

I went back in the house and got busy cleaning and organizing. In what seemed hardly any time, Diane called to say that they had arrived safely at the campsite.

"You're there already?" I asked, delighted.

"I told you it's not very far," she said.

We chatted a little, and I felt a wash of relief that the weekend had started smoothly. Knowing all was fine, Warren and I decided to enjoy the night and went off to join our close friends Brad and Melissa Katinas, who were having a lobster bake in their backyard. We danced under the stars as our friends all had a good laugh about Warren's outfit. For some reason, he had decided to surprise me that night by wearing pink plaid shorts with a white belt and a pink button-down shirt. White loafers completed the look. Knowing I'd be sad without the girls home, he wanted to make me laugh. It worked.

Nothing special happened that night—we just had a good time with friends. But I sometimes look back on that night and wonder if we will ever have an evening like it again. The very normalcy is what I can no longer imagine, the simplicity of a happy evening not marred by a backdrop of loss, emptiness, and pain.

On Saturday morning, Warren got up early and I lay in bed, my mind whirling. Although I knew how lucky I was—my girls were happy and well loved—I wanted even more for them. Like so many mothers, I thought endlessly about what would make them happy, and even when my life revolved around camp and car pools, I enjoyed all the tasks of motherhood. But my head never stopped focusing on "What next?" and "Am I doing this right?" Without them home this weekend, needing me to cook and counsel, I found myself focusing on their futures.

We lived in Floral Park on Long Island, in the house where Warren had grown up, which his great-grandfather had built. Warren liked the sense of deep-rooted tradition in the walls, but Emma and Alyson shared a bedroom and Katie's room wasn't much bigger than a closet. Was it time to move? Did they need their own rooms? And then came the question of schools. Several of our friends had already moved to a nearby town where they had a middle school, which Floral Park didn't. Katie was only in kindergarten, but shouldn't we be thinking ahead?

The phone rang a few times with friends calling, but I didn't answer. My friend Jeannine Votruba texted to see how Warren and I were doing on our own. She and I had met at the Mothers' Club in town years ago, and with her high energy and take-charge attitude, Jeannine could probably run any corporation in America. But right now she focused her executive skills on her four young children and her many friends, me included. Her daughters Sydney and Nina were as close as sisters with Emma and Alyson.

"We're having a great time!" I quickly texted back.

Let her imagine laughter, great sex, and a romantic second honeymoon. If I admitted to her that I had sunk into a blue mood without the girls around, she'd rush over and tell me to snap out of it. And she'd be right. I knew I should try to enjoy this private time with Warren.

You have a wonderful life with three beautiful children, I told myself. *Just appreciate it.*

I knew I was blessed. My girls had a gleam about them and seemed to glow with joy. Though still young, they had big hearts and enough confidence to help the underdogs. Emma's third-grade teacher told us how incredibly kind my daughter was to an autistic boy in her class. He responded to Emma better than to anyone else—probably because she always took the time to talk to him and give him special attention. I was proud of that. Loving my daughters and having fun with them was having the right effect.

A few days earlier, a woman I didn't know had come up to me at the beach club where the girls attended day camp.

"Are you Alyson Hance's mother?" she asked.

"I am."

"I just wanted to meet you," she said, extending a hand. "You have such a happy child, I figured you must be a really great person."

Remembering that as I lay in bed on that Saturday morning, I smiled into my pillow. Yes, I had happy children. And what could be more important than that? Everyone admired Alyson's ease and her smile embraced the world. I didn't have to worry about her. And Katie, though only five, expected the world to be good to her, and so far, she hadn't been disappointed.

Emma was the Energizer Bunny of the group—she loved being active. Her days this summer started with an 8 a.m. enrichment program at the school, then at 9:30, I drove all the girls to camp for a full day of swimming, sports, and playing at the beach.

Every day at 4 p.m., when camp ended, the other girls carpooled home and Emma hopped into my car, scarfed down a snack, and changed her clothes while I drove her to travel soccer practice. Two hours later, we zipped to another town (requiring another change of clothes) so she could rehearse for a play with a church theater troupe. Emma was one of the youngest in the cast, and since the adults couldn't get to the stage each evening until after work, the rehearsals went on until 10 p.m. The production of *Beauty and the Beast* would surely be terrific, but really, was all this worth it?

"I'm so tired," Emma groaned one morning when I woke her at 7 a.m.

Uh-oh. What had we gotten into? I didn't want her feeling stressed and pressured.

"You're doing a lot," I said, stroking her head. "Maybe you should give up something. Should we stop the enrichment?"

"No!" she said, sitting bolt upright. "I got picked special for that."

"Travel soccer?"

"Not travel soccer!" she said. "I tried out for the team and I made it. I can't quit."

"Camp? You don't have to go to camp."

"Nooooo! I love camp!"

Well, that was that. I didn't have to ask about rehearsal. Neither of us would want her to give up the play. Emma was transformed when she stepped onstage. I loved watching her and could easily imagine her becoming a talented actress one day.

Warren, who believed in strict bedtimes, didn't like how the days and nights were getting longer. The girls needed their sleep. Or maybe Warren was trying to keep his little girls from growing up too quickly. Emma was only eight—how busy would she be when she was fifteen?

"But Daddy, I want to do the play," Emma said, overhearing us discussing it one night. "I know it's late, but I'm going to sleep right now. I won't complain."

Too much? Just right? Was Emma overscheduled or getting exactly the stimulation she needed?

Thinking about the girls now made me want to hear their voices.

I checked the time and called Diane. My girls were too young to have their own cell phones, so Diane handed hers over to them and we chatted briefly about their plans for the day. Boats! Swimming! Hikes! Their excitement came through the phone. We blew kisses good-bye, and for the rest of the day I smiled as I pictured them happily playing together at the campsite.

When we spoke again that evening, Alyson proudly reported that they had gone swimming and paddle boating. She and Emma had swum far out in the lake and then clambered up on the dock, where they practiced their dives and cannonballs.

"I didn't get to the dock, Mommy, but I went in the lake," Katie reported when it was her turn to talk.

"That's great," I said, smiling at the delight in her voice. "And by next year, I promise you'll be swimming all the way out with your sisters."

The campsite had an arcade, and as soon as we hung up, they were going to head over for a round of games.

"I packed quarters for you," I reminded Emma. "Make sure you share them with your sisters."

"I know, Mom, I'll share," Emma said good-naturedly. "And after the arcade, we're going to roast marshmallows."

I didn't have to worry about Emma. She always took charge of a situation and helped her sisters. I was happy that the girls were having experiences with their aunt and uncle that they wouldn't have had with Warren and me.

Sunday morning I woke up in a rush of good spirits. I could see the end of the weekend. The girls would be home soon.

Anxious as I had been about the children getting to the campsite safely, I never thought twice about their trip home. Maybe worry is more an emotional reaction than a response to reality. Watching them drive off, I felt helpless to safeguard them. But now that they were coming home, I assumed they were out of harm's way, that my sister-in-law was only hours away from delivering them safely to my doorstep. Maybe that wasn't rational—but when is worry ever rational?

In the late morning, Emma called Warren at his office to say that Aunt Diane had gotten a late start, but they were all in the car now and heading home. It was like Emma to worry about the time. Like her daddy, she was very punctual and must have been concerned about missing play practice. Warren phoned me to relay the message, and I started figuring out how to reorganize the day. A little after noon—12:08 p.m., as records later showed—I spoke to Diane to check what was happening. Just a late start, she explained. No problem and no reason to worry.

We then launched into the kind of conversation you might have a million times with friends or family. Two moms chatting about logistics. We talked about what time they'd be home and about plans for the week ahead. Diane wanted to attend Emma's play, but since she worked full-time, could she get tickets for the following Sunday? Sure. We went over how many tickets she'd need. Let's see, Erin could sit on her lap and Danny and five-year-old Bryan would stay home, so one ticket should be enough.

"I'll make sure to come to that performance, too," I promised.

"Great," she said.

I called my friend Melissa to tell her about the schedule change. Melissa, a pretty blonde with a perfectly decorated house that looks like she has a staff cleaning it 24/7, keeps everything in such meticulous order that her husband, Brad, jokes that they live in a museum. But she's one of the most warmhearted people I know, and she and Brad, a successful Wall Street guy, were among our closest friends. Our oldest daughters were the same age and shared the same name, and both Emmas had been cast in the summer play.

"Emma won't be going to play rehearsal today," I told Melissa, explaining the situation. "The girls are getting home late."

"Is everything okay?" Melissa asked.

"Everything is fine."

But by 12:58 p.m., it wasn't fine.

The phone in the house rang, and when I answered, Emma said, "Something is wrong with Aunt Diane."

"What? What's wrong?" I asked.

"I don't know." Emma was crying and she sounded scared. I heard Alyson in the background, also crying. My heart began to pound. What was happening?

Diane took the phone from her.

"They're just being silly," Diane said. "They're playing." But her words were slurred, almost incoherent. I assumed that they were on the road heading home, pulled over somewhere.

"Are you okay? Where are you?" I kept asking.

I couldn't get an answer.

"Let me talk to Emma again," I said.

Diane continued talking, her sentences muddled, and I looked around for my cell phone to call Warren. My strong, capable husband could take care of this. He'd talk to his sister and straighten it out. Diane hung up just as Warren walked in the door.

"I just spoke to your sister and she's slurring her words. She sounds drunk," I said, growing more nervous.

"Impossible," he said.

"I know, but she sounded strange. Maybe she had a seizure. Or a stroke."

He grabbed the phone and called her right back. She answered and Warren immediately knew something was wrong. She couldn't have a coherent conversation. Scared as he was, he went into action. He would go over and get them.

"Stay right where you are," I heard him say. "Do not move. Do you understand, Diane? Do not get back in the car. Do not move."

He asked to speak to Emma, trying to figure out exactly where they were.

"Tell me what signs you see on the road," he said to our eight-year-old. "Read me all the words you can."

Instead of getting overwrought, I felt unexpectedly calm. A problem, yes, but Warren would handle it. Diane must have made it to a rest stop, which meant other adults would be around to comfort the children. I pictured them at McDonald's, many people nearby, the girls in safe hands. Someone was surely helping them.

Warren listened as Emma carefully read from the road signs, spelling out the words she didn't know. My good girl. She wasn't crying anymore and apparently sounded composed. As near as Warren could tell, they had stopped at a rest area near the Tappan Zee Bridge in Tarrytown.

"I'm on my way," he said, rushing toward the door. He called his dad, asking him to come with him. If Diane couldn't drive, they'd need two people to get the kids and the Windstar back home. As he left the house, he called back to me, "Call the police. Call 911."

I went over the conversations in my mind again and concluded that Diane had suffered a seizure. That was the only reasonable explanation. I knew something about seizures because Danny had been struck with one out of the blue not long ago. And one of my oldest friends from nursery school was regularly coping with her husband's seizures from a brain tumor. I had heard all the symptoms. Diane's seemed to fit the pattern.

I punched in the emergency police number and blurted out the story. We needed help. My sister-in-law was driving my kids home from a camping trip, and something seemed to be wrong.

"I think she's sick or having a medical emergency," I said.

I stressed that there were five children in the car. Five children. As far as I knew, the car had pulled over at a rest area in Tarrytown, but I couldn't say exactly where.

The cop listened politely but responded laconically. "You don't know where they are?" he asked.

"No. From what my daughter said, they're at a rest stop in Tarrytown," I repeated. And then for good measure, I added, "She's eight years old." Whether I meant Emma's age to give validity to the report or express the urgency of the situation, I'm still not sure.

"Well, you'll have to call the police in Tarrytown," the cop said. "Maybe they can help. It's outside our area." He gave me a phone number to try.

I hung up and suddenly felt my sense of calm disappear as a wave of helplessness crashed over me. Call Tarrytown? I needed to rally help however I could, but I realized how vague my story sounded. At a loss, I called Melissa and filled her in, telling the disconnected details one more time. Brad's brother was a cop, so maybe he could give some suggestions. What was I supposed to say to the police to get their attention?

"I'm coming right over," Melissa said.

"You don't have to," I assured her.

I tried to reach my cousin Liz, who lived near Tarrytown. Maybe she could get to the car quickly. But I just got her voice mail. I called my mother in New Jersey to see if she knew how to get in touch with Liz.

"Should I come to you?" my mom asked, her voice quavering slightly.

"No, Mom, everything is going to be okay. The girls are at a rest stop. I'm sure somebody is taking care of them. There must be a lot of people around. Warren is on his way there right now."

I tried the number in Tarrytown and got transferred a couple of times, repeating my story to anyone who would listen. I got through to a cop who asked me my license plate number and registration. I couldn't remember the number. Maybe I was more anxious than I realized. He couldn't help without the information, and I hung up in frustration.

Melissa showed up at my door and came into the living room. She knew how to keep her house perfect, but right now, even she couldn't sort out this mess. After my call to her, Brad had called 911 for me. Eventually, the police went to the only big rest area on a highway in Tarrytown, but didn't find anything that matched our description.

Melissa called Diane's cell phone. No answer. I didn't know that Warren had been trying the number over and over.

"Diane's probably in an ambulance," I told Melissa again. "I think she had a seizure."

I slipped into a practical gear, anticipating what I had to do. With Emma's play and Alyson and Katie's activities, the week ahead was already crammed with responsibilities. But if Diane was in the hospital, I'd pitch in and take care of Erin and Bryan. That's what family did. The whole thing seemed like an inconvenience and maybe a good story to tell later.

What else can I do? I wondered. Danny had been the last one with them, so maybe he knew something. Diane and the children had planned to leave the campsite first, with Danny staying back to pack up the camper. But everything seemed unclear now. I didn't have Danny's cell phone number, so I called another relative to get it. When I finally reached Danny, he sounded groggy. He had gotten home a while ago and fallen asleep before he had to go to work that night.

"Diane's not there?" he asked sleepily. "She should have been home by now. I'm going to go find her. I know the route she takes."

Warren called me from the car. He'd contacted his friend Doug Hayden because he was a lawyer and a judge in town and knew a lot of people. Warren had made Doug one of his first calls, thinking he might have some advice. But nobody knew where to go. Diane wasn't at the rest stop where she was supposed to be, where Warren had implored her to stay.

By now Melissa's husband, Brad, had come to the house, too. Not knowing what was going on, Jeannine called from Lord & Taylor and started describing a dress she was trying on. Instead of giving an opinion, I told her what was happening.

"I'm coming over," she said. "I'll try these later."

"You don't have to," I insisted. "Melissa's here. We're fine."

"Too late," she said. "I'm already heading to the parking lot."

What was going on? It was a beautiful Sunday afternoon and my friends were interrupting their plans to come over. I couldn't understand why. Maybe Diane had gotten sick, but I kept telling myself that everything would be fine. I wouldn't allow myself to see the urgency that other people did.

Una, the wife of our lawyer-judge friend Doug, walked in at some point.

"Oh gosh, what are you doing here?" I asked when I saw her.

"Doug told me about Warren's calls," she said. "I thought I'd better come here."

I started to get increasingly anxious. Jeannine, Melissa, Una—why were all these people coming over? Was I missing something?

Everybody seemed to be on their cell phones. Melissa kept trying to call Diane's cell. Una spoke to Doug and tried to get updates. Meanwhile, Warren was at the police barracks in Tarrytown. At his suggestion, the police were trying to tap into Diane's cell phone, and they needed Danny's permission.

Somehow, word came that there had been an accident. More calls, more confusion. I was uneasy, but I still wasn't panicked. Car accidents happened all the time. The girls would be scared and probably shaken up a bit, but nothing we couldn't fix.

"I know Emma broke her leg," I said, hopping around the room. "I know it, I just know it."

For Emma to have broken her leg would have been karmic. I'm a terrible liar, but I'd needed a dramatic excuse to get out of a commitment a few weeks earlier, and I'd fibbed and said that Emma had broken her leg. I'd felt guilty at the time. Now I was convinced it was coming back to haunt me. If Emma had a broken leg from this accident, it would be my fault. "Emma broke her leg," I moaned, worried about retribution. But no, everyone was going to be all right. Mild injuries. A broken leg. We'd deal with it.

Then my mind jumped way beyond that. "Please don't let anyone be brain-dead," I whispered.

Una patted my shoulder. "Jackie, don't even think that. It's going to be okay."

But she got on the phone, calling a nurse she knew at Westchester Medical Center, hoping to find out some details.

I leaned over Una as she held the phone, grabbing her arm with two hands. "Tell me, is anyone hurt? Is someone brain-dead?"

She had no information. "My friend doesn't know anything," Una said. "Stay calm."

I began pacing up and down the kitchen, into the living room, then around in circles through the den. Back and forth, back and forth, like a dog chasing its tail, I kept going, seeking something I couldn't find.

"They're okay, they're okay, they're okay," I chanted to myself, clasping my arms together and moving my hands from side to side.

Someone told me that Warren was racing to the hospital, so we'd know soon enough.

"They're okay, they're okay, they're okay," I said, continuing my chant. "I know they're okay."

Then I saw Brad on his cell phone and I heard him say, "Warren?" Fear and concern resonated in Brad's voice, as if the person he was talking to on the other end was hysterical.

In the frenzy of the last couple of hours, time had sped by. But now it came to a grinding halt. My eyes were fixed on Brad and all the buzz around me seemed to stop.

As he listened to Warren try to give the full report, Brad stood straight, then slumped against the wall. I saw him drop his head once. Twice. Three times. The wall could barely hold him up. Then he put down the phone and came over to me. His face looked stricken.

"Jackie, they're all gone," he said.

"No," I said evenly.

The words didn't penetrate. I just kept looking at his tortured face.

But Melissa understood what his words meant.

"Brad, don't say that!" she yelled. "Don't say that!"

"They're all gone," he repeated. "Jackie, I'm so sorry . . ."

I don't know what else he said because I ran out of the house shrieking. Screaming, shrieking, yelling. No words, just horror. I ran fast, because maybe if I got away from the house, from my friends, from the phone, it wouldn't have happened. I charged down the street howling like a wild animal, feral cries resonating in the quiet afternoon. Neighbors started coming out of their houses at my horrified screams and people called out to me, but I kept running and didn't stop.

Without thinking where I was going, I headed toward Salvina's house. The matriarch of a big Italian family, Salvina had babysat for Emma, Alyson, and Katie in their first years. I would drop them off at her house when they were small, sometimes three days a week, and she cared for them like her own. Her house always seemed to me like a magical place, filled with cousins and sisters and extended love. Even as tiny babies, the girls never cried around Salvina—she had the secret potions to soothe upset stomachs or calm colic. As she watched my children grow, I watched hers. When Salvina's daughter got married, Katie walked down the aisle, a flower girl.

Now Salvina opened the door. Since it was Sunday, she was cooking gravy for the big family dinner she served each week. The smell of food that would normally make me feel so good now hit my stomach and a wave of nausea took over.

"Jackie, what's the matter, what's the matter?" she asked in her heavy Italian accent. A tiny woman with short black hair, she waved me inside. But instead, I just grabbed her arm.

"Salvina, the girls are dead. The girls are dead," I said.

"It's not true," she said placidly.

"No, that's wrong. Couldn't be," said her husband, coming to join us.

Sal, another neighbor, who was an undercover cop, had followed me but I sat down in Salvina's living room.

"It's true, Salvina. There was a car accident," Sal said. If anybody knew anything it was Sal. Not only a cop, he volunteered in the fire department and as an EMT.

But like me, Salvina couldn't process the words. She began screaming and rushed over to the couch to sit beside me, holding me and moaning. We rocked back and forth together and I sat there for what seemed like hours. I heard Jeannine come in and say we should go back home, but I didn't want to leave.

Maybe if I never left the sofa in Salvina's house, I could make my own truth. Brad would be wrong. The girls would come in the door. Emma would be upset about missing play rehearsal but Alyson would comfort her. They would tell me about the fun they'd had camping and we would hug and kiss and talk about how scary it had been when Aunt Diane got sick. Salvina would give them delicious pasta, and I would tell them that they had been brave and now we were all together, which was all that really mattered and exactly what we all wanted. What I wanted desperately.

TWO

don't know how I got back home from Salvina's. Swarms of friends and neighbors had already gathered inside and outside our house, and several of the men had gone to the hospital to get Warren. I was in our living room when he arrived home, and the moment he saw me, he crumbled. His grief was already crushing, but once multiplied by mine, it became unbearable. He put his arms around me and we both fell to the floor, reeling and helpless, grief rolling over us like a locomotive.

Warren had always been my rock, his solidity a perfect foil to my more emotional responses. But now we were both in shock. Even his efforts to show superhuman strength might not be enough to sustain me.

At some point, I looked out the window and saw news trucks and camera crews.

"What's going on?" I asked.

"The reporters are all trying to talk to you," one of my friends said. But she pulled the shades down and kept the curtains closed.

By the next day, the police had cordoned off our street, but television producers and news reporters clambered across our lawn, looking for an interview. Friends went outside to shoo away bookers from *Dr. Phil* and *Oprah* and the network morning news shows. Producers from a dozen or more talk shows and local news stations left notes asking for me. Were they joking or just unbelievably callous? My tragedy as a lead-in to Lindsay Lohan on Fox News?

· · ·

I got the story in fragments and didn't fully grasp what had happened until much later. In the immediate aftermath, all I knew was that Diane had put the children back in the car, then driven from the rest area where Warren had begged her to stay. Not answering her phone, she headed north instead of south on the major road, then drove onto an off-ramp for the Taconic State Parkway. For nearly two miles, she drove the wrong way on the highway.

Drivers who saw her beeped their horns and called 911.

Many reported that she held the wheel firmly and seemed serene. Even if she had gotten onto the ramp by mistake, there were several places along the highway where she could have pulled over. She didn't.

After 1.7 miles, she plowed headlong into an oncoming SUV.

Diane and her daughter, Erin, died. Emma, Alyson, and Katie died. Katie was still alive when she got to the hospital but doctors couldn't save her. The three men in the SUV died. Only Bryan, Diane's young son, survived, with two severe injuries and broken bones.

Eight people dead. Police called it the worst car crash in the county in seventy-five years.

The newspapers dubbed it the "Wrong Way on the Taconic Tragedy" and splashed it across their front pages. Local TV couldn't get enough of it, and the story went viral on the Web and got national attention.

But none of it could bring back my girls.

My daughters were gone.

Warren hadn't seen Emma, Alyson, or Katie at the hospital. Ever the good person, he had gone to be with Bryan, since his father, Danny, hadn't yet arrived. That's how close our families had been. Only later would the goodwill become just another source of pain and confusion.

At some point that evening, I slipped away from the concerned friends and neighbors and went to the bedroom Emma and Alyson shared. I retreated into their closet and closed the door. I could hear the swell of voices downstairs, the anguish and the sobs. But I covered my ears and just rocked back and forth in the corner. My girls, my girls. In their dark closet, I could breathe their air and feel their presence. Friends came upstairs to get me, talking to me from the other side of the door. But why should I come out? Why would I ever come out again?

A psychiatrist I had seen in the past came by our house the next day, as did another doctor in town, and suddenly I had a fistful of pills to take every few hours—antianxiety drugs and antidepressants, drugs to help me sleep and others to help me cope. I didn't know what I was taking and I didn't care. Anything to dull the pain, the unbearable empty feeling that had suddenly taken over my life. If someone had suggested general anesthesia, I would have clamped on the face mask and breathed deeply.

Our friends marshaled forces and took over whatever arrangements they could. They set up a tent and tables with coolers at the end of the driveway for all the gifts of food that were pouring in. Someone made a schedule in which friends signed up to be in the house twenty-four hours a day. The whole community rallied around us, and even through my haze of shock and grief, I felt the goodness of the people around us holding me together.

Isabelle and Mark, our close friends and back-door neighbors, had been away on vacation, and they rushed back to be with us. Their children, Ryan and Kailey, were the exact ages of Emma and Alyson—and were like two halves of the same puzzle. We never closed the gate between our yards because the children traipsed back and forth, treating both families as their own. I was as likely to find Kailey in my kitchen as Kate. Now Warren whispered to me how terrible it must be for Isabelle and Mark to tell their children that their best friends were dead. A horrible conversation to have, he said. He couldn't imagine having to give our girls that kind of news.

In truth, we would have given everything we owned to have one more conversation with our daughters, whatever the topic. But we were too shattered to think rationally. I nodded at Warren's comment, sharing his regret that our friends and their children had to endure such pain. I felt that somehow, it was my fault.

The next few days were filled with questions no parent should have to answer—about caskets and burial plots and eulogies at the funeral. Warren took control, handling all the specific arrangements. Picking where the girls were laid to rest mattered deeply to him. I didn't know how he was coping, but maybe staying busy helped him avoid the avalanche of grief that would otherwise overwhelm him—and that was currently crippling me.

Two days after the accident he came to me with the news that Father O'Farrell, our local parish priest, was able to get us into Holy Rood Cemetery.

"What? What does that mean?" I asked, not focusing.

"It's a beautiful place for the girls, Jackie. You're going to love it there. It's right near Jeannine's house."

"Oh," I said, still not really grasping what he was talking about. "Okay."

"It's good news," Warren persisted, "because it's basically sold out and impossible to get a plot. But they took care of it."

Two days ago, I had been focused on what school I wanted my girls to attend. Now I was competing to get them into a cemetery.

Father O'Farrell had called on the bishop to pull some strings at Holy Rood, and with the path cleared, Warren had been able to buy a double plot big enough for twelve—six for our family and six for Diane's family, the Schulers. The expense was huge, but we weren't thinking about that now. Nor did we have enough information in those first days after the accident to realize that burying the girls next to Diane would eventually become a constant source of pain for us.

Once the plots were decided and a funeral date was picked, a friend came and gently asked what I wanted the girls to wear in their coffins. They were going to be God's little angels. I was dressing them for eternity.

I wanted to scream that they weren't God's angels, they were my baby girls. But instead I mumbled something about white sweaters. Pretty dresses. Bows in their hair and their diamond crosses.

Would the girls approve? In real life—only two days before—they were little fashionistas with their own ideas about style. We loved shopping together and talked about the right outfits for every occasion. I knew what they liked to wear to parties, school, beach club, and camp. But we never discussed what to wear for eternity. As with so much else now, I was on my own.

• • •

Nobody would get to see the girls in their pretty dresses because at the wake on Wednesday, the caskets stayed closed. Caskets are usually kept open at a Catholic wake, but everyone agreed that in this case, the sight would be too unbearable. The real problem, though, was that I hadn't seen the girls, either. Right after the accident, Warren's father, my brother Stephen, and a police officer friend named Lou had identified the girls at the hospital before they went to the funeral home. Trying to protect me from the unimaginable anguish, friends had kept me away. They didn't want me to open each Pandora's box of pain.

But the attempt to preserve my sanity had backfired. My mind conjured horrible images that haunted me constantly; I had to see the girls myself. When at last I saw the girls in their open caskets before the wake, I was stunned. The girls looked perfect. Pretty and unmarked. The accident hadn't left them marred or visibly injured, and their minor bruises were covered. How could they be so perfect—but so lifeless? The girls had smooth faces and soft skin. Every fiber of my being said it didn't make sense. How could they be gone? Diane was the only one who looked like she had been in an accident. How could this have happened?

Five coffins lined the room of the funeral home, evidence of a titanic tragedy. The proper term for a wake is a vigil, but if we couldn't protect the girls in life, how could we watch over their souls in death? All our vigilance had not been enough. A Catholic wake is meant to have a positive spirit, but now that innocent children had been yanked from the earth, all the talk of souls coming home seemed warped and wrong. Home for Emma, Alyson, and Katie should be in Floral Park with the parents who loved them. Nothing else made sense.

Hundreds of people came to the wake, friends and family members and neighbors. The whole community of Floral Park seemed shocked and shaken, and they came to offer whatever comfort they could. Seeing familiar faces, from local cops to shopkeepers to friends from the Mothers' Club, at least made me feel less alone. As I wandered through the room greeting everyone, I felt like the macabre hostess of the worst party in the world. Childhood friends from New Jersey and classmates from high school arrived, and several who knew my mother gathered around her. I wanted my mom to take care of me, but she had lost the three grandchildren she adored and could barely handle the depth of her own loss.

Danny came into the funeral home and we hugged. It was the first time he and I had seen each other since the accident, and instead of being comforting, the touch destroyed us both. We fell to the floor in a tangle of tears and screams, holding each other and sobbing. The emotion was overwhelming, but I eventually managed to stand on my feet again and make it through the rest of the vigil.

I felt the outpouring of emotion from the whole community as people asked how they could help us, so Warren and I suggested donations to the Hance-Schuler Family Foundation. At the moment, it was just a mailbox at Jeannine's house, but I had a vague sense that great good could eventually emerge. Almost immediately, people devastated by our loss and wanting to express their support sent notes and cards and emails, checks and cash and generous donations. It was the first inkling I had of how generous people can be. The depth of human kindness would continue to overwhelm me again and again in the coming months.

The superintendent of schools arrived at the wake, her expression frozen tight with anguish. She came over and, taking my hand, spoke warmly about the girls—how smart they were and how kind; the great spark of joy they brought into a room.

Many others had expressed similar sentiments, but her memories of my happy daughters were especially meaningful to me. School is where children spend most of their time and feel connected. I pictured Alyson swinging happily across the monkey bars during recess.

"Maybe we can donate playgrounds to the schools," I said spontaneously.

"That may be a bigger project than you realize," she said, with a smile that briefly wiped the pain from her face.

"Well, something like that. Maybe I can plant a tree," I said. I immediately liked that idea. At least I would have something to nourish, something of mine that would grow.

• • •

The next day, Thursday, was my children's funeral.

I suppose I got up that day and brushed my teeth, took a shower, and combed my hair—all the little daily routines that would suggest I was alive and functioning. But I wasn't, really. What was happening was beyond comprehension, and my mind completely shut down, refusing to take in the scene. I survived the day by not really being there.

In newspaper photographs from that day, I am in dark glasses, my face puffy and pasty. Warren is on one side of me and a police guard is on the other. Warren looks blank but determined. In survival mode, he feels the burden of making sure the day goes right.

The costs for the funeral had soared, and a few people suggested using some of the donations that were coming in, or asking for others. But I came out of my stupor long enough to issue an ardent "no." We would pay for the funeral. We would bury our own children.

I had grown up as a devout Catholic, so the familiar traditions of the Church brought some comfort when everything else around me was crumbling. Having gone to church every week for most of my life, priests and blessings and hymns were the right source for consolation. All of us fall back on ritual to smooth over grief, letting rules and traditions be the guide through a time of uncertainty. Funerals become grand exercises, a kind of pomp and ceremony to mark graduation from one world to the next. Since Emma, Alyson, and Katie would never get to graduate from high school or college—or even grade school—this was all we had.

I remember looking out the window of the limousine taking us to the church, hearing music, and wondering, *Where did the bagpipes come from?* Two rows of bagpipe players lined the road, blowing their mournful tunes. The four black limousines bearing our family and Danny's pulled up behind the five white hearses. Grim-faced men hefted the white-and-gold coffins and brought them into the redbrick Our Lady of Victory church. Once they would have thought of themselves as our friends, brothers, and uncles. Now they would forever remember being pallbearers at my daughters' funeral.

More than a thousand people filled the pews in the church.

Hundreds more waited outside.

Floral Park is in suburban New York, but it is an old-fashioned town where everybody knows one another. I suppose you could plunk it in rural Wyoming or Idaho and the small-town spirit would feel the same. Warren and his siblings—including Diane—grew up here, and the family's roots go back more than a century. Since our house had generations of history, the tangle of interconnected relationships could fill a soap opera.

The hundreds of people who knew us or had been touched by the girls came to the service in shocked disbelief. The tragedy had seeped into their homes, and they reacted as if it were their own family. A small town like ours functions in some ways like an extended family—everyone watches out for one another. The gossipy chatter that can sometimes feel intrusive turns, in times of trouble, into a saving grace. Even people who didn't know us lined the streets or stood on their front lawns, offering prayers and support. I didn't realize until much later how much I was buoyed by the strength and support of the community. Warren and I felt like we had lost everything, like we had only each other. But now a thousand people wanted us to know that we had them, too.

As we walked into the church, part of me kept thinking, *This isn't really happening*. I would wake up tomorrow and get my life—and my girls—back. This nightmare would be over and we could get on with our plans for summer camp and church plays.

One newspaper reported that as the coffins were wheeled into the church, music played softly in the background and "Jackie Hance placed a hand over her mouth, hugged her husband, covered her face and placed a hand over her heart."

How theatrical that makes me sound, as if I had planned each gesture for fullest effect. But this wasn't a movie with Meryl Streep playing the part of the grieving mother. Instead, it was real life, and the grieving mother—me—was disappearing into a black hole of woe.

Warren had decided to give the eulogy, knowing that it would have been impossible for me. I couldn't imagine how he would do it.

"I have one chance to tell all the people at the funeral about the girls and what's in my heart, and if I don't do it, I'll regret it the rest of my life," he had told me right after the accident. Those words came back to me as he walked forward to give the eulogy.

Warren had never done much public speaking, and he avoided the television cameras that were everywhere. He wanted to talk only to the people he cared about—and they were all gathered at the funeral. As he stood at the front of the church, he spoke calmly, his voice steady.

"What we ask all of you going forward is when you see us on the street, please don't look the other way," he said at one point. "Please don't be afraid to talk to us. You don't have to offer any more condolences, you don't have to tell us how sorry you are."

Our own sorrow was already so relentless, pressing down so heavily, that any more might crush us completely.

He talked about our girls and he talked about Bryan, the "miracle child" who had survived. Only at the very end did he lose his composure.

"Cherish your children," Warren said. "Hug your children. Kiss your children. And don't forget—"

But he couldn't finish the sentence. As he gave in to his grief, the whole church seemed to be rocked by sobs. Parents clutched their children and held them tightly. The girls' friends had tears streaming down their cheeks. When people finally left the church, some of the children sat on the curb, too stunned to move. I look at pictures from that warm, sunny day and feel sad for the pretty little girls in their summer clothes whose lives had suddenly changed. They had always felt safe and protected in our suburban community, surrounded by parents and adults who loved them. But now they had discovered the truth they shouldn't have to face: Mommy and Daddy love you, but they can't always protect you.

After the funeral, hundreds of children, parents, townspeople, and mourners streamed over to Trinity Restaurant, a popular spot in Floral Park. With everybody wanting to show their support, the owners had put up a big tent outside and asked all the local restaurants to donate food. Warren wanted to attend.

"We can't go to a party," I said, horrified.

"We have to," Warren insisted. "All these people are trying to do something nice for us."

He headed over to the restaurant, but I couldn't stay in public a moment longer. I was thoroughly drained from the funeral, and didn't want to see anyone. My Catholic traditions got me through the wake and funeral, but enough—I had to be alone.

A phalanx of loyal friends ushered me back to the house and I collapsed on my bed. The wails and sobs I had held back in public erupted now and ricocheted through the house. My life had been ripped away from me and I thought I would cry forever because I couldn't think of any reason to stop. Later, neighbors would tell me that they could hear my howls of grief through the open windows, that they shivered at my pain and at the helplessness they felt when faced with the prospect of comforting me.

But finally I stopped and lay there, as limp as a rag doll, too drained to move. Is there a limit to how many tears your body can produce? Do you ultimately cry so long that your body withers like a dried leaf and all emotion is gone?

"I'll go to the restaurant," I said, getting out of bed. "I changed my mind."

I wasn't sure why I was going, but I wanted to be near Warren. And I felt a wave of guilt—all these people had arranged the lunch in honor of my girls and to be kind to me. However I felt, I needed to show I appreciated their generosity. The friends who had come home with me were surprised, but I got dressed and we walked the few blocks to the restaurant, where everyone had gathered.

With everyone from town present, the scene at the restaurant seemed as unreal as everything else that had happened in the last four days. I had a profound sense of dislocation, as if I had stepped out of my life and gone through a wormhole. Maybe, in some parallel existence, the life I had begun with my three daughters was still going on. At this very moment, in another dimension, I was helping Emma get into her costume and telling her that she would be wonderful in the premier of the play next week.

But in the only reality I had, I was sitting under a tent in the long driveway of a nice restaurant on Jericho Turnpike, while throngs of people dug into the platters of pasta, salads, sandwiches, and cookies that had been so generously provided. Food donated in love and grief and helplessness.

Around me, I heard people laughing and talking. But I didn't want to talk. I couldn't laugh.

What am I doing here?

I got up to leave. I didn't belong at a party, however kindly it was meant. Frankly, I didn't belong anywhere anymore.

Three

Everyone told me that my girls were in heaven.

On most days, I agreed.

I grew up attending mass every week, and whether out of belief, comfort, commitment, or guilt, the Church had remained a central part of my life. The girls always came with me to mass and sometimes Warren would join us, too. He knew how much prayer meant to me.

But after Emma, Katie, and Alyson's funeral, I stopped going to church. How could I believe that God had been listening to my prayers? I had prayed fervently for my children's safety, their health, their happiness, every night. Even before they were born, I didn't stint on grand gestures. While pregnant with Emma, I wore every crucifix I owned and put twenty pins on my bra strap each morning, in honor of my favorite saints.

One evening halfway through that pregnancy, Warren and I went out for dinner and I had three rosaries draped prominently around my neck.

"Jackie, you have to stop. This is getting embarrassing," he said.

"How could it be embarrassing to protect our baby?" I asked.

I felt a huge responsibility to shield my children from harm. If that meant putting aside my own ego and needs, I didn't mind. Ferociously protective, I called on the saints to help me watch over my girls, and I continued wearing crucifixes and pins with each pregnancy.

I had followed all the tenets of Catholicism and done everything right. But now my whole belief system had been spun on its head.

Rosaries and crucifixes and pious prayer had not been enough to safe-guard me or my children from the randomness of life. I couldn't believe that killing three innocent children was part of any divine plan.

But religion and rationality aren't a good mix, and it is hard to shake free of what you have always believed. So I comforted myself with the thought that I would see the girls again in heaven, that we would be reunited.

The sooner the better.

"I'm going to be with the girls soon!" I started telling my friends, flashing a big smile that reflected my sense of relief. It was more than just a way to make myself feel better; I truly believed it. My little girls would not spend eternity without the love of their mother. I needed to be there to take care of them in heaven as I hadn't been able to on earth. I clung to the promise of our reunion as my only chance of feeling happiness or joy again. And, in my deranged state, I thought the sooner I joined them in heaven, the better for all of us.

My closest friends, who were still keeping watch at our house twenty-four hours a day, faced the reality of what I would have to do to make this heavenly connection happen. They didn't want to keep me from the girls—but they wanted to keep me alive until I could think straight. Though I'd always been high-strung and anxious, I'd never had suicidal thoughts before, but the circumstances had dramatically changed my entire outlook on life.

So, without telling me, my friends quietly removed anything from the house I could use to harm myself. Sharp knives disappeared from our kitchen. Long scarves were gone from my dresser. Getting dressed one morning, I couldn't find my favorite belt. I went to cut something out of the newspaper, and instead of my usual kitchen blades could find only children's safety scissors.

Since the Church had been the foundation of my life, I began look-ing for answers through religion. I grew up believing that priests knew the answers to all the mysteries of life. They could tell me what God ex-pected of me; all I had to do was follow their rules. I had turned to priests when I was pregnant with Emma and an early sonogram suggested she might have cystic fibrosis or Down syndrome. The doctor recommended an amniocentesis but I didn't know what to do. I would never terminate the pregnancy—I had bonded to my baby from the first moment—but Warren said he wanted to be prepared. I worried about the risk of miscarriage that accompanied the amnio. What if I lost my baby? I had sworn to myself to protect her under any circumstances.

"I'm so confused," I had moaned to the priest. "I'm not giving up on this baby no matter what. Why would this happen? What do I do?"

He didn't ask for medical specifics—he just told me to follow my heart. "Do what makes you and your husband most comfortable," he said.

It took two weeks for the amnio results to come back. While I waited, I kept going back to the church and praying that my baby would be healthy.

The test came back fine. Emma was healthy. I thought then that my prayers had been answered.

After the funeral I made appointments with several different priests, visiting them and asking questions, looking for explanations as to why the God I had always trusted could turn on me with such vengeance. Nobody had answers for me that I could understand. As priests, they offered theoretical theology instead of honest, simple answers.

"How could God do this?" I asked one.

"It wasn't God, it was Diane," he said. He then went on rhapsodically about fate and destiny and free will.

"So this was supposed to happen to me?" I asked, getting increasingly confused. "It was my destiny? I was born for this tragedy?"

"No, no," he said, getting slightly flummoxed. "As I mentioned, we have free will."

Of my own free will, I decided we were getting nowhere and I'd better leave.

I visited a priest at another nearby parish. Like all clergymen, he had dealt often with sadness and grief, and he offered carefully practiced words of kindness and comfort. But in the face of numbing grief, platitudes are pointless. They slide off your skin like dewdrops from a leaf. I wasn't seeking solace—I needed answers. So I began again, asking him the question that had been tormenting me.

"Why were all three girls taken? Couldn't one of them have been spared? It seems so unfair."

Danny still had his son, Bryan. The girls had each other. But Warren and I were completely alone and bereft. All three of our daughters gone? How could that be? What meaning could possibly emerge from such misery? I gazed at the priest through my haze of sorrow, hoping that he would have the bit of wisdom or ethereal insight that would pierce the balloon of pain that surrounded me.

But he answered too quickly.

"They needed to be together," he said.

I felt the anger rising in me since I'd already heard that same response over and over. The very idea infuriated me. What did it mean that they needed to be together? Didn't the girls need to be together here on earth with Warren and me?

I left again, disappointed in another collared cleric who couldn't help.

Reeling from pain, I told my friend Tricia, a mother of three and an executive at a big company in Manhattan, that I was losing faith in the Church. Tricia always found solutions, and she gave me the number of a young priest she knew, Father Brian Barr.

When I called him, he'd already been briefed by Tricia.

"I'm so sorry," he said as soon as I told him my name.

"You have to help me," I blurted out. "You have to tell me this pain is going to go away. God won't let me live like this, right? If you're sick, you get pain medicine, so what do I get? I need to know he'll take me quickly, otherwise I'll have to kill myself."

He waited until I finished, then spoke firmly. "Jackie, everything is chaotic right now, but we need to stop the bleeding first. Then we can figure things out. It's like triage. The bleeding is so severe that you can't think rationally."

"If I kill myself, would I go to hell?" I asked, getting right to the point.

He stayed on the phone with me for almost two hours, as I barraged him with questions.

"All your questions are reasonable," he said finally. "I need to get back to you. Please don't do anything until I come talk to you. In the meantime, remember that the pain you feel now won't be the same you feel in six months."

I thought that was ridiculous. Of course this pain would never cease. And how could this priest know, anyway? He wasn't a mother. He didn't understand.

But I promised Father Barr I wouldn't do anything drastic until we spoke again. After all, I needed to confirm that taking my own life would reunite me with my girls. I got through the next few days by waiting for him to arrive. Without solid answers, I was afraid to act.

He pulled up to the house one afternoon in a Jeep, wearing khaki shorts, an open-necked shirt, and flip-flops. Like all the others, he didn't have an explanation as to why all three girls had been taken. I moved on to my next series of questions. My plan to see Emma, Alyson, and Katie made perfect sense to me, but I needed to confirm the entry requirements to the Kingdom of Heaven.

"You can't enter heaven if you commit a mortal sin," he said.

"God would send me to hell for wanting to be with my children?" I asked in disbelief.

"Suicide is a mortal sin," he reminded.

"Isn't God kind and compassionate and forgiving?" I asked, near tears.

"Yes, of course."

"Well, wouldn't a forgiving God understand that a mother needs to take care of her children? Are you telling me God would keep me from my children?"

"I can't answer that," Father Barr said finally.

"But this doesn't make sense!"

"You're speaking like a very rational person," he said. "If you're rational when you commit suicide, then you won't go to heaven."

"But I'm crazy, I really am. You're just not here when things get really bad!" I said ardently.

How did it get to this? Did I really have to convince a priest that I was crazy in order to assure my passage to heaven?

My search for straightforward answers seemed to leave all the priests I confronted shaken and uncertain. Catholicism is based on belief, not careful reasoning. If you try to treat the articles of faith like a mathematical equation, you discover they just don't add up. The priests were willing to offer comfort, but they didn't want to engage in carefully calibrated conversation. They balked at offering literal assurances that heaven existed—and that the girls and I would find each other in that better spot.

Was it really better? When my father got sick and quickly died of cancer, a year before Emma was born, the priestly intonement that he had "gone to a better place" made sense. We all nodded compassionately. However sad and painful his death, I liked thinking of him smiling down at me from heaven. And I got pregnant so quickly after he died that I was sure Emma was Dad's gift to me.

But with my daughters, none of the bromides about a "better place" made sense.

To add to the heartbreak—and my confusion—Katie had survived the crash and was the only one still alive at the hospital. At first, I had thought it was Alyson who had fought on, which made sense to me because Alyson had the biggest heart—one so big and open and generous that it would keep beating forever. But then Warren told me I was wrong—our little Katie had been the one who struggled for life in the hospital.

Thinking about that sucked the air out of my lungs. What had happened to Katie in those moments when she teetered between life and death? I remembered stories I had read of people on the precipice of death choosing whether to stay on earth or go to heaven. One man who had suffered a heart attack described that he was on his way to the other side when he suddenly realized how sad his wife and daughter would be. He fought back to be with his family.

Had Katie had that experience? Did she elect to be with her sisters instead of with me?

Katie and I had always been inseparable. I loved to find special ways to bond with her, and one day when the big girls were in school, we went off to get manicures together, giggling from start to finish. When Emma and Alyson saw our sparkly nails, they'd begged to get their nails done, too, so I set up another date for all of us. I couldn't deny Katie that second round of laughing together with me and her sisters. She must have been the only five-year-old in town who got two mani-pedis that week.

As close as she and I were, Katie also adored her older sisters. Emma and Alyson always carpooled to school with their best friends and neighbors, Kailey and Ryan. On days that I drove, Katie of course came along, happily sitting in the car for the round-trip to school and back. But even on the other days, Katie didn't like to be left behind. She'd walk next door with her sisters, and Isabelle would pop her in the car to take her along—then drop her back at our house. She kept a car seat longer than she needed to just so Katie could ride in the car with her.

Katie had always been inseparable from her sisters. I couldn't shake the idea that after the accident, she had been given a choice. On some level, I understood her wanting to be with her sisters. I wanted to be with them, too.

With these thoughts of ending my life to see the girls, I thought that I'd hit the absolute depths of despair. Then I learned that I hadn't even come close to rock bottom.

The next blow happened the Tuesday after the funeral, as Warren and I sat in the Long Island living room of a woman named Elaine Stillwell. We had connected to her through Compassionate Friends, a national organization for grieving parents. She was telling us about her own loss many years earlier and the comfort and support her local bereavement group could offer. I'm sure she ran a warm and sympathetic group, but I already knew that Warren and I couldn't join. The meetings were open, and we needed to protect our privacy. Our story—and our pain—had already been made too public.

In the midst of the conversation, Warren got a call on his cell phone and stepped out of the living room to take it. When he came back, his face was rigid.

"We have to leave," he said.

"Why?" I asked. It had been a long drive to get here, and I wanted to stay in Elaine's living room, hearing her comforting words, for a while longer.

"Now, Jackie," he said. His whole body was tense and I heard the urgency in his voice.

We made a quick exit.

"The toxicology report is going to be released," Warren said as he led me to the car. "It's not good."

Up until now, the police had been calling the accident a "mystery" and saying that alcohol didn't seem to be involved. Diane had driven down an exit ramp to the Taconic Parkway that was isolated and poorly marked. Local residents had long worried about people getting confused. But once on the highway, with cars whizzing by, Diane could have pulled over to one of the grassy areas along the side of the road. Drivers who passed her honked their horns and tried to gesture. Some said she was staring straight ahead, holding the steering wheel in the correct 10-2 o'clock position, and seemed calm. Others said she straddled lanes and seemed erratic.

Why did she keep driving?

Warren and I had been too dazed and distracted to come up with any theories of our own. Seizure or stroke, probably. Some other neurological disruption. Something must have happened to leave her muddled or disoriented.

Now police had an answer so shocking we found ourselves tumbling down another rabbit hole. A state trooper had hinted to Warren a couple of days earlier that horrifying findings might be released, and Warren had tried to warn me of the possibility. But we had both stayed in a state of denial.

"The toxicology report says Diane was drunk," Warren said.

When I gasped, he added, "And high on pot."

Diane's blood alcohol level had been 0.19 percent—more than twice the legal limit. Police described it as the equivalent of ten shots of vodka in an hour. She had six grams of undigested alcohol in her stomach, and police found an opened vodka bottle in the wreckage. There was also evidence that she had been smoking marijuana just an hour before.

"No, no, it's a mistake," I said.

"It's an official report," Warren said.

"But it must be a mistake. Diane doesn't drink. It's impossible."

This latest news was almost too horrifying to handle. Diane drunk with five children in the car? Was that why Emma had been crying? Is that what she meant when she said that something was wrong with Aunt Diane?

Warren and I were not yet capable of going anywhere on our own, so our dear friend Isabelle had driven us to the meeting at Elaine Stillwell's house. Now as we hurried back into Isabelle's car, she told us that reporters were mobbing our neighborhood again. Police had closed off our street after the accident, and they might have to do it again. The previous week, the "Wrong Way on the Taconic" story had grabbed newspaper readers and tabloid TV viewers with its anguishing human tragedy. Now the disaster had America's other favorite element: scandal.

Instead of driving us home, Isabelle decided we would head in a different direction. Looking for someplace safe to escape the press, we went to the suburban retreat of our friends Brad and Melissa, in the neighboring town of Garden City. Suddenly we were fugitives from our own lives. Too many times this week we had evaded reporters by having Isabelle take us to her house and help us get inside undetected. Then we would slip out her back door, sidle across the two yards, and sneak into our own home from the back. The furtiveness unnerved me. We were the good guys in the story, not the villains. We hadn't done anything wrong. But I suddenly realized how the toxicology findings would sound to the rest of the world.

"We have to make a statement," I said, panicking now as we pulled up at Melissa and Brad's house. "People are going to think I was an irresponsible mother."

Despite the powerful eulogy he had given at the funeral, Warren didn't consider himself a public speaker, and he felt wrong talking to reporters. "I don't owe them any explanations," he said stoically. "I talk to the people I care about."

We called my brother and asked him if he would speak for the family. Three years older than me, Stephen had been the person I turned to when we were growing up. My mom suffered from postpartum depression, but the problem was so little understood forty years ago that she was hospitalized and given shock treatments—which only made it worse. My parents separated quickly and divorced when I was ten. Though I saw my dad every day, my mom and Stephen and I formed a tight threesome. When Stephen went to Annapolis for college, I was devastated. Now he lived in New Jersey, not far from where we grew up, with his beautiful wife, Caroline, and my nieces and nephew.

Since Stephen had a job getting bigwigs positions in the financial sector, he was used to public speaking and agreed to appear at a press conference where he would read our statement but not take any questions. The reporters pounced. Like hungry birds, they were determined to peck at whatever they could get.

In front of a throng of cameras, reporters, and commentators near our home, Stephen explained that he was speaking for Warren and me—but not for Danny. He said that we were "shocked and deeply saddened" by the information in the toxicology report, and that it was "the absolute last thing that we ever would have expected." Then, speaking in our voice, he made the most important point of all:

"We would never knowingly allow our daughters to travel with someone who might jeopardize their safety."

Never, under any circumstances. Never ever. I wanted him to repeat that line a thousand times. He continued with the words we had carefully chosen:

"Because we have never known Diane to be anything but a responsible and caring mother and aunt, this toxicology report raises more questions than it provides answers for our family."

Listening intently, the reporters immediately sensed the first hint of a rift. And they were right. The Hances and Schulers had grieved together last week when our family bonds promised to trump all. But the toxicology report changed everything. Diane was buried alongside my girls, so we were connected to her forever, and realizing that brought a new, unexpected wave of pain and confusion.

Four

People began asking how I felt about Diane. No one can imagine how complex that question is. How does a person go from being like a sister to me, loved by my girls and cherished by my husband, to being the person who ruined our lives? Diane treated the girls like her own children—calling them before the first day of school, sending loving cards for Valentine's Day, and stopping by just to see them and say hello. How could this person I loved and trusted have done something so unthinkable? Not to have any answers was torture.

Grief is an overpowering sensation that fills every crevice of your heart and every synapse of your brain—and doesn't leave room for anything else. But now another emotion began to creep in.

Anger.

The encroaching rage was like a surprise intruder on my grief, demanding a response I didn't have the strength or emotional resilience to give.

If the toxicology findings were correct, my children didn't just die—they had been murdered.

I began to discover that as torturous as grief may be, it doesn't claw at your soul in the same way that anger does.

"Why couldn't they have just been in a regular car accident?" I whispered to one friend. "Then I could deal with the grief without having all this anger, too."

People began talking to me about "healing," but the word rang hollow. It wasn't as if I had scraped my knees and would start feeling better with some Band-Aids and lollipops. My life had essentially ended. Everything I cared about had been ripped away, and I grew increasingly angry at God for leaving me in this position. Our friends started looking for therapists who might help us, but many of the professionals didn't even want to talk to us. Our tragedy was too much for them. They couldn't begin to be helpful. Like the priests, they didn't have any answers.

After the toxicology report became public, we wanted to take the high road, looking for answers while also expressing our sorrow and sympathy for everyone involved. Danny, meanwhile, fell prey to loudmouth lawyer Dominic Barbara, who had offered to represent him. That's when the small rift between our families became a chasm.

In the part of New York where we lived, Barbara's name would always be linked with Joey Buttafuoco, the unsavory car repairman who had an affair in the 1990s with Amy Fisher—a teenager who shot and seriously wounded Joey's wife, Mary Jo. Dubbed the "Long Island Lolita" by the media, Amy went to jail for seven years, and Joey got six months for statutory rape. The story was a favorite in tabloid TV for years and was even made into a movie, with Dominic Barbara fanning the flames however he could.

In other words, he was not the person you would turn to if you wanted to prove your family's high moral integrity.

Dominic Barbara called a press conference almost immediately. Danny asked Warren's father and his brother David to be there at his side, but they declined. Danny was upset—not understanding how sordid it felt to the rest of us that he was going on TV. He wanted to defend his wife, but recklessly spinning the story just added fuel to the already-burning press fire.

Famously flamboyant Barbara seemed delighted to play master of ceremonies at the press conference, chatting happily and setting rules. He said a few sentences about what a terrible tragedy had occurred, but the words rang false. Standing outside in the sunshine, he told reporters that Diane Schuler could not possibly have been drunk. He turned to

Danny for confirmation. "I never saw her drunk since the day I met her," a tearful Danny announced.

Barbara suggested that something else must have caused Diane to go the wrong way. "Something happened to her brain," he said. He talked about a possible stroke and raised the issue of a tooth abscess that caused her pain. He didn't say that the toxicology report was wrong, but he introduced his investigator, Thomas Ruskin, who had been on the case only twenty-four hours but confidently announced that what happened was "so out of character for this woman, [there] has to be some other explanation."

Danny seemed slightly out of it. He looked uncomfortable, staring off into space as he spoke, but his lack of eloquence at least made him sound genuine. Rumors had swirled that Danny and Diane had fought the morning of the accident and that she was distraught driving home because he told her he wanted a divorce. "Not so," the lawyer declared.

"I love my wife, we loved each other," Danny said on cue. "She was a perfect wife, outstanding mother, hard worker, reliable person, trustworthy. I'd marry her again tomorrow. She's awesome. The best."

When Danny faltered a few times, he was helped out by his sister-in-law Jay Shuler, who is married to Danny's brother Jimmy. Angular, slim, and well-spoken, Jay was supportive—and sounded smarter than Danny. Barbara quickly pulled Jay in front of the microphone, where she said all the right things: Diane had been a nanny before she became a Cablevision executive. She treated her nieces as if they were her own girls. Family was the most important thing to her. There was no way she would jeopardize the children.

Except that Diane *had* jeopardized the children.

Danny wouldn't apologize for his wife's actions. Whatever the reasons behind the tragedy, the results were horrific—eight people dead. Instead of acknowledging that, he made it worse.

"I go to bed every night knowing my heart is clear," he blurted at the end. "She did not drink. She is not an alcoholic. My heart is resting every night when I go to bed."

The words curdled in the warm air. His wife and baby daughter were dead, and his heart rested comfortably every night?

Dominic Barbara seemed oblivious to the blunder. Pleased with the press conference, he decided to take his sleazy show on the road. With Jay as his new foil, he showed up on *Larry King Live* and CBS's *The Early Show*. Hearing about the media circus, I felt vaguely nauseous. Barbara was a clown, happy to perform, and I couldn't bear to watch or listen. Why would Danny be doing this? Could he really prove that the toxicology was wrong and something else had been behind the accident?

But I also felt just the tiniest speck of relief. Though it wasn't the way I would have handled the situation, or how I would want to investigate, I desperately needed to believe that something else had happened. I didn't want to be angry at Diane, and any explanation that could release that fury and make sense would be okay with me—whatever its source.

One comment, though, jumped out at me and I couldn't make it go away. Barbara had begun the press conference by announcing that Danny would not answer any questions about marijuana use.

Which immediately caused everyone to jump to their own conclusions.

I knew Danny had problems with anxiety and he'd had a bad reaction to the antianxiety drugs a doctor had prescribed. Was he self-medicating with pot? I could believe that, but Diane was a different story. She was a hard worker who took care of everything in the family.

Danny said he and Diane had a couple of cups of coffee together the morning of the accident. Everything was fine. A few hours later, Diane had done the unthinkable.

We all wanted to know what could possibly have happened between that last cup of coffee and Emma's call. Days later, the cell phone would be found, discarded at the side of the road, near a small truck stop. I had envisioned the children at a busy McDonald's when I last spoke with Emma, but that wasn't quite right. At that point, Diane had simply pulled over at an unattended spot by the side of the road.

The police investigation found she had made two other stops. First, early in the trip, she went to a McDonald's to buy everyone breakfast. Everyone remembered her because Bryan had wanted Chicken McNuggets and the guy at the counter insisted they didn't serve them that early.

Wanting to make sure that the children all got what they wanted, Diane asked to talk to a manager. She had been completely rational—and determined—in the conversation.

Later, she stopped again at a gas station and went into the convenience store. She left the kids in the car, and the surveillance tape at the store showed her walking through the aisles. She left without buying anything.

And that's all we knew. We would keep coming back to those scraps of information over the next months, twisting them into different shapes, trying to make them tell a story. But the evidence didn't add up to anything that ever made sense, so we kept going around in circles with no escape.

Five

Extreme stress does odd things to the mind.

I have no factual explanation for the temporary amnesia that kicked in right after the accident. Every time I woke up, I had forgotten what happened. More specifically, I didn't know that the accident had occurred or that my children weren't coming home.

One morning I got out of bed, stumbled out of my room, and found Jeannine sleeping in the hallway.

"Why are you here?" I asked, bewildered.

"I slept here," she said.

"Where are the girls?" I asked, looking around at their empty rooms.

"Jackie . . ."

"Oh, that's right. The girls are on a camping trip." I felt slightly dazed. The girls would be home soon, right? Sure they would. This morning, maybe this afternoon. But why was Jeannine here? And if she needed to sleep over, why had she stayed on the floor outside my room?

In movies, amnesia is the basis for charming entertainment—like a perky Drew Barrymore in *50 First Dates* waking up in Hawaii each morning, unable to remember that Adam Sandler has been wooing her. My amnesia wasn't quite so endearing and nobody would sail off happily into the sunset at the end. Whenever I fell asleep, my brain reset, knocking me back to the Sunday morning of the accident. Whether I jerked awake from a midday nap or got up from a fitful night's sleep, I would wander around, asking for my daughters. Sometimes I drifted into the street, as if looking for them. I'd go to the kitchen and start making lunch for them or find treats to put in their backpacks. My unconscious apparently wanted to keep repeating the day until I got it right. But, unlike a character in a movie, I could never get it right. I couldn't alter the ending.

Did I know what had happened and just refused to believe it? Even in retrospect, I can't begin to explain the tricks my mind played. I wanted so deeply and desperately to change that day that my brain wouldn't hold on to the truth. My subconscious self simply refused to accept the reality.

My friends, including Jeannine, tried to drag me back to reality. They kept newspapers in the house from the day of the accident, which they showed me repeatedly. Since two people would usually sleep over each night—curled up on the couch or outside my bedroom door—my friends had written instructions, explaining what to do when I looked at them blankly and couldn't remember anything. They all came to understand that the story of what happened to Emma, Alyson, and Katie would get written on the blackboard of my mind, then erased just as fast.

One morning, about two weeks after the accident, my friend Tara was in the house when I woke up. Then eight months pregnant but still sleeping over to be there for me, she had braced herself for the ritual of nudging me into the present. As kindly as possible, she told me why the girls weren't there, and as usual, I remained slightly hazy. She patiently read me the newspaper account. I listened. She read it again. But I wasn't the only one listening. As she described the tragedy for the second time, Warren's frustration suddenly boiled over. Struggling with his own torment and grief, he found my denial, however subconscious, too much to bear.

"Enough!" he yelled. "I don't want to listen to this anymore!"

"Why are you yelling?" I asked him, bewildered.

"Jackie, snap out of it! The girls aren't here!" he shouted.

"What do you mean?"

"Jackie, there was an accident. You know that."

"What accident?" I gazed at him, my expression blank and uncomprehending.

"The girls are not here. The girls are dead!" Warren shouted.

"Why would you say something like that?" I asked, my voice trembling.

"Because it's true."

"How can you say that?"

"It's the truth, Jackie. Look at the paper. Read it again. They're dead." He threw the frayed newspaper on the table and slammed out of the room.

I'd like to say that his fury snapped me out of the amnesia. But it didn't. Trying to speak rationally to a person who has become thoroughly removed from reality does no good. For weeks, we continued the same dance.

Warren continued to suffer from my unhinged state, and so did my friends. "Imagine how horrible it is to tell your friend that her children have passed," my dear friend Jeannine said months later, after I'd begun to comprehend what I'd put them through. "Now imagine how horrible it is to have to tell her that a hundred times."

I still feel guilty that I added to others' anguish, but the memory loss wasn't willful. Denial may be a survival mechanism that kicks in when events are more than we can bear, an evolutionary tic that guarantees we go on despite overwhelming circumstances. Doctors had also prescribed heavy drugs for me to help with depression, anxiety, and sleeplessness, and the combination of Xanax, Ambien, clonazepam, and a few others might have caused a chemical disconnect.

Warren didn't typically have to face my confusion in the morning because I regularly woke up before dawn, while he was still sleeping, to go running. For years, I had been part of a running group of five or six moms who met most mornings before the sun rose to exercise. We'd start texting each other at about 4:30 a.m.—who's in, who's out. "Was up all night with crying baby, so too tired to run," an apologetic text might read. Or "Count me in! Got some sleep." Those early-morning beeps on my phone made me smile and gave me a sense of belonging.

Once the group gathered, we'd take off for six miles, chatting and sharing stories all the way. A kaffeeklatsch on steroids, we ran fast and gossiped endlessly. Even with a stop at the local deli afterward for actual coffee, I'd be home by 6:15 a.m., heart beating and endorphins soaring. It had long been my favorite way to start a day.

I didn't plan to start running so quickly after the accident, but it seemed the most natural thing in the world. Friends and family packed our house for days after the funeral, but I was disoriented and had stopped eating. Wandering through our living room on Sunday night, I noticed my friend Bernadette. In her mid-thirties but with the looks and energy of a teenage rock star, Bernadette was one of the linchpins of the running group. She had married early and had four children, the two younger ones in the same grades as Alyson and Katie.

I knew the next day was Monday, but what did I do on Mondays now, in this post-accident world? What could connect me to the person I had been just a week ago?

I tapped Bernadette on the shoulder. "I'm going running tomorrow, right?" I asked her, completely out of the blue.

"Sure you are," Bernadette said without hesitation. She smiled at me, as if she'd never thought I'd do anything else. "But Jackie, if you're going to run, you have to eat."

I had no taste for food and couldn't imagine how I would ever swallow anything. A tightness perpetually clutched at my throat. Nothing tempted me, and I'd lost several pounds in the week since the accident. For some people, that might be good news, but I'd been slim to start with and didn't have a lot of reserves. Bernadette immediately made a new rule: If I wanted to go running, I had to gulp down three cans of Ensure. In coming weeks, that simple rule might have saved my life. It was the only thing that got me to ingest any calories at all.

My friends knew that I'd battled bulimia from the time I was a teenager. Trying to cure the condition, I'd met with specialists in eating disorders and tried various healthy eating regimens. I'd had individual counseling and gone to group therapy sessions. But combating the disorder was a difficult challenge, and finding a remedy proved elusive.

"If you know it's a problem, why don't you just stop?" Warren asked me once, when we were dating. However bewildered he felt, he remained supportive and had come over to New Jersey to drive me to a doctor's appointment.

"I don't know," I said. "It's not that easy." Why don't overweight people stop eating cookies? Why don't diabetics stay away from candy? I've heard about people who pay thousands of dollars for a week at a weight-loss spa, then sneak out at night for a pepperoni pizza. Our short-term impulse controls and long-term goals don't always match up.

The bulimia stopped during my pregnancies but kept coming back. I never let the girls know about the problem and hid from them when I threw up after binges. Nobody has quite figured out what really causes bulimia, but it's generally understood that feelings of inadequacy definitely play a part. So does a desire to please people and keep your life under tight control.

After the accident, my subconscious must have finally accepted that however much I monitored what I ate, life would spiral in its own direction. I could never control what really mattered. In fact, trying to control anything now seemed pointless. The bulimia disappeared and never resurfaced.

Members of our running group usually drove to Bernadette's house in the early morning to start the run from there. But now they changed the plan to make it easier for me. I set my alarm for 4:30 a.m., and whichever friend had stayed over at our house groggily got up, helped me find running clothes, and walked me outside to the street corner. The group gathered there around me—and we took off.

Some mornings I kept pace with the group and joined the conversation. Other times I bolted ahead by myself, going so fast that nobody could keep up, as if I wanted to outrun my own pain, leave the past behind and go to a different, distant place.

When the worst has happened, how do you go on? Sometimes all you can do is put one foot in front of the other—quite literally. Running was a bit of normalcy I could hang on to when everything else had become tangled and twisted. I had run before the accident and now I was running again. Tying on sneakers and going into the cool morning air was something I had always done without the girls at my side, so, unlike most of my activities, it wasn't haunted by memories.

Coming home from the run at 6:15 a.m. used to be ideal. After getting the day off to an exhilarating start, I had plenty of time to wake the girls, make them breakfast, and pack their lunches.

Now I came home to unbearable silence.

The quiet in the house hit me like a sledgehammer every single morning, after every single run. Instead of excited chatter bouncing off the walls with my three girls dashing around getting ready for the day, I faced only silence. The noiselessness had an almost palpable presence—a looming, gloomy headstone marking all the words that weren't being uttered, the laughs not laughed, the footsteps not landing on the floor.

In the silent house, I looked at the clock and felt myself sinking even lower. What did I have to do all day? The hours ahead stretched endlessly. After the girls were born, I had quit my office job and become a full-time mom. I had worried about losing a bit of my identity, but being a mother gave me a sense of purpose. Now, without my girls, I had no purpose, no reason for being.

As I floundered, Warren tried to stay strong, talking to lawyers and handling all the tangled legal and financial problems. I had always wanted him to go to church with us and now he was attending mass twice a day. I had wanted him to exercise and now he was running and riding his bike a lot. He walked the dog. One day he bounded into the kitchen where I was sitting and I looked up and felt that flush of adoration, like when we were first together.

How great to experience that again. But it didn't last long. With the girls ripped from me, my heart had been torn out—and how could I care about anyone if I had no heart? I couldn't say "I love you." If Warren tried to hug me, I stood there limply until the embrace ended. I had turned to cold stone, which probably isn't what any man wants in a wife.

Late in the summer, Melissa and Brad invited us to their vacation house on Long Beach Island in New Jersey, and Warren and I decided that a sandy beach and new scenery might do us good. The getaway had an effect I wouldn't have expected.

On the second day of the vacation, Warren took a shower after a day at the beach. I looked at him as he dried off with a towel—and felt a twinge of our old attraction. For the first time since the girls died, I imagined having sex with my husband. Just as quickly as I felt the pull, I was racked with guilt. Was it wrong to feel desire? Even though I wanted to be close to Warren, I couldn't let myself want to, I couldn't give in to it.

A strong physical attraction had been a part of our marriage from the start. Warren had complained once, years ago, that I never initiated sex, and all I could do was laugh.

"How could I? The minute I walk into the bedroom, you're all over me," I teased him.

Since the accident, we often stayed far apart, going to sleep at different times or in separate places. Alone together in the bedroom we were more likely to fight—or cry—than to make love. But something about the beach house—the fresh air, the freedom from the oppressive silence in our own home—let us both remember what used to be. That night in bed, I was drawn to him, and he responded. As the beach breeze wafted through the window, Warren forgot that he was a man in torment and remembered only that he was a man.

"Warren, we can't do this," I said, suddenly feeling uncertain and pulling away.

"Yes, Jackie, we can. We have to," he said.

"But the girls—" I began to protest.

"This isn't about the girls. It's about us."

Having sex that night, I let myself be distracted for a few minutes from the black horror I couldn't otherwise escape. It was nice to feel my husband close, but I felt guilty about experiencing pleasure and wouldn't let the connection unfreeze my heart. I remember that night on Long Beach Island so strongly because it didn't happen again for a long, long time.

Six

I n my unhinged state throughout August, I felt that I had two mysteries to solve. The first was why Diane drove onto that highway. The second was how Emma, Alyson, and Katie had died in the car. Maybe it was obvious to other people that a horrific car accident could snuff out three little girls. But it made no sense to me. I kept thinking of how normal and pretty they looked when I gazed at them before the funeral.

"I want to see the autopsy reports," I told Warren.

"No you don't," he said.

"I do. I swear I do. I have to know what happened to the girls."

"The autopsies won't give you any answers."

Warren had the autopsy reports but kept them hidden from me. I knew exactly where they were—and one day while he was out, I finally got the courage to read them.

I could feel my heart pounding as I slowly took the official documents out of the drawer. Would the medical examiner's findings tell me some secret that I hadn't yet known or imagined? Would I finally understand what my daughters felt during those final, horrible moments?

I held the autopsy reports in trembling fingers, stunned at first by how short each seemed. Three skimpy pages, one for each girl. Barely one tiny paragraph on each page. How could the girls be dead with so little wrong with them?

I read the few sentences over and over, but the words just blurred in front of me. I called my friend Maria, a hospice nurse, and she rushed over to help me understand the clinical lingo. Emma and Alyson had

died at the scene, Katie at the hospital. The dry report blandly enumer-
ated the findings of head trauma, broken clavicles, and internal injuries.
Clearly this wasn't the grandiose explanation I wanted.

"It doesn't make sense," I said, calling Jeannine later that afternoon.
"The girls looked so perfect at the funeral home. Something else must
have happened."

"Like what?"

"I don't know. But how could they all die?"

"The force of the trauma from the car accident caused internal injuries," Jeannine said simply.

An instant, an accident. How could that one moment end everything that mattered in my life, everything that defined me? Our lives
are supposed to go on a straight path, and when they veer so dramatically, how can we grasp that what has been so vital and alive is no longer
here? I still wanted to believe in an orderly universe, to find bigger forces
at work that would give meaning to what right now felt so completely
meaningless.

I called our pediatrician, Dr. Ana Dellorusso, and asked to see the
girls' medical records.

"Jackie, they were healthy children," she said gently. "What are you
trying to find?"

"Maybe they all had a heart disease. Something genetic that they
were born with," I said, trying to sound rational.

"Why would you think that?" she asked.

"Because it doesn't make sense that they all died. Maybe there was
an underlying reason I don't know about. I want to see their records."

She could have told me to stop being silly, but instead she let me take
the thick files that had accumulated over the years as the girls came in for
vaccinations and well-child visits, for the occasional cold or strep throat.
I didn't find anything suspicious because there was nothing to find. All
three girls had been perfectly healthy. The car accident—nothing else—
had killed them. "What happened in that car was just the laws of physics," Dr. Dellorusso explained, trying to give me an answer.

Physics. Others had said the same thing to me, talking about trajectories and impact and force. But how could something so cold and mathematical explain what had happened to three warm and vibrant girls?

Not completely convinced, I turned my attention to the girls' teeth, conjuring mysterious dental problems from thin air. Danny's lawyer had raised the possibility that a gum abscess had somehow been involved in Diane's actions. The theory might have been a reach, but since we had all resorted to grasping at straws, I wondered if something comparable could have weakened the girls. Is that why they had died?

Emma had already started going to an orthodontist and wore a palate extender as a first step to the braces she would eventually get. We had a drama every night as I took the tiny key and turned it in the appliance, per the orthodontist's instructions.

"I'm gagging! You're choking me," she'd complain some nights, when she leaned back for me to make the adjustment.

"I know it's uncomfortable," I would say, struggling to do it right. "But you look so pretty now when you smile, and you want to have a beautiful smile when all the grown-up teeth come in, too."

"I still don't like it," she grumbled. But because she was such a good girl, she always took good care of the apparatus, even when she woke up the next morning with her mouth aching. She brushed carefully and worried about hygiene. The orthodontist had warned us to stay away from certain foods that could get stuck in the wires, so at the movies, she walked by the popcorn and only allowed herself Tic Tacs as a treat.

"What kid goes to the movies and only buys Tic Tacs?" I'd ask, teasing her. "You'd be okay with a chocolate bar. Can I get you a Kit Kat instead of Tic Tacs?"

"No, this is fine," she'd say, always cautious. Alyson and Katie made up for their abstemious sister by loading up at the concession stand and walking happily to their seats with popcorn in one hand, candy bars and a soda in the other.

Now I felt yet another pang of despair. I couldn't bear to think that I had asked Emma to put up with a moment's discomfort for the grown-up smile she would never get to show.

But maybe something else had gone wrong tooth-wise that I didn't even know about. Once I started obsessing about the subject, Jeannine agreed to drive me to the dentist's office so I could examine the girls' records.

"You're not going to find anything," she warned me, trying to find the right balance between being supportive and sensible.

"I might," I said, not ready for rationality.

But, sure enough, the dentist's records showed that the girls had good teeth, no abscesses, hardly even a cavity.

"I'm sorry," Jeannine said. "I know you wanted a different answer. But I guess it's physics, just like everybody has been saying."

Physics. Even if Albert Einstein gave me a personal lecture on energy and force fields, I still wouldn't accept the answer.

I knew my pursuit of the autopsy reports and the medical and dental records lacked logic, but I had a desperate drive to find a sensible story that could explain the absolute senselessness of what had happened. I wanted a practical reason that I could repeat to myself at night as I lay in bed forlorn and sobbing. Fighting with Warren and at wit's end about how I could go on, I needed a narrative that put all the facts in place.

Having grown up in the Catholic Church, I was used to homilies and simple stories where all the facts lined up: good and evil, an orderly world, God's reason for everything. But my story now was all disorder and chaos. Good and innocent children were dead, and unless I could understand why, it felt like the world had gone completely off its axis. My nagging Catholic guilt kept insisting that God must be punishing me, which just added to my anguish. I had no idea what I had done to deserve such outsize wrath and vengeance.

In my search for answers, I suppose I also subconsciously hoped to absolve Diane of blame. Maybe that sounds backward. The media had already condemned her, and I could have joined right in, dumping all the culpability for the tragedy on her vodka-swilling. But I just couldn't reconcile the kind Diane I knew with the evil Diane depicted by the tabloids. And I suppose self-protective mechanisms kicked in again, because if I'd allowed myself to believe that she had done this on purpose, I would simply have gone crazy.

Dominic Barbara's investigator Ruskin started talking about exhuming Diane's body to search for more clues. I understood the impetus, but I also knew it could backfire. Who knew what they would actually find in the quest to clear Diane's name.

One day I called Jay Schuler, Danny's sister-in-law, who shared my fascination with plumbing the depths of the tragedy over and over. For hours, we would ponder the possibilities.

Theory #1: Diane had a tooth abscess.

Diane hated dentists. One of the surveillance tapes at the convenience store showed her walking in, talking briefly to the clerk, then walking out when she couldn't find what she wanted. Police speculated that she had been looking for pain medication.

Neither Jay nor I quite knew how to link the theory of the throbbing tooth to the final result. Jay thought Diane might have begun drinking to ease the pain, but I couldn't see her chugging vodka in front of the children.

The facts pointed in one direction, but my heart pointed in another. I knew all about the toxicology report and the bottle of vodka found on the scene. But I kept thinking of the quote attributed to Albert Einstein: If the facts don't fit the theory, change the facts.

When it came right down to it, I didn't believe Diane had been drunk. On the phone before the accident, she had slurred her words, but that could have meant a stroke or a seizure. And when I had spoken to her forty minutes earlier, she had been fine. The police report might have concluded that she had gone from fine to deadly drunk in forty minutes, but I couldn't fathom it.

In one of our endless conversations, Jay reminded me of a case she'd heard of in which a fireman died in the line of duty; when tests showed a high blood alcohol level, experts testified that at scorchingly hot temperatures, blood sugar can morph to mimic high alcohol levels.

Theory #2: Someone in McDonald's drugged her.

After Diane insisted on getting what the children wanted (lunch at breakfast-time), she made a fuss and spoke to the manager. Was it possible she annoyed someone—either behind the counter or in front—

enough to take revenge? Some version of the date-rape drug would have knocked her out in the car. Maybe it sounded unlikely, but was anything in this whole event probable or predictable?

Jay spun some stories that seemed too far out even to consider. She told me about a drug bust at that McDonald's involving some employees just a few months earlier, and a police officer, somehow related to the events on the Taconic, who had died under strange circumstances. She talked about the possibility of conspiracies and cover-ups.

No matter how far-fetched or realistic our theories were, we still had nothing but conjecture, and the bottom line remained: no simple explanation fit.

Maybe what kept the tragedy so alive in the media was its mystery.

"I know you need to find answers," I told Jay. "But if you're ever one hundred percent confident that Diane was just drunk, please don't tell me."

"Why?" she asked.

"Because I can't think like that," I said. "I need to be in a good spot with Warren, and hating Diane won't help. I have to believe that she was the person I knew."

I needed even the merest sliver of hope that something else had happened that day, otherwise I'd hate Diane and I'd hate Warren and then I would not be able to go on. Still, no matter what the explanation, the fact remained that Diane had been behind the wheel in the accident that killed my girls.

Seven

Warren went back to work in September, about two months after the accident. He owns a real-estate appraisal company, and since the mortgage crisis hit, he hadn't been quite as busy as before. But he had a job, a place to go. In general, he wanted to get through each day with as little emotion as possible, and work allowed him a mental checklist to get through. When he got home, he'd have dinner, watch sports on TV, and go to sleep—another day without the girls completed. By staying regimented, he didn't have to think.

I could do nothing but think. Endless questions spun through my mind, tormenting me. Had the girls suffered? Did they know what was happening as the car sped along the Taconic Parkway? What were their final thoughts? Were they scared?

I played and replayed each horrible moment in my mind. I needed to talk. I wanted someone to help me take the pain away. But how could Warren do that for me when he was struggling with his own anguish? Our approaches to the overwhelming grief were miles apart. I looked to him for strength, but all I saw was heartache. We were both broken, but in different ways.

Love should be a balm in times of grief, but instead, being together just caused us more hurt. Every time I looked at Warren, I thought: *It was your sister who did this. Your sister destroyed our lives.* I couldn't blame him for her actions, but there was nobody left to hate. Warren was in front of me every morning and night, and the anger burned. When I saw the misery in Warren's eyes, I knew he couldn't silence the chorus of guilt ringing in his own head. My anger and his guilt—the tensions between us grew in every way. We began fighting so ferociously that our friends felt uncomfortable about leaving us alone together. Anger, grief, guilt, and resentment are a toxic combination.

Warren started working long hours again, feeling better when he could keep himself distracted and his mind occupied. But his office is near our house, and one afternoon, I found him napping on the couch.

"Why are you here?" I asked when he finally woke up.

"I was tired."

"You're tired because you stay up at night," I sniped.

"What do you want me to do?" he asked.

"Take sleeping pills at night so you can work during the day."

"Leave me alone. I'll nap when I want to."

A ridiculous fight? Of course—they all were. On some level, the argument about his nap revealed my escalating fears about money. I didn't have a job and was worried that Warren wouldn't be able to work as hard as he had before. The deeper problem was that I had always turned to my husband for strength and now he had none to give. The early burst of courage and fortitude he'd shown had seeped away. He wanted to help, but he couldn't take care of me anymore, since it was all he could do to take care of himself. As a man, he liked to fix problems. But this was beyond fixing.

One reason grieving couples break up is that simply seeing each other is a constant reminder of heartbreak. Warren would get up in the morning and hear me crying or see me upset and the rest of his day would be ruined. Sometimes I pretended to be asleep until after he left for work so that he didn't have to face my despair. People told us we should work on our marriage and communicate better, but that just made us laugh. Work on the marriage? We barely had the emotional energy to work our way through a bowl of oatmeal.

What's worse, being happy—even for a few minutes—seemed like a betrayal of the girls. Happiness became as dangerous an emotion to avoid as any other.

A few Sundays before the accident, Warren and I had gone with the girls to a baseball game at Citi Field. An ardent Mets fan, Warren had season tickets at the old Shea Stadium, and once a season, he'd treat each girl to a father-daughter date of baseball, hot dogs, and happy time together. Then Shea was torn down, and when the fancy new stadium went up, so did ticket prices.

That Sunday afternoon, Warren wanted to do something memorable with the whole family for the Fourth of July weekend. And for him, that meant the Mets. He asked our friends Mark and Isabelle if they wanted to join us, and when they agreed, he rushed to get tickets. It was last-minute, and he sprung for wildly expensive seats.

"Who cares, let's do it," he said.

"If it costs so much, shouldn't we do something the girls really like?" I asked.

Too late. He had the tickets in hand.

"They'll like this," he promised.

We ate lunch at the fancy Acela Club at the stadium and cheered all afternoon from our up-close seats. The children jumped up and down and waved to their favorite players. It was the kind of happy-go-lucky experience that leaves you wrung out from sheer pleasure by the end. Warren's enthusiasm percolated through all of us.

"An expensive day, but the best day," Warren said as we fell into bed that night.

Looking back to that day after the accident, I suspected that I'd never feel such lighthearted elation again. And I'd probably never go back to a Mets game, because the associations would be too painful.

But in September, we returned to Citi Field. One of our friends, Paul Asencio, worked as an executive for the Mets, and he and his wife, Heather, had become intertwined in our lives since the accident. We sought comfort in them, as we did with so many others, and they responded. Paul and Heather must have looked at their own three energetic daughters and felt extraordinary empathy for us. With great warmth and generosity, Paul invited us and all our friends to be his guests at the game.

On a lovely fall evening, we arrived at the stadium and were ushered into a prime suite. No ballpark franks for us tonight—there was a bartender serving drinks and gourmet food piled high. As our friends milled around laughing and talking, Paul arranged for third baseman David Wright, Alyson's favorite player, to come by and say hello to us.

David Wright! It was like being face-to-face with George Clooney. The All-Star slugger posed for pictures and chatted for a few minutes. Warren was over the moon. And then it got even better. Paul took us down onto the field.

For a big baseball fan like Warren—and even for me—it was like stepping onto hallowed ground. Warren's dad came with us, and we all had silly smiles plastered across our faces.

Oh my gosh, I thought, my head spinning from the lights, the excitement, and the famous players tossing balls a few feet from us. *I'm having too much fun!*

I looked at Warren, and we both grinned. For the first time since the accident, we were having a good time. We wanted the night to go on and on. When the ball game ended, we hung out with our friends awhile, letting the high spirits linger. Several of our friends offered to come home with us, but we said we were fine. Not just fine, happy for once! We could go home by ourselves, no problem.

Still slightly euphoric from the excitement of the ballpark, we arrived back in Floral Park after midnight. When we had the girls at home, we always rushed back from an evening out so we could pay the babysitter and drive her home. And maybe we had that image in our heads as we went inside. But of course there was no babysitter to greet us.

Nobody. Nothing. Emptiness.

Just that sledgehammer of silence.

The pain smacked against me and I ran to the girls' room, crying and wailing and unable to talk. Going from being so happy and light at the ballpark to such misery at home was almost unbearable. Was it worth going out if we had so much pain when we returned?

Warren tried to stay positive.

"At least we had one good evening," he said, following me upstairs. "Aren't you glad we went?"

"No!" I screamed, sitting on Alyson's empty bed and rocking back and forth in agony. "This is much worse than if we had just stayed home alone."

We began to fight—vicious, horrible accusations thrown back and forth. The pain morphed to anger that we couldn't contain, and we screamed and raged at each other.

Isabelle and Mark came over to alleviate the tension and wisely stayed on, seeing how our spirits, which had soared so high, inevitably dropped so low. Yes, the emotional swing was almost unbearable, and so was the penetrating guilt. How did we dare allow ourselves to laugh and be happy and enjoy a ball game when our children would never have fun again?

After that outing, I once again resisted leaving the house. Big excursions didn't end well and small ones produced their own kind of torment. Even going out for simple errands was fraught. The girls had so often been at my side for jaunts around town that every store I walked into evoked ghostly images. Looking in a window one day, I saw a shoe display and suddenly Emma stood next to me, pointing out the clogs she wanted as we laughed together about how cute they'd look on her. She wanted them right then, but instead I promised to buy them next week.

What was I waiting for?

As I stared at the clogs, my heart began pounding and I felt my throat closing up and the air squeezing out of my chest.

Should I buy them for her?

Unable to tell reality from fantasy, I started gasping and clutching at my chest. A woman called out to me to see if I needed help, but I ran away, arms flailing, and escaped down the street.

Yes, I need help, I thought. *I need my daughters. I want to die and be with them.*

I knew the symptoms of a panic attack—the pounding heart and the closed throat—because I'd had them before. Hyperventilating makes you feel like you'll have a heart attack or die. For most people, that's frightening and they breathe into a paper bag to get the oxygen flow under control. But I had no paper bag and I wanted to die, anyway.

Take me right now and I'll see the girls!

I already felt like a freak, and panic attacks like this one just aggravated my sense of not belonging in normal society. Better to stay home and avoid the embarrassment.

Also better not to bother eating meals than to risk going into a grocery store, where every aisle was a minefield of memories that could blow up in my face. The girls and I had always shopped, cooked, and baked together; the joy of that had been so central to our lives that I couldn't bear getting anywhere near the kitchen now. Right after the accident, I packed up my Cuisinart and KitchenAid and mixing bowls and gave them all away. I'd cook only for the dog. Friends still brought over dinner for us—opening the door to the baskets and casseroles that were left was a nightly treat—but our cupboards were bare. One night at about eleven o'clock, I heard Warren call Isabelle, our next-door neighbor, and ask if he could come over and get a snack.

"There's nothing to eat here," he moaned. "I'll take any junk food you have."

The next day, I thought about going to the small, local grocery so he'd have fruit or cookies. Then I flashed back to the Sunday afternoon just a few months earlier when I'd asked Warren to stay with the girls so I could make a quick trip to the market. He'd agreed, but as I headed out the door, I heard Emma's little voice.

"Mommy, can I go with you?" she asked.

"Sure," I said, smiling to myself. The trip would take longer, but it would be more fun with her along.

"Mommy, can I go, too?" Alyson asked, jumping up from the sofa.

And before I could say yes, Katie had piped in, "Mommy, me, too!"

So we'd all headed out together and left Warren in peace to enjoy a baseball game on TV. At our favorite market, the girls had grabbed for one of the portable scanners. They liked the high-tech shopping method of selecting a product off the shelf, scanning it, and then dropping it in the bag. The personal devices were meant to make shopping quicker, but with Emma, Alyson, and Katie each clamoring "My turn to scan!" at every item, a jaunt through the aisles took forever.

But how could I complain? The grocery store was like a giant playground for us. Sometimes Katie liked to ride on the end of the shopping cart, but generally the girls wanted to help. That day, as usual, I gave them little tasks.

"Can you go to that case and get milk?" I asked—and then watched as they raced off together to decide on the perfect carton.

At some point, Alyson and Emma dashed to the end of the aisle to pick out the spaghetti they wanted. I got distracted with something else, and when I rolled the cart to where they should be, they had disappeared.

"Emma? Aly?"

No answer. I panicked.

"Emma and Aly? Where are you?"

Fright ripped through me like a thunderbolt. I searched frantically but no little girls were playing by the pasta. I was just about to raise an alarm for help when they veered back around the corner of the aisle, giggling at the surprise treat they'd found for me.

"There you are," I said, my voice shaking.

"Did we do something wrong?" Emma asked, worried.

"Only that I couldn't see you," I said weakly, pulling them close in a double hug. My heart had been pounding so hard at the fear of losing them that I could hardly breathe. It had taken me a few minutes to recover my high spirits.

Now I knew that if I stepped into the supermarket again, I would be looking for the girls to reappear around every corner. And they never would. It wasn't worth steeling myself against the haunting memories just to buy a loaf of bread.

Going into any public place also meant worrying about the stares and whispers of strangers and casual acquaintances. I'm still not sure it really happened, but I imagined that people who recognized me from TV news reports gaped at me in shock and curiosity. Did they hope I'd cry? Did they want me to be courageous? Maybe they just wondered what somebody looks like when everything that matters has been ripped away. Some people would come over and touch my arm.

"Oooh, Jackie. How are you?" they'd ask, with that look of sadness.

I appreciated the sympathy, but I always wondered whether people thought poorly of me as a mom. I didn't want to have to defend myself to strangers or offer an explanation to try to counter what they'd read in the newspapers. In an odd way, I was embarrassed, horrified at being linked to the sordid events of the "Taconic Mom." I wanted people to acknowledge the girls and remember them, but I didn't want anyone to focus on me.

"I'm praying for you," people often said.

"Don't pray for me. Pray for the girls," I always replied, rushing away.

Still, I understood the fascination. The worst had happened to me. For years, I had been just like every other mom in our town dashing around with her kids, and now I was the walking embodiment of every parent's bleakest nightmare. From being an ordinary woman, I had become a marked woman, with a metaphoric scarlet letter: *T* for Tragic, or *L* for Lost Everything.

When a tragedy of this magnitude occurs, people instinctively scramble for reasons why it could never happen to them. If someone whose very existence has been devastated by disaster is really no different from you, that means you're vulnerable, too. Finding an explanation (however false) for what the other person did wrong makes you feel more in control of your own destiny.

One day when I was out walking the dog, a woman I barely knew walked by and stopped in her tracks on seeing me.

"I don't know how you do it," she said, bursting into tears. "If I were you, I couldn't go on."

Never had admiration been so misplaced. She saw me as some hard-shelled other who had been chosen for tragedy because I could cope with it. But I was just another mom, exactly like her. I didn't want to go on. I still thought of killing myself every day, but that took courage, too. I had no maps or guideposts. Nobody had written a book I could read on how to behave. I was simply an ordinary woman thrust into a situation far outside what any of us expect or imagine.

You are me, I wanted to tell her. *I am you. This could happen to any of us.*

My life stood as scary proof that you can do everything right—follow all the expected paths of college, marriage, children, community—and still be shattered. Being a good person doesn't protect you from the randomness of life and death. My children were innocent victims. Warren and I had done nothing wrong—certainly nothing to warrant pain of this magnitude. Strangers could look at me with derision or disdain or doubt, but that didn't change the fact that tragedy had landed on our household for no obvious reason.

I suppose people felt safer about their own futures if they could list all the ways I was to blame. Vicious blogs appeared online, postings by people who didn't know me or any real facts. Their opinions should have been meaningless, but I couldn't stop reading them. Warren would find me sobbing at my computer at 2 a.m., crushed by some callous comment from an anonymous attacker. Warren eventually took down the Wi-Fi in our house and shut off the Internet. But it was too late. The cruel remarks were already ingrained in my mind:

She must have known Diane was an alcoholic.

She never should have let her kids go in that car.

Somebody could have stopped Diane after Emma called crying.

Rationally, I knew the answers to all of those "should-haves."

First, we had never seen Diane drink anything more than a single beer or the occasional piña colada and had certainly never ever seen her drunk.

Second, Diane was family, and we trusted and even relied on each other. To people who seemed dubious, I wanted to say: Think about your own sister or sister-in-law. Would there be any reason to worry about her behind the wheel? If I'd had any inkling that something might go wrong, I would have tied myself to the fender before letting my three innocent girls drive away in that car.

And finally, once we realized something was wrong on the drive home from the campsite, we did everything we could to stop Diane. Warren begged Diane to stay where she was. He got all the information he could and raced out to rescue his family. We called the authorities. We asked for help.

We did everything we could.

In the midst of crisis, all you can do is act honestly, openly, and with the purest of motives. That's what we did.

Warren and I never spoke publicly or tried to defend ourselves. Truth isn't always a deterrent to what others choose to believe. People wanted to find reasons why we must have been responsible, and their need to blame played into our own irrational guilt. In my darkest moments, I believed I was responsible. My job in life had been to protect my girls, and I had failed.

Fortunately, my friends had a completely different reaction. I'm told it's common for friends and acquaintances to run away when a tragedy happens—they're not sure what to say or how to react, and they struggle with the uncomfortable feeling that bad fortune is contagious. But my crowd did the opposite. My friends became superfriends. They rallied around Warren and me, completely supportive and nonjudgmental.

Most of us had children the same age and, since they liked being together, we bonded through their activities. Our lives were constantly intertwined. My friend Deana taught all the children religion, and she and Isabelle and I were Girl Scout Daisy leaders together. We had way too much fun helping our littlest Scouts earn their "petals." Isabelle and I and several other of our friends banded together to cheer at soccer games or gymnastics practice. With sports, Scouts, and religion, and all the kids feeling like one family, we could have been mistaken for a revival of *The Brady Bunch*.

The moms' supportive spirits must have set a good example for the children, because they always looked out for each other. For instance, one little girl in our circle didn't like to be away from her mom. When she found herself alone one afternoon, I saw Alyson stepping in to hold her hand.

"You'll be okay," Alyson told her. Seeing that kindness in my girls made me so proud.

After the accident, however, a veil of shock descended on all the families. We heard about some children who started having nightmares; others who refused to let their parents out of their sight. One of Alyson's close friends sobbed hysterically when the family set off for a vacation, and it took awhile for the parents to realize that she was terrified about being in the backseat of their minivan on the highway.

Since most of our friends had young children, their first instincts must have been to protect them and try to make them feel secure. But they never wavered in their stalwart support of Warren and me. Isabelle made a schedule so somebody was always in the house to answer the phone, make sure we had food, keep us from sinking into the abyss. Or that was the goal.

We sank, but at least the house stayed clean.

"Dude, who are those two with all the enthusiasm?" my laid-back half brother, Mark, asked in wonderment one day. He had happened to come over when two of my friends, dizzying dervishes of energy, spent the day scrubbing, polishing, and putting things away.

Mark didn't have to clean or organize to be welcome. Even though he was much younger than me and the product of my dad's second marriage, I'd always been close to him. He lived in New Jersey and now tried to visit as often as he could.

My friend Karen—the whirling dervish whom Mark admired—had moved to another town awhile before the accident and we saw each other less. But now she came back into my life like a much-needed shot of 5-Hour Energy. After signing up on the schedule to be with us on Tuesdays, she loyally showed up at the house every week. One Tuesday, with all that energy, she didn't want to sit around.

"Come on, I'm taking you out," she said matter-of-factly.

"To do what?" I asked.

"It doesn't matter. Shopping. A grown-up playdate. We're getting out of the house."

For some reason, I numbly agreed. I didn't know how I would fill the days and weeks that stretched endlessly ahead of me, so to have one taken care of seemed a strange relief.

And not just one—one day every single week. Tuesdays with Karen became an inviolable part of the schedule. Every week, she arrived at my door with a plan for the day. Since she had three children of her own, the exact same ages as Emma, Alyson, and Katie, she could easily have found reasons to skip a week now and then. But she never did. Even during school vacations, she arranged for babysitters so she wouldn't have to let me down. I felt guilty—I didn't want to disrupt anybody's life. But she never gave me a choice.

"I don't feel like going out today," I moaned one Tuesday, huddled on the couch in sweatpants, with no intention of moving.

"You'll feel better once you're out," she said brightly. "Get dressed. We're going shopping."

"Not today."

"Yup, today!" She grinned and clapped her hands, a combination friend, guru, and personal shopper. She wouldn't take no for an answer. Karen, like so many of my friends, seemed instinctively to understand how to help someone sunk in depression:

1. Get them moving.
2. Plan something they can look forward to.
3. Insist they engage in the world.
4. Talk to them.
5. Be a constant presence.

Karen's depression-fighting strategy usually involved retail therapy. We would go to a mall, browse through stores, buy a few things, have lunch. For those few hours, I'd feel like an ordinary person again rather than a tragic freak. *I'm shopping for sweaters! I must be just like everyone else!*

One day in Lord & Taylor, a tall, flamboyant makeup artist for one of the major companies stopped us as we wandered down the cosmetics aisle and introduced himself as Sterling.

"Ladies, come on over here. How about a makeover?" he asked, mincing around us. "I can make you even more bee-you-ti-ful."

I shook my head no, but Karen gave me a little nudge. "Go. Do it."

"Oh yes, let's do it!" Sterling said. His prancing was already making me smile, so I let him lead me over to the makeup chair. As I sat down, he studied my face for a moment, then showily whipped out his brushes and pots of color.

"Keep it very natural," I warned him as he started in.

He nodded and, with a grand gesture, started applying cover-up to the dark circles under my eyes. He moved with such exuberance that a scout for the Alvin Ailey dance troupe would have grabbed him on the spot.

"Oh, what a nice life you ladies have," he burbled as he made broad strokes across my face. "You get to spend the day lunching and shopping."

Nice life? I looked over at Karen and we exchanged a smirk. He had no idea; it was such a relief.

When Sterling finished, he held up a mirror for me. His idea of "natural" included red lipstick, bright pink cheeks, and smoky eyes. Not my usual look.

"What do you think?" I asked Karen.

"Bee-you-ti-ful," she said, and we both laughed.

Maybe I didn't like the eye shadow shade, but Sterling had given me the perfect makeover. I'd been able to forget who I was for a few minutes—and even laugh. I couldn't imagine a better transformation.

The excursions with Karen gave a measure of consistency to my week, and I looked forward to Tuesdays with an excitement way out of proportion to what we actually did. The jaunts gave Warren some peace of mind, too—for several hours each week he didn't have to worry about me, and I wasn't likely to call.

Since shopping with a friend seemed like the definition of normalcy, I felt a surge of satisfaction at taking out my purchases at night. Warren took a different view—particularly when I came home every Tuesday for four weeks straight with a new hat and scarf. To me, nothing is more comforting and homespun than a knit scarf, and my heart was so cold that any sensation of warmth gave me pleasure. Small purchases, but the pretty layers of bright-colored yarn made me happy. I liked the textures of the nubbly knits, and wrapping myself in a snug new scarf gave me a feeling—both literal and metaphoric—of being cozy and protected.

After seeing me unwrap my new knits every week for a month, Warren grimaced when I opened up another shopping bag one Tuesday evening.

"Another hat and scarf?" he asked. "What do you need them for?"

"I like them," I said, my voice rising.

"Okay, but you've bought one every week. How many hats and scarves can a person wear?"

"Why do you care?"

"It just seems like a waste of money."

I felt ready to explode. "Really, Warren? My kids are dead and you're going to question me about a hat and scarf? If I want a thousand hats and scarves, who the hell cares?"

"Jackie—"

"I mean it!" I screamed. "My kids are dead. Don't talk to me about a hat and scarf!"

The conversation ended quickly.

Maybe it wasn't my most shining moment, but I felt a bit of vindication later that week when the argument came up again in front of the couples therapist we had started seeing once a week. Dr. O'Brien was usually nonjudgmental and didn't give opinions, but this time, he took my side.

"You have a lot to be angry about, Warren," he said. "I understand that. But do you really want to fight with Jackie about a hat?"

"Not one hat," Warren grumbled. "Four weeks' worth of hats."

But then he let it go, and I half smiled at Dr. O'Brien. I suppose I was grateful I had won that one. But for some reason, I didn't feel very victorious.

Eight

Doctors talk about depression as a chemical disorder of the brain, which is why antidepressants can often lift a funk. But bad situations like death or divorce or job loss can trigger depression in anyone, no matter how chemically balanced you otherwise may be. I'd battled depression at other times in my life, but nothing like the feeling that hit me after the loss of the girls.

I took antidepressant medication every day, but my doctors reminded me that my own actions made a difference, too. Exercise is a great way to relieve melancholia, and the endorphin rush I got from running always made me feel better. I'd also read articles claiming that if you make yourself smile, you'll feel happier. It sounds crazy, but there's a connection between mind and muscle: if your face muscles are pulled into a cheerful expression, your brain starts to think you're happy.

My brain wasn't so easily tricked. But I've always believed that when you look good, you feel better, so most days, I tried to make myself get dressed and comb my hair. When you're depressed, wearing makeup and high-heeled shoes isn't a sign of vanity or wastefulness—it's a symbol of hope.

Trying to pull myself up from a frightening slump one day, I got dressed in black jeans and a pretty embroidered blouse, dabbed on makeup, and searched my jewelry box for my favorite rings and earrings and necklaces. I already had a stack of pretty bracelets on my wrist that I wore all the time—each of them with the girls' initials, EAK. Some of them had been made for me—by schoolchildren in one case, and by a woman I didn't even know in another.

The bracelets were my way of keeping the girls close at hand, and the stones sparkled in the sunlight when I went outside. I made myself go to a local store, and as usual, people stared at me as if I were a celebrity. One woman I didn't know very well hesitated and then came over.

"Oh Jackie, you look so pretty," she said with exaggerated warmth. "It's good to see you all dressed up. Jewelry and everything."

"Um, thanks," I said. My fingers fluttered unconsciously to my face and I twiddled my earrings. Something told me that "you look so pretty" wasn't meant as a compliment. However kind she meant to be, I imagined her voice held an undertone of reproach. Seeing me out in public with a plastered-on smile, she had no way of knowing about the depression, the despair, the utter blackness that seemed to make up 99 percent of my life now. Her eyes fluttered to my bracelets, and I could almost hear her thinking:

"If my children were dead, I wouldn't be worrying about makeup and jewelry."

Devastated that anyone might suggest I'd forgotten the girls, I rushed away from the store and back to my silent house, where I crumpled in sobs on the sofa. Everything I tried to do backfired. Looking good seemed wrong. But was looking bad any better? If I went out gray-faced, wearing sweats, my unkempt hair pulled back in a ponytail, people would whisper about how drained and careworn I looked. Probably that's what they expected—Jackie as a walking ghost of grief. I've always cared too much about what other people think, but looking haggard only fed my depression, and right now, I knew that if I sank any lower into my pit of despair, I might never be able to emerge.

Before the accident, my daily schedule was set by my children's needs—school, summer camp, sports practices, play rehearsals, and playdates defined where I was and when. One child or another was always with me. Once Katie started school, I had a few hours to myself and I thought about taking more cooking classes, or getting a job. Free hours felt like a gift.

Now I had nothing but those free hours—and they felt more like a prison.

The success of "Tuesdays with Karen" reminded me that I needed to keep my days full. Empty hours would only hang heavy. As usual, my friends provided a solution. Another Mothers' Club friend named Kathy Power had been a regular in a Thursday-morning bowling league and insisted on signing me up. I dragged Isabelle in, too, getting her to join us at the lanes. I'm not much of a bowler, but since it was a team competition, I had to show up or I would put everyone at a disadvantage. No matter how low my spirits, my sense of obligation to the team won out and I'd drag myself to the lanes for a couple of hours. Wearing funny-colored shoes and swinging an eight-pound ball down a glossy lane does tend to be a good distraction from real life.

Mondays, my friends Denine and Laura came over for TV Night. Both of them were die-hard fans of *The Bachelor*, and though I'd never watched it before, we now curled up weekly in front of the show with ice cream and bowls of snacks. Many Monday nights, my neighbors Tia and Desi and Gina swarmed into my den to join us, too. Suddenly there was a houseful of women.

"What's going on?" Warren asked, coming home from work one night and finding us all there.

"Just watching TV," someone called out cheerfully. "Want to join us?"

"No!" he said, fleeing upstairs.

If *The Bachelor* wasn't on, we'd watch *The Real Housewives of New Jersey*—or whichever version of that franchise happened to be available. For us, any of those shows were like *Monday Night Football* must be for a group of guys—we cheered and screamed and were very loud.

"Don't kiss her!" I screamed during one episode of *The Bachelor*, covering my face at a too-romantic close-up. "Oh, gross!"

We hollered our opinions at the TV and booed the contestants we didn't like. Not the highest intellectual activity, but always fun and a way to forget.

• • •

Even though I could fumble my way through the weekdays, Saturday and Sunday loomed as unbearable black holes. Our friends were with their families, going with their children to soccer games and dance recitals and gymnastics shows.

Warren and I had nothing to do.

We'd always followed the women's magazine rule of Saturday night as date night. When the girls were here, we'd get a babysitter and go out with our friends on Saturday nights, our one chance to let loose and act like grown-ups. To regain some slice of normalcy, Warren insisted that we start having those date nights again. Since the evening activities had never involved the girls, he figured we wouldn't be overwhelmed by memories.

But everything had involved the girls.

One Saturday night, trying to get ready to go out, I stood desultorily in front of the mirror, staring at my makeup. It had been a long, empty day and maybe Warren was right to try to add some distraction. Half-heartedly, I picked up a lipstick.

And suddenly I had an image of the girls swarming into the bedroom, as they usually did on Saturday night. It was so vivid that it seemed real.

"Oooh, Mommy, you look so pretty!" Alyson said. Always happy, she made me feel happy, too.

She leaned close to me in the mirror, asking to try on the lipstick, and of course I grinned and handed it to her. And then Katie pushed in, asking for blusher for her naturally rosy cheeks.

"Is it a Gersham night?" Emma asked as she, too, began applying my makeup to her already smooth face.

And that memory brought me up short.

On evenings Warren and I expected to have a few drinks, we used to hire a local guy named Gersham to drive us. If he wasn't available, we arranged for a cab or assigned someone in our crowd to be the designated driver. From a very young age, the girls knew that Mommy and Daddy would never drink and drive. Nobody should. It was too dangerous.

Thinking about that, I dropped the lipstick and stared into space.

Explaining the open vodka bottle that the police found, Danny insisted that Diane was simply transporting it home—an excuse that caused eye-rolling from most people but made some sense to me. Diane once told me that with a lot of teenagers around the campsite, she left only fishing equipment in the camper during the week, worried that somebody would break in.

"That's all I need—kids drinking in my camper," she had said.

But the facts seemed to point in a different direction. Open vodka bottle. Drunk driver. Wasn't it all obvious? The problem was, I could not imagine Diane swigging vodka in front of the children.

And thinking about Emma and Gersham and our getting-dressed-before-a-date conversations, a new thought struck me.

If Emma had seen Diane with a vodka bottle, she would have said something. She knew you didn't drink and drive. She knew.

The very thought made my head spin.

Are you saying an eight-year-old should have stopped her? a more rational part of myself retorted.

No! I argued back. *But Emma knew the danger, so she would have said something on the phone.*

But she didn't. Are you trying to blame her?

Of course not! But maybe that proves something else happened. Maybe Diane wasn't drunk. Because Emma would have mentioned it.

Somehow, I managed to stop perseverating long enough to put on makeup and get dressed. My mind far away, I added chandelier earrings, a few necklaces, and the stack of EAK bracelets I always wore. I smiled, remembering how Dr. O'Brien had teased me that I might be suicidal, but I still accessorized.

I tried to put myself in a better mood as Warren and I drove silently to a local restaurant called Fiore. Often Melissa and Brad, Jeannine and Rob, or Isabelle and Mark would scoop us up and take us out on Saturday night, hoping that a couple of hours of laughter and good food would be some relief. Tonight, they were all there, along with several other couples, at a noisy table dotted with wine and beer bottles. Warren and I sat down to join the revelry, and the owners came by to make sure we felt comfortable.

"I just want you to have a good time," one of the owners said generously. "Anything you need, just tell me."

"Oh, thanks, we're fine," I said, lying.

Someone put a beer in front of me, and I looked around nervously, feeling self-conscious about the people at nearby tables. If I thought it wrong to be having fun, how much more judgmental would others be? Everyone must be gossiping about us, shaking their heads in surprise to see me laughing or holding a beer.

You shouldn't be partying, the ever-chiding voice in my head warned.

I looked across the table at Warren and saw him trying to put on a brave show. Okay, we could smile for a couple of hours, enjoy our friends, act like normal people. I let my spirits lift ever so slightly.

Later, when Warren and I got home, a toxic mix of guilt and gloom descended on us the moment we closed the front door.

"You really didn't eat very much tonight," Warren said as we walked into our empty living room. Maybe he meant to be nice, but it was enough to start a fight.

"I don't know how you could eat," I retorted. "The girls don't get to eat. Why should we?"

"Not eating won't bring them back."

"It's disrespectful. If you had a child in a wheelchair, would you dance in front of her?"

"It's different, Jackie!"

"It's not. If they can't enjoy food anymore, why should we?"

"We have to accept what's happened and try to live," Warren said, trying to be reasonable.

"I don't want to live," I said bluntly. I folded my arms across my chest, loneliness enveloping me like a shroud. Warren stood very still. He wanted to make things better for me, and I knew of a way he could.

"One of us has to be with the girls," I said, thinking I sounded very rational. "They're so little. They need a parent to take care of them. You kill me and I'll go to heaven and be with them."

"I'm not doing that, Jackie," Warren said sadly. "I refuse to make this story any worse than it is."

"Then I'll kill you," I said earnestly. "I don't care if I go to jail. What difference does it make? I'm glad to sit in jail if I know you're in heaven with the girls."

"Nobody is killing anybody. We've had enough death."

"Please, Warren! Kill me or I'll kill you! I don't care which! One of us has to be with the girls!"

I started sobbing. I didn't expect Warren to hold me, since that wasn't in our repertoire anymore. He couldn't make the pain go away, and sometimes being with him only made it worse.

I ran up to the girls' room and slammed the door. It was swelteringly hot but I wouldn't turn on the air-conditioning. Forget the glorious images I liked to envision of heaven—the girls were lying buried in the ground. They were probably hot. And I would sit here in their room, hot, sweating, crying, alone. It was the only way I could be close to them.

Nine

Birthdays had always been big events in our family. I liked throwing parties at our house with throngs of friends and outsize buffets. I loved to cook and bake and people always raved about my food. Even more important, I knew how to make pretty displays that got lavish praise before anybody even took a bite of the goodies inside.

In September, as Emma's birthday approached, I started planning her party. Whether the girls were with me or not, I was their mother. Nothing could change my dedication. Even though she was gone, Emma deserved a celebration on September 9, the day she would have turned nine.

Emma's first birthday had been my best bash ever. We had rented a big tent for the backyard, which we put next to the brand-new swing set our friends had chipped in to buy, one big gift instead of many smaller ones. Already seven months pregnant with Alyson, I whipped up pastas and salads and a prettily decorated cake. I convinced one of Warren's longtime friends to get into an Elmo costume I'd rented, and he wandered around entertaining the little ones. I'd also hired a clown I found through an ad. She arrived cheerfully dressed in a jester's costume but turned out to be a slightly weird middle-aged woman who kept fanning herself and complaining about hot flashes.

After Emma's first birthday party, I had envisioned all the birthday fetes yet to come—and went out and bought a party tent. Warren had gasped at the $2,500 price tag.

"It'll be worth it!" I promised him. "We won't have to rent again. It's a great investment."

Just for fun, I bought a popcorn machine, too.

My purchases paid off in pleasure in those early years and even led to a catering business that I launched after Katie was born. I got hired for a few big functions like christenings, showers, and an engagement party, and the girls always had fun pitching in. For one Communion brunch, Emma helped me take little baby quiches off the baking trays and we arranged them together on platters, with pretty tomato rosettes between them. I remember looking up at her, hands sticky and face streaked with flour, and thinking how lucky I was to have such a perfect assistant.

People loved my parties, but I spent so much making everything look special that I lost money on every gig. I switched to cupcakes-only-catering, and once again, the girls were my secret weapon. We decorated cupcakes with candies and gumdrops and streaks of sparkle sugar that were a big hit at children's parties. I got hired for a wedding shower, and I was excited until the bride announced she wanted different-colored hydrangeas on each cupcake. Hydrangeas? I didn't know enough icing tricks to make elaborate flowers, so I bought premade fondant blossoms to scatter across the frosting. Sure enough, guests cheered when I brought out the trays, but my bank account suffered.

The girls and I loved to watch cooking shows on TV, and one night we all sat together, giddily watching *Ultimate Cake Off* on the Food Network.

"You should be on this show!" Alyson had said.

"You bake better than anyone," Katie agreed, giving me a hug.

Eager to make them proud—and have a thriving business that would make us all happy—I signed up for a cake-decorating class at the Institute of Culinary Education in Manhattan. With some training, I could do hydrangeas or daisies or roses. Katie was about to start first grade, and I was about to start my cooking classes. We could learn and grow together. But then the accident happened and I couldn't imagine going to the classes.

The morning of Emma's ninth birthday, Warren and I went to mass and then drove out to the cemetery. Friends tried to cheer up the grim scene with balloons and flowers and stuffed animals, but Warren and I cried as we left the presents we had bought our Emma—pink sneakers and a pretty bracelet, her favorite peanut butter, and some magazines she loved. We wanted her to be happy, but the silence of the cemetery seemed to scream a different story. Warren and I walked away without a word, in our own private worlds, with our private tears.

In the afternoon, about forty children and adults came to the house. I felt completely numb. Emma's friends clambered merrily on the swing set like they always had, and watching them, my head began spinning in confusion. How do you have a happy birthday party when the birthday girl isn't there to enjoy it?

I hadn't moved any of Emma's or Alyson's toys or clothes since the accident, and the room they shared remained exactly as it had always been. The beds were made and the duvets fluffed. The eye masks the girls liked to slip on at bedtime waited neatly on the pillows and their slippers were tucked by the side of their beds. Their jackets hung tidily from the coatrack. The familiarity of the scene made their friends comfortable. As they swarmed into the girls' room to play, I pushed aside my own agony. It would be nice if I could still make the other children happy.

"If you like that, you should take it," I said to one little girl who was admiring a kooky pen on Emma's dresser. The pens with faces on them were a big fad then and Emma had a huge collection.

"Really?" she asked, picking it up carefully.

"Sure. Emma would want you to have it," I said, with a smile on my face and a lump in my throat, thinking of how generous my daughter had always been with her friends.

"Oh, thank you!" she said happily.

Almost on autopilot, I repeated similar offers and watched as children walked away clutching little mementos of their lost friends. Even though the offers were genuine, part of me wanted to scream "No, give it back!" each time a child danced off with one of my daughters' possessions. Handing over their toys confirmed that they would never be here to play with them themselves.

I kept up my friendly charade for the whole party. Having so many children dashing through the house and yard and basement was both heartening and heartbreaking. All our families had been so close over the years that I had come to adore many of these children and care about them as my own.

But they weren't my own. My own weren't here.

After everybody left, I fell apart, the facade shattering into shards of grief. And it didn't get better. For a full week after, I barely left my bed, crying mournfully and hoping each time I went to sleep that I would never wake up again. The school year stretched ahead of me, and all the usual high points now loomed as nadirs of unmitigated misery. I couldn't face another birthday party, not to mention Thanksgiving, Christmas, or Mother's Day.

But as Alyson's Communion date approached, I couldn't ignore it. Emma had enjoyed the big party we threw at her Communion, and now Alyson deserved the same, right? Food, music, catering hall—we'd do everything just as Aly would have wanted. In the dark of night, I reeled at the thought of smiling through another party that was missing the guest of honor, but I didn't think I had a choice. I didn't know how to change the track that my life had been on, and despite the accident, I didn't want to. I'd continue to shop for the girls, buy them presents, celebrate big events like Communion.

"If a party is going to be too much for you, don't do it," one of my friends said.

"How could I not?" I asked. "Aly was so excited about her Communion. She'd been talking about it."

"You don't have to, Jackie. Maybe worry about yourself."

I shook my head, troubled and dazed. I couldn't think like that. I didn't ever want to think like that. My friend meant to be kind, but how could she suggest I give up on Aly? As a parent, you may get frustrated and tired or even despairing, but you always put your children ahead of yourself. You sign up to be a parent forever, and the connection never ends. Your children are your children, whatever happens to them.

So I started planning the party.

Communion is a sacrament, but like a Jewish bar mitzvah, the ritual includes both ceremony and celebration. Going overboard seems to be part of a lot of coming-of-age observances, and Emma and I spent a lot of time before her party discussing what white dress she should wear. We knew girls whose families had spent hundreds of dollars on elaborate Communion outfits and then made them a family tradition. But we figured Alyson and Katie would each want their own Communion dresses, rather than a hand-me-down.

"If you're going to wear it once and then outgrow it, why go crazy?" I asked. "We can spend money on something else."

"Okay with me," said ever-practical Emma.

My mom made a special gift of a headpiece, veil, and shawl that all three girls would be able to wear at their Communions. Then Emma and I went shopping and found a beautiful dress that was under $100. She looked like a princess dancing at her party, and when she spilled a Coke all over it and started to cry, I told her not to worry. And I meant it.

And now it was Alyson's turn.

I didn't get to buy a dress for Alyson, but I wanted the party to be just the way she'd like it. I booked a gala room at the New Hyde Park Inn and hired a DJ to get everyone dancing. I sent out invitations, but instead of presents, I suggested our guests donate art supplies to the nearby children's hospital. Aly had been a good artist and wanted to be an art teacher, and she would have liked knowing that other children would get to paint and draw because of her.

The day of the party, I took more antidepressants and antianxiety pills than usual. I'd become masterful at turning myself into some automated version of myself in public, stripped of feeling, able to smile and function. I knew my ever-smiling Alyson would want everyone happy at her party—including me—so I put on my best false front and danced to the music. Alyson's sweet friends gathered around me and we all danced together, with arms swinging and bodies moving. My animation gave them permission to have fun, too.

Alyson would have liked the party. She would have been proud of me.

Warren, though, was responsible for the most memorable moment of the night. Just as the party was beginning, he stepped to the dance floor and took the microphone.

"Thank you all for coming," he said to the gathering crowd. "Before this party starts, I'd like to take this moment to dance with my wife."

I didn't quite know what he had planned, but he guided me gently toward the dance floor and put his arms around me. He had arranged that the first song the DJ played would be Michael Bublé's touching and emotional "Hold On." All the guests gathered around, swaying to the music and overcome by the words that seemed written just for us.

Didn't they always say we were the lucky ones?
I guess that we were once,
Babe, we were once.
But luck will leave you 'cause
It is a faithless friend . . .

As Bublé's mellow, romantic voice filled the room, I leaned my head on Warren's shoulder and held him tightly. All around me, I saw our friends weeping, but I disengaged myself from the moment and refused to cry. I didn't want to hear the lyrics about how once we'd been so lucky and now life had turned. If I managed to hold myself together through this song, then I'd be okay for the whole party—and I could go home later and collapse in private.

And in the end, when life has got you down,
You've got someone here that you can wrap your arms around.
So hold on to me tight . . .
We are stronger here together,
Than we could ever be alone.

I let the music wash over me, knowing that if I looked into Warren's eyes, we would both dissolve. Like Sinatra, Bublé has a crooning, worldy-wise style, and Warren had chosen the song carefully. However much we had been fighting, however much our anger and grief threatened to incinerate our marriage and destroy us, he wanted me to believe in him. Most of our guests must have agreed with Bublé that even though life had gotten us down, we were stronger together than apart. Because as Warren and I clung to each other, there wasn't a dry eye in the crowd.

The sad truth, though, was that Warren and I didn't make each other stronger. He couldn't stand to see me constantly upset, and I had such loathing for Diane and the cruelty of what she'd done that I couldn't stop myself from lashing out. The accusation I kept promising myself not to make eventually slipped out.

"Your sister killed our kids," I hissed in the midst of a fight one evening in October. I knew the comment was rude and wrong, but I couldn't control my venom.

We launched into the kind of pitched battle that occurs only when you think there's nothing left to lose. Grief is harder to handle than rage, so transforming one into the other had its purpose.

"Do you think Emma died scared?" I asked Warren. "Do you think they all did? Every time I close my eyes, I hear her crying." Her sobs from our last phone conversation persistently rang in my head.

"I don't know. We'll never know. But she wasn't crying when I talked to her," he reminded me, as he always did. He had spoken to her after I did.

"They must have known what was happening when Diane drove onto the highway," I persisted, tormenting us both, and beginning to sob. "Can you imagine? They probably looked out the window and started screaming. But they were helpless."

"Jackie . . ."

"Why wasn't I there to hold them? Did they cry out for me?" Now my whole body was shaking in anguish.

"You have to stop."

"I can't stop!" I screamed. "My children are dead and I don't know what happened to them!"

"We can't keep going over this. It doesn't help."

"I need to talk about it!"

"There's nothing more to say. We've said it all."

"Why won't you talk to me, Warren?" I yelled, my anger and anxiety spinning out of control. "Is it because you know your sister did this to us?"

"I'm not my sister!" he roared. "I'm not responsible for this!"

"Then, who is? What happened? They're dead, Warren. They're dead."

I sobbed hysterically and trembled and screamed, and Warren hollered in frustration and pain. I was consumed with reliving every torturous moment, while Warren wanted to block out the torment and not think about the horrifying details.

We had plummeted into a black, ugly place so oppressive that neither of us could imagine there would ever be sunshine again. When Warren couldn't take the hammering argument and emotional hysteria anymore, he stormed out of the house.

"Where are you going?" I screamed, charging after him. However crazed I might be, I had a sudden flash of fear. His bolting in a deranged state after midnight didn't bode well. We had made a pact early in our marriage that if either of us headed out fuming after a fight, we couldn't take the car. If you want to kill yourself, okay—but you couldn't hurt anyone else.

Now Warren raced down the driveway on foot, his flip-flops slapping against the blacktop like shots in the night.

"I've had it!" he shouted. "Enough! I'm going to go jump in front of a train!"

Warren didn't threaten or say things he didn't mean. Would he really do it? If Warren quit on life, his dad and brothers would fall like dominoes right behind him. I had believed Warren when he said he didn't want to make this story any worse. But maybe he didn't care anymore.

I tried to follow him. "Come back," I called, the intensity of his despair somehow penetrating my own blackness. "Don't do that, please! Please!"

"Good-bye, Jackie."

Bloody images flashed into my head. I pictured Warren on the tracks, a train bearing down. I could almost hear the whistle, the screams, the end of the father of my children.

He fled down the dark road, and I followed but couldn't keep up. I was in better physical shape, but tonight he was the more desperate one, and the adrenaline seemed to give him Olympic speed. Turning around, I staggered back to the house, shivering in fear.

Normally, I called friends when things got bad, but this time I just crawled into bed, shaking and sobbing. I had done this to Warren and nobody could change that. I talked about dying all the time, but Warren couldn't be the one who finally quit. Sadness and guilt overwhelmed me. I was supposed to love him, but I had driven him away.

I don't know how much time went by. Much, much later, I heard the front door opening and footsteps on the staircase. Warren came silently into the room and lay down in the bed next to me.

We didn't talk about what happened or where Warren had gone for so long. We knew that confronting such depths of despair could only bring more pain.

Ten

One day when the girls were little, we sat together, talking about their futures. I wanted them to have careers and be moms, too. Although I had given up my career to be a mother and didn't regret it, I realized that their lives might be better with some balance.

"You could be doctors or teachers or lawyers," I suggested.

"I want to be an art teacher," Alyson said firmly. "I love art. Anything with art."

"Good plan," I told her. "As long as you love what you do."

Emma thought she wanted to be an actress or singer, since her passion was performing.

Katie, only four at the time, had the firmest plan. "I'm never leaving you and Daddy," she said. "I'll be with you forever."

"You still need a career when you grow up," I told her, smiling as she climbed into my lap.

"Then I'll help you make cupcakes, Mommy," she said. "Nothing else."

We all laughed. Maybe it was a little early for Katie to make a plan, but as a devoted full-time mom, I tried to stay on top of everything in my children's lives. I plotted birthday parties months in advance and family vacations years before they happened. I envisaged proms and weddings and talked to the girls about what lay ahead. Or what I imagined lay ahead. I had confidence in the power of our orderly, organized life. The future wouldn't surprise us because we prepared for it.

After the accident, I understood that all those preparations didn't add up to much. Control is just an illusion. The children had been my whole life, and now that whole life was gone.

Warren and I had always been careful about money, but now part of me felt like I might as well spend on anything I wanted. What reason did we possibly have to buy bonds or stash money into a retirement account? Warren and I had put money in college savings accounts and never considered a world where the girls wouldn't head happily off to freshman year with new clothes and dorm furnishings from Target. But all those college savings had gone to pay for a funeral.

Our moods swung dramatically, but Warren, nobly, still wanted to be a good husband. He kept looking for things that would give me some passing glimpse of pleasure. My car had been smashed in the accident, but for a long time, I didn't need a new one because I wouldn't get behind a wheel. Warren drove or friends took me wherever I needed to go—which was just as well, because I was too fragile to face the world on my own, anyway.

But eventually I realized I would have to drive again. However generous my friends were with their time, I needed to start taking some first tentative steps back to independence. I didn't really care what kind of car I got. I didn't need an SUV or a minivan anymore. A fancy car felt meaningless—even tasteless. But then I remembered that my stylish girls had always wanted me to have a convertible.

"You'd look so great driving with a top down," Alyson had said one day when a neighbor drove by with her hair blowing in the breeze.

"And you'd have fun," Emma agreed. "What do you think, Mommy?"

I thought they were right. But who puts kids in a convertible? Practicality won out and we stuck with a minivan.

Sometime in the late fall, almost as a joke, I suggested a convertible to Warren.

"The girls wanted me to have it," I said. "They used to tell me how pretty I'd look sitting in the front seat."

"Then that's what you should get," he said simply.

I told him the car had to have a retractable hardtop and a full back-seat. I never even thought about price—because I didn't really expect him to buy it—and we dropped the subject. But, eager to prove that life could still have its bright moments, Warren asked his friend Chris to visit car dealers for him. Like me, Warren still felt awkward going out in public where people might recognize him. Our pictures had been in the newspapers a lot, and he felt safer having a good-natured friend make the rounds for him. Chris had my dream requirements tucked into his front pocket as he did his test drives. Finally, he brought Warren to see what he thought was the nicest car with the best price.

Unaware of all that had gone on, I was out with Melissa one day when Warren called my cell phone to ask what time I'd be back.

"I don't know, we won't be too long," I told him. "Why?"

"Oh, just wondering," he said. He sounded slightly odd, but I didn't pay much attention.

When Melissa and I got home, Warren stood in the driveway waiting for us. Rain swirled around him, but he didn't seem to care. He wanted to see my face when I got the first glimpse of what he had driven home—a light blue Volvo convertible with a cream interior.

I jumped out of Melissa's car and ran over to it.

"Really? For me?" I asked, a huge smile plastered on my face. Warren broke into a genuine grin. This was the Warren I had first fallen in love with—always surprising me with something special and making the extra-thoughtful gesture that most men wouldn't try. I felt a brief flash of the giddiness I used to experience when we were dating and I knew I had found a man who loved to make me happy.

"Do you like it?" he asked, wanting confirmation for what he already knew.

"It's perfect! I can't believe you bought me a convertible!" I said, bouncing around delightedly.

His grin got even bigger. For months now, nothing Warren tried to do eased any of my anguish. The only expressions he'd seen me show were grief and pain and anger. This flash of happiness must have felt like sunshine breaking through the clouds. And in fact, the literal and metaphoric happened together that afternoon, because as Warren opened the door so I could sit in the car, the rain stopped and the sky turned blue.

"I love it!" I said, sliding onto the leather seat. It's probably hard-wired in guys to want to please their wives, and my enthusiasm made Warren puff out his chest just a bit.

Once Warren and I finished admiring the new car, I drove around the corner to show off to Isabelle.

"What fun!" she said excitedly. She and Kailey and Ryan piled into the convertible and we all drove through the neighborhood laughing and talking.

And then I got panicky. What was I doing? Given my constant fears of how other people perceived me, I suddenly dreaded the thought of anyone seeing me with the top down.

How awful! She traded in her kids for a convertible!

The crazy voices in my head always imagined what other people would be saying, and now they screamed that Grace Kelly could ride around with her hair blowing (or neatly tied with a scarf) in *To Catch a Thief*, but I had no right. I was a mom in mourning, not a Hollywood starlet.

The pleasure of the new car disappeared almost as quickly as it had come. Fortunately, Warren had gotten the hardtop, so from the outside, nobody could tell that the square Volvo sedan could morph into a racy convertible. I never put the top down around town and figured everyone would assume that I'd appropriately moved from a minivan to a safe, smaller car.

But then a funny thing happened. On one of our Tuesday outings, Karen and I were shopping at a mall far away from Floral Park. Going where nobody recognized me allowed me some feeling of release, so when we started driving home and she goaded me to put down the roof, I figured, What the heck. Why not.

But transforming from sedan to convertible wasn't as easy as I thought. It started off okay. When we stopped at a red light, I put my foot on the brake and held down the button. I felt like the captain of the starship *Enterprise* as the roof lifted slowly, going straight up, before beginning its descent into the trunk, which had also smoothly opened. Then the light changed to green and I started driving again. Big mistake. Safety features don't allow that. Once I took my foot off the brake, the whole action stopped.

The roof was straight up in the air at a 90-degree angle, like a sail-boat mast. It was a windy day, and given the awkward angle of the roof, the wind gusts slammed against it with unexpected force.

"The roof is going to fly off!" I called, almost screaming.

"Can't happen! Swedish engineering!" Karen shouted back, starting to laugh.

"Well, if it does, you're going to explain it to Warren. This was your idea!" I said, also laughing.

We were on a one-lane road with no place to pull over, so I drove slowly, not going above 20 mph. With the gusts pummeling the up-right roof and the cars behind us honking, the whole situation struck me as hysterically funny. It felt like the car might just lift off the ground—a Volvo version of the Flying Nun.

I laughed louder and Karen did, too. By the time we pulled safely into a parking lot by the side of the road, our gales of laughter blew louder than the wind.

"Ohmygodohymygodohmygod!" I said, trying to catch my breath.

We laughed so hard that we both started crying, and happy tears streaked down our cheeks. It was one of those unexpectedly exuberant moments that gives a jolt of sheer silly pleasure, making us forget everything else in the world. Given all the tears of devastation I'd shed—usually accompanied by howls, wails, and sobs—I didn't mind these tears at all. They certainly felt different.

We finally steadied ourselves, put the roof back up, and drove home. That night, I tried to tell the story to Warren, but except for my giggling in the retelling, it didn't sound very funny anymore.

"I guess you had to have been there," I finally said lamely, almost to myself.

Falling asleep that night, I realized that a car, great jewelry, new furniture—they're all just things at the end of the day, and they offer no lasting feelings. Children—and the memories of children—are what endure. A home, Warren, family, friendship. I needed to find what mattered again, to understand what had happened to my life and how to rebuild it when all that had truly sustained it was gone.

Eleven

Some of my friends say that Warren and I make an unlikely pair. We are simply wired differently. He's always evinced an easy contentedness, while I get restless. I don't need much sleep, and I never relax, even on vacation. The summer we joined a beach club, friends joked that I could never sit for very long.

"Anyone need anything?" the cabana boy asked one day, coming over to where my friends and I were lounging.

"We're good," I said. Then a minute later, I jumped up and dashed off to get some water or suntan lotion.

"Why didn't you ask him to get that?" Melissa asked when I came back.

"I needed to get up, anyway," I explained. I have a lot of energy—and a lot of anxiety—that I need to release, whether in useful activities like running or planning, or fruitless ones like worrying.

Warren and I grew up with different backgrounds, which partly explains our contrasting styles. My Italian family was emotional, voluble, and dramatic—so it's natural that I want to talk about everything. Sometimes too much. Warren has the more steadfast approach of his Germanic father. Mr. Hance, a retired postal worker, seemed resolute and resigned in the face of tragedy. He tried to keep his life orderly and unemotional, getting done what he needed to without a lot of fuss or fervor. He lost his only daughter and four of his grandchildren in one inexplicable accident, but he didn't talk about it much. Instead, he trudged to the cemetery every week to water the plants and tend the plots.

I sometimes wonder if men who maintain a pragmatic approach

have emotions roiling underneath that they cover up with a solid facade. Or is the facade really the truth? Mr. Hance never talked about the
breakup of his marriage decades earlier, but the pain must have reverberated. When Warren was fifteen, and Diane, the youngest, only eight,
their mother had an affair and left. After Eileen moved out, Mr. Hance
stayed behind to raise the four children on his own. Warren and his siblings had very little contact with their mother.

Warren became a pillar for his family, the one his siblings—his twin
brother, John, their brother David, and the youngest, Diane—could rely
on. The parents made a plan that when Diane reached twenty-one, they'd
sell the house and split the proceeds. But as that birthday approached,
Diane and Mr. Hance still lived there and Warren, ever the good guy,
didn't want their lives to be disrupted. He bought half the house and
let them stay. He eventually moved in with them while we were dating.
When we got married, they left and Warren and I made it our home.

It's not surprising that Warren felt deeply connected to the house,
but I just considered it the place we currently lived. He had strong
roots, while I floated around, always imagining the brick-and-mortar
that might make us happier. Once the girls hit preschool, I talked about
house-hunting in the nearby town where Jeannine and Rob and Melissa
and Brad ultimately moved.

"Garden City has a middle school the girls would attend, rather than
going from elementary school to high school," I said.

"The local schools were just fine for me," Warren insisted.

"I don't like that the girls have to share a room," I said, trying another angle. "The house is too cramped for three children."

"When I grew up, we had four children here," he said.

Try to argue that one.

Emma, Alyson, and Katie loved the house and our big backyard, too.
I was the only one who had a problem with it, who wanted to move on.

I knew he was right about the town, though. Friends and neighbors
cloaked us in love and support. I don't know if every community is like
ours, but people gathered around us with extraordinary warmth and caring. Warren and I joked that we had an open-door policy, and we meant

it quite literally. We never locked the door, happy to have anybody stop by, and fortunately, people popped in regularly.

We've always been lucky with our friends, and now several couples in our closest circle seemed to put everything else aside to be with us. They never made a fuss about it—they just showed up. The five women in my running group bolstered me daily. Friends I had grown up with—many of them still in New Jersey—checked in regularly, and those from Warren's early years—many of them still in Floral Park—recharged their bonds. My cell phone rang constantly with women from the bowling league or prayer group that I had joined. Neighbors and fellow parents from town came by on unexpected evenings with food or funny stories.

"Hello, Hances!" our ever-merry friend Bob GaNun would call out when he sauntered in, a couple of nights a week. "It's Uncle Bob." He would sing a song or do an Elvis impersonation so good that he could be onstage in Las Vegas. For a few minutes, Warren and I would smile and feel safe from our endless arguments.

Warren's brother David got a leave from his air force posting in Korea for the funeral and then, not wanting to abandon Warren, asked to be transferred to New Jersey. We converted our basement into his weekend bedroom, and having him nearby was good therapy for Warren. The two of them bonded over drill bits and chain saws. Warren had many home-improvement ideas, and David, a great hands-on guy, actually knew how to do them. Typical guys, they didn't have to talk to get comfort. Pounding nails and climbing ladders seemed to do the trick.

David became the weekend cushion between Warren and me, keeping us from turning volatile on those long Saturdays and Sundays when other people were busy with their families. I loved David and appreciated what he did for Warren. But he was a Hance, a brother of Diane, yet another reminder of what had happened.

"I can never get away from your family!" I yelled at Warren one afternoon. "Diane is dead, but she won't leave us alone!" When I went to visit the girls at the cemetery, I saw her tombstone. When I talked to Warren, Mr. Hance, or David, I glimpsed her face. No matter what I did, I could never get away from her.

Feeling ambivalent about family was new for me. Warren and I had always kept blood relatives close. Emma, Alyson, and Katie had adored my mom, who babysat for them often. Mr. Hance—Poppy—was a daily presence in their lives, and many aunts and uncles and cousins came by frequently. When the girls had questions about other relatives, we answered them simply.

"Mommy's daddy is in heaven," I told the girls, and we visited him in the cemetery often.

"What about Daddy's mommy?" Emma asked.

Eileen might have wanted to reconnect with her children and grandchildren now, but before the accident, Warren couldn't see the point.

"Daddy's mommy didn't want to be a mommy anymore," I explained.

They accepted the statement with the innocence of children. The explanation made sense to them, even if it didn't to me.

Now when I was feeling sympathetic, I could admit that Warren hadn't had an easy time with the women in his life.

His mother left him.

His girls were gone.

I never wanted to be another woman in his life who left him. That's at least one of the reasons I stayed after the accident, when it might have been better for both of us to be apart.

My childhood wasn't nearly as complicated as Warren's. I grew up in a moderately affluent neighborhood in New Jersey where my dad owned the Town Pub, where I eventually met Warren. It was a popular hangout, and my dad loved being the center of the social scene. He hired many of my school friends to work there nights and weekends, and my first real job was at the restaurant, too. My mom didn't have a job until I reached high school, but my dad took good care of her even after their divorce, and we always had what we needed.

About the time I went off to college, the restaurant took a downward slide and finances got tight. My dad didn't mention the problems, but his checks started bouncing. I got called to the registrar's office at Boston University and was told that I needed to provide a cashier's check if I wanted to stay enrolled. My grandmother paid the tuition, and I got a job to pay rent.

When the debts became too much to handle, my dad lost the restaurant and took a job at another one. I needed to earn a salary in the summers, and while many of my friends continued to work at the Town Pub, I loyally went to the restaurant where my dad now worked. The only problem was that I couldn't make enough money there.

My dad must have had the same problem, because eventually he gave up on restaurants and started driving a cab. At first I felt embarrassed for him. He knew everybody in town. What if he ended up with someone in the backseat of his cab who had been a friend? But he didn't worry. He liked driving and talking to people, and he had no ego invested.

I admired him for losing everything yet still finding a way to go on.

Dad also didn't mind when I went back to working at the former Town Pub. Whatever the new owners had done, I still got good tips there, and as Dad saw it, money was money. One day, I got off work at the restaurant early and was heading out with my longtime friend Cortney, when her car broke down in the parking lot. We went back inside to wait for help. A guy we knew called out "Hi!" and invited us to come join the crowd of pals around him. I went over reluctantly, grumpy about the delay and the broken-down car. I didn't pay too much attention when one of the guys introduced himself as Warren Hance from Long Island.

"Long Island?" I asked, snarkily. "How do you get all the way to Long Island?"

"It's not so hard," he said, missing—or ignoring—my sarcasm and instead spouting off driving directions specific enough to get me directly to his house.

"Okay, but why did you come all the way to New Jersey tonight?" I asked, as if he'd just circumnavigated the Atlantic in a rowboat rather than driven across the George Washington Bridge.

"I came to see the restaurant," he said. "My friend's brother bought it."

"Really? My dad used to own it."

Somewhere in that tangled web was a connection. And it wasn't long before we both felt a deeper connection, too.

In the next few months, Warren came to New Jersey so often that he probably *could* have circumnavigated the globe. I guess you could say our relationship started with my waiting on him, because he returned to the Town Pub for dinner the night after we met—and sat at a table where I was the waitress. It took a few dates before I realized he'd become my boyfriend. Two years later, we were inseparable.

"I want you to move somewhere closer to me," Warren said at that point.

"Where would I go?"

"I'll find you a place," he promised.

I still lived at home, and though I'd been on my own in college, I'd always relied on my dad. Now, classically, the role subtly shifted to Warren. He located an apartment in Queens, and when I worried about how I could afford it, he had the apartment furnished for me. He made it easy to move from my past in New Jersey to my future in New York.

After I met Warren and moved to New York, I began working in the catering department of Barnard College. I'd often arrive at 5:30 a.m. and work until late evening—long hours of running around, nonstop, but I loved it. Food and menus had always been my passion and an idea started to nudge into my mind that maybe someday I'd have my own catering company.

When I wasn't working, Warren and I spent all our time together. We were friends and lovers and shared everything, but he never asked me to marry him. I was young when we met, and maybe he wanted me to grow up a little bit. We were clearly going to be together forever, but I couldn't understand his reluctance and threatened to leave on a regular basis.

"I probably won't be here next year if we're not engaged," I told his family one year at a Christmas party.

"This is the last Easter party I come to without a ring," I said at another family gathering.

But the years went by and I kept showing up, wearing only the rings I'd bought for myself. I talked about marriage regularly, but Warren never responded. Maybe he didn't have much faith in the whole concept because he'd never really seen it work. Why risk the hurt he'd watched his father go through?

I finally stopped thinking about a proposal.

Which is exactly when I got one.

"What makes you want to get married now?" I asked him one day, after I'd said yes and he'd slipped a beautiful diamond on my finger.

"Because you stopped asking," he admitted. "And I love you."

It had taken us six years from that night at the bar to the evening at the altar.

Once we got married, in April 1999, I quit my job and went off the pill. I wanted a baby—babies—immediately. Children gave life meaning.

Back then it never occurred to me that they could be taken away, devastating all the meaning in life, too.

Twelve

ragedy turns everything upside-down. Occasions that once made my life good now made it bad. Events I once looked forward to I now faced with dread.

Like Halloween. Isabelle and I had made a tradition of getting dressed up in costumes and going to school to watch our children in the Halloween parade. I loved the year Emma had decided to be a pirate with a bandanna around her head, a fake sword at her side, and black tights with skulls on them. Alyson had looked incredibly cute as a fairy and Katie pranced proudly as a mermaid. Our stoop always had three pumpkins that we'd carved with the girls and lots of lights and decorations to welcome the trick-or-treaters.

Jeannine threw an annual Halloween costume party for the grown-ups—and she took it seriously, with contests and events and over-the-top outfits. For one party, a group of us were characters from *The Wizard of Oz*: Isabelle was Dorothy, Mark was the Scarecrow, I was a Munchkin, and Brad dressed as the Mayor of Munchkinland. Melissa, who always dressed up as something pretty, got to be Glinda, the Good Witch.

For my first Halloween without the girls, I stayed in bed all day crying. As evening fell, I left a spread of candy on the stoop for any children who stopped by, but didn't turn on any house lights. Huddling alone in the dark seemed the only way to get through the night. Jeannine canceled the annual blowout Halloween party because all of us were haunted by real ghosts and didn't need anything else to scare us.

By the next morning, I could check another painful day off the fall holiday hit parade. But there were more to come.

As the leaves fell off the trees and the days got colder, I shuddered at the thought of going to our traditional family Thanksgiving dinner at my brother Stephen's house in New Jersey. Sitting at his festive table without the girls in their normal places would be more than I could bear.

"Come to our house for Thanksgiving," Jeannine offered, always stepping forward in the crunch. "We'll start a new tradition."

"What about the extended family you usually go to?" I asked.

"We'll skip it. Being with you and Warren is more important."

In typical Jeannine fashion, she cooked up more than dinner. Her town had an annual Turkey Trot, and since one of Warren's friends wanted to organize a running club for the Hance Family Foundation, this seemed like the place to launch it. A small gang of friends and neighbors would run five miles in honor of Emma, Alyson, and Katie—wearing T-shirts to show their support and raising money with every step. Warren insisted that he and I should run, too.

"Ugh, no," I groaned. "Do I have to?"

"Yup, you do," said Warren, an advocate of tough love.

"I only run with my running group," I protested, looking for any out. I wanted to stay in bed and cry on Thanksgiving morning, far away from any crowds. I didn't want to wear a T-shirt with the girls' picture and have people stare at me in public as I ran down a street.

"Well, everyone's going to be there, so you have no choice. You're running."

When Warren and I arrived Thanksgiving morning, the crowd running for the foundation had grown to forty or fifty. Everyone was wearing white T-shirts with a logo commemorating the girls. The warmth and enthusiasm were overwhelming, and as we took photos in our matching outfits, I started to cry. Emma, Alyson, and Katie had brought everyone together, and the race would be infused with their spirits.

I couldn't get too emotional, though, because Bernadette and Tara and all the other women in my usual running group surrounded me and brought me to the starting line. As we took off along the route, I heard bystanders cheering, and though I was sad, their goodwill seeped into my heart. I didn't think I had much to be grateful for on this holiday, but I suddenly felt very thankful for the goodness of the people running with me and the kindness of those lining the road.

Warren and I had one place to go between the run and Jeannine's dinner—the cemetery. I couldn't let a holiday pass without spending time with the girls, but so far, the visits had been difficult. The grave sites remained stark and I had cried on Emma's birthday, upset that people going there would see such a barren plot.

"The headstones aren't ready yet," Warren had said shakily, trying to explain.

"I don't care about excuses," I had said, sobbing. "We can't do this to them. The girls always looked so pretty when they went to school. The cemetery has to be pretty at all times."

So, on Thanksgiving, I walked tentatively toward the girls' graves— and then stopped, feeling another surge of gratitude.

"It's so beautiful!" I said, turning to Warren.

He smiled, pleased and relieved. The headstones had finally been finished and laid, and our friend John Power, who is a landscape architect, had planted graceful trees and shrubs all around. The whole scene looked so peaceful and appealing that I felt a tiny bit of comfort. I fell to my knees and touched the fresh soil where John had done his wondrous transformation.

"I can't buy the girls dresses now or put ribbons in their hair," I said, brushing a smudge off the headstone. "All I can do is make sure it's beautiful here. This is the only place I can still take care of them."

Warren's eyes filled with tears. "John did a good job," he said. "He knew what it meant to you."

We lingered longer than usual, and for the first time I felt some peace being at the burial plots. I knew I would start spending time here with my girls again. John had turned it into a haven where I could come to be close to the girls, talk to them or read to them or leave them little gifts.

I managed better than I expected during Thanksgiving dinner at Jeannine's. She kept the mood casual, which took away some of the sting, and with just her immediate family, I didn't feel like a freak. But as I looked around at her very normal family, I wondered—as I so often did—who else had ever been in a situation as extreme as mine. I knew of other people who had lost one child, but to have a whole family wiped out seemed leagues beyond any probability. I was like a triple amputee—mutilated so severely that others wanted to look away. I felt like an oddity, an aberration, an abomination.

My pain was so deep that I couldn't imagine others had ever survived anything comparable. But I realized that through the centuries and across different parts of the world, mothers' hearts beat much the same. In thinking about the first Thanksgiving celebrated by early settlers, I realized that those Pilgrims must have lost children during the harsh conditions of the first brutal winter in the New World. The loss must have been as devastating for those seventeenth-century mothers as it was for me. But the Pilgrims had chosen to look forward and celebrate the good. As I took a bite of Jeannine's sweet potato casserole, I wondered how I could possibly do the same.

Thirteen

We had money pouring in right after the accident from people who had heard about Emma, Alyson, and Katie and wanted to do something. There are only so many flowers to send. Neighbors and friends had an urge to give, as did strangers from around the country who sent sympathy cards with unsolicited contributions. Often cards contained a crisp five-dollar bill or a wrinkled twenty. Older people sent shakily written checks and children put in coins from piggy banks. Personally, I could imagine being touched by a tragic story on TV and feeling sorry for the people involved, but to find their address, buy a card, write a note, put in money? It seemed stunning to me that so many people made the effort to show compassion for our family.

Warren worked hard to get the foundation started, and my running friend Bernadette pitched in with her usual energy. They set up an official board with friends and advisers. I initially stayed on the outskirts of the action, glad to have the foundation but still too dazed to do much thinking. The generosity was overwhelming. A Wall Street firm sent us $20,000—which left me jumping up and down in delight—and a middle school organized a book sale and gave us the $200 proceeds. We got a letter from a mom who said her five-year-old set up a lemonade stand with her cousins and raised $50 selling drinks, cookies, and brownies. She sent the check to the foundation along with a note: "I didn't know the family personally and I am saddened each day for them. They are amazing people to take such a sad ordeal and turn it into something positive to help others."

Another contribution came with a letter that read, "My heart goes out to Mrs. Hance. She is a role model of how to stay strong and brave throughout a tragic situation."

Strong and brave? Not a chance. Amazing? No way. I cried every day. I had meltdowns on a regular basis. Reading all the notes made me feel like a fraud. I didn't want to be a role model, I wanted to be a regular mom. Why would anyone look up to me when I stumbled at every step?

Though I struggled, coming up with projects for the Hance Family Foundation gave Warren a great sense of meaning and purpose. "You need to come to the meetings," he said to me one night when he came home, invigorated by what was being planned. "It's impressive what the foundation is doing."

"Okay."

"I mean it, Jackie. We can do a lot of good."

"Great. Good. Great that we're doing good," I said.

Meetings were hard for me and the whole business aspect—the bureaucratic lingo—made me shudder. For me this wasn't a business, it was about the girls.

But Warren was right on one level. With the mystifying twist our lives had taken, we had the chance to do good. But how? Families who lose a child to illness often want to help find a cure for the disease. We had happy, healthy children to memorialize, so it seemed natural that we help other children lead happy, healthy lives.

The foundation made its first contributions in the early fall following the accident. I remembered talking to the school superintendent at the wake and thought about how important learning had been to the girls, so we came up with the idea of providing books and supplies and school trip expenses for children whose families struggled to afford them. Our town had three elementary schools—two public and one parochial—which seemed perfect. Three schools, three girls, three hearts.

I also wanted to support a summer camp because the girls had loved their own camp experiences so much. Emma and Alyson had gone to

camp at our beach club for three years and Katie for two. Brad and
Melissa recommended a camp for disabled children that they knew
about because they had volunteered there when they were young. I liked
the idea immediately. Emma had been admired by her teachers for her
constant kindness to the other children in her class, and this seemed a
great way to honor the respect and understanding she offered everyone.

Just two months after the accident, Emma, Alyson, and Katie—
through the foundation—were already giving a boost to children in
need.

A woman in town named Kate Tuffy came to me with an idea that the
foundation launch a program to help build self-esteem and positive
thinking in girls.

"I like that," I said.

"We can call it Beautiful Me," Kate suggested. I was in no condition to question anybody's plans, so I nodded dumbly and told her to go
ahead.

Without knowing it, Kate had hit a topic dear to my heart. I grew
up without much self-esteem, and I was determined that Emma, Alyson,
and Katie wouldn't have the same problem. From the moment they were
born, I tried to help them feel good about themselves—and about how
they looked. I knew that for girls, unfair as it may be, the two are more
closely linked than they should be.

Emma was naturally tall and thin, and during the summer, she
would bop around the house in a bikini. One morning when she was just
six years old, Alyson put on her own bathing suit, and when she looked
in the mirror, her eyes filled with tears.

"I don't look like Emma," she said, rubbing a hand on her round
tummy. "I have a belly like Poppy."

"Your belly isn't like Poppy's," I said, hugging her. "Everybody has
their own shape. You don't look like Emma. I don't look like Daddy.
Part of what's wonderful is that we're all individuals and we look like
ourselves and nobody else."

"But I don't look good in the bikini," Alyson said.

"You're gorgeous," I told her. "But you don't have to wear a bikini just because Emma does."

"Then what should I wear?" she asked.

"Let's go find a bathing suit that you feel good in."

We went out shopping and Alyson picked a tankini that covered a little more of her tummy but was still a two-piece. She felt good in it and went to the beach proudly.

Giving my girls a positive self-image was high on my Mom To-Do list—and I kept at it every day. Our house was always happy and upbeat and I made sure the girls knew how much I loved them. I didn't want them struggling with body image the way I had. Now, with Beautiful Me, I could help other girls gain confidence.

Kate Tuffy worked with a therapist named Liz Munro to organize a three-class curriculum, and almost immediately, dozens of girls signed up. The first sessions were held at a local church.

"You should get involved," Kate urged me, sounding a lot like Warren.

Much as I liked the program, I didn't really want to get involved, but I hated letting people down.

"I'll make the snacks," I promised Kate.

I made a big fruit salad and assembled goodie bags that included a photo of the girls for everyone to take home. Kate and Liz tied every aspect of Beautiful Me to my girls. The mission, they said, was "to extend the lessons Emma, Alyson, and Katie taught through their examples—that being comfortable with who you are makes you a better sister, daughter, and friend."

"Come to the first session," Kate urged. "You can give out the gift bags and talk to the girls. It will be something to do."

Of course, I couldn't turn her down. The girls were ages five through ten, about the same age range as Emma, Alyson, and Katie, and since the program was held in Floral Park, I recognized all the girls. Seeing children I knew involved in a program that gave them confidence to succeed should have been a great satisfaction. And on one level, it really was.

On another level, it was a buzz saw to my heart.

One thought hummed endlessly in my head: *My girls would love this program. Why aren't they here?*

I made it through to the end of a class with a smile on my face, then raced home and fell into my bed sobbing. I couldn't get up again for days.

When I mentioned that Kate would be doing another Beautiful Me soon, Warren, who saw how it had immobilized me, said, "You're not going back there."

"I have to. She needs help. And this one's in a different town."

I thought being in a class far away where I didn't know the children would be slightly better. But it backfired.

"Are Emma, Alyson, and Katie the girls who died because they didn't hold their mommy's hand when they crossed the street?" one five-year-old asked me, looking at the picture of them.

"Uh, no," I said, shocked. "They died in a car accident."

She looked at me skeptically. I could only look back in disbelief. I didn't know where she got the idea; maybe her own mom had used the story as a threat when they crossed a busy street together. The little girl's confused comment shouldn't have mattered, but it threw me into a tailspin. Once again, I went home from the session and dissolved in a puddle.

"How are you doing with Beautiful Me?" Jeannine asked when she came over later and found me barely able to move.

"Everybody loves it," I said. "But the whole time I'm sitting there, I keep thinking that the only reason it exists is because my girls are gone."

Never one to sugarcoat, Jeannine nodded. "It's a mixed blessing," she admitted.

"I'm happy that it does so much good, and I even like watching the girls gain so much confidence during the course. But . . ." I dropped my head back onto a pillow, unable to continue.

"But your girls aren't there, so it's hard to care about anything else."

"Does that make me a bad person?" I asked.

Jeannine shook her head. "Just an honest one."

• • •

Bernadette and I had taken over responsibility for a Youth Council run in town a couple of years earlier, and we'd expanded it dramatically. Now Bernadette had the idea that by connecting the run with the foundation, we could make it monumental. The more we all talked about it, the bigger the idea grew. We'd organize several races for children and adults, as well as games and activities—a Hance Family Fun Day that would take over the whole town.

We picked a Saturday in May and put the date on the calendar.

Planning became a big deal during the fall. Committees were formed and assignments were made. People volunteered to organize events, coordinate with the town, and collect major donations for an auction. With so much to do, a lot of busy people got even busier. I started to feel a little guilty about how hard they were working—and how disconnected I felt.

In rational moments, I knew I couldn't change that the girls were gone. If I had to be on this earth without them, I might as well try to make other children happy. I wanted the girls to be remembered, and we expected that on Family Fun Day, hundreds would come out in their honor. But when a child dies after five or seven or eight years on this planet, what legacy can she leave? It would be nice to see smiles on children's faces and know that in some way, Emma, Alyson, and Katie helped put them there.

As the foundation grew, I wanted to love the raft of positive programs we were sponsoring. Theoretically, I did. One nice activity called Grow With Me gave fifth-graders a full-day outing to the local park and garden where they planted seeds and learned about nature.

As with Beautiful Me, I went along as a tribute to the girls. The first field trip went off perfectly—a sunny, beautiful day and the fifth-graders smiled as they dug their hands in the dirt and tenderly touched the shoots of new plants. Their faces lit up with excitement when botanists explained the cycles of growth and specialists taught them about butterflies and snakes. It was sweet and inspiring. But my heart boiled with anger and resentment.

These are Emma's classmates. Why isn't Emma here? I thought.

I cared about the other children, and I knew they liked the program. We were doing something lovely in the girls' memory.

But all I really felt was pain.

These children are having a wonderful day because my daughters are dead.

I kept my unworthy feelings to myself and pushed on.

Fourteen

Our house always had a beautiful glow at Christmas, our happiness shining as brightly as the lights that we strung from every beam and banister. I festooned the downstairs rooms with garlands and wreaths and children's drawings, and Warren liked to buy a tree so massive that it scraped the ceiling. In the interest of preserving the paint job, we eventually bought a graceful artificial tree that looked perfect when we decorated it with ornaments and twinkling lights. Three stockings hung on the mantel and presents quickly piled up under the tree.

But the year the girls died, I never unpacked the lights from their storage boxes and I didn't want a tree. I couldn't muster an ounce of Christmas cheer. I didn't even go to church. God obviously hadn't listened to my prayers in a while, and I wasn't in the mood to offer any new ones. We had a tradition of going to the home of our friends Maria and Anthony every Christmas Eve. They lived about thirty minutes away. Warren and Anthony had grown up together, and our children, who were the same age, liked celebrating together.

But there was no celebrating this year.

Trying to bring us some cheer, my friend and neighbor Laura and some others on our block bought a little pink tabletop tree that they decorated with ornaments and bows and a pink skirt.

Somewhat abashed, Laura brought it to the house.

"Oh no, what's this?" I asked when I first saw it. "You've got to be kidding me."

The tree was adorned with soccer ball ornaments, pictures of the girls, lots of angels, and a big EAK strung across it. "We all decorated it with the things the girls like," Laura said.

I put it on the end table in the living room. When it lit up, I sometimes laughed and thought how cute it was to have a pink Christmas tree. At other times, I reflected on how far my life had sunk—from the glorious holiday festivities I used to have, I was now left with a sad little Charlie Brown tree and no children to laugh with me.

Others in town wanted to give us some cheer, too, and I heard rumors that a big group planned to come caroling at our house on Christmas morning.

"I don't want that," I said to Isabelle one morning. She had come over with coffee and was sitting in my kitchen. "No way. Make them cancel it."

"I didn't have anything to do with it," she said plaintively, taking a sip from her cup rather than looking at me.

"Can't you stop it?"

"I don't know. An email went out and—"

"Oh no, don't tell me," I said, rocking back in my chair in shock. "An email? So how many people are going to show up?"

"Maybe a lot," she admitted. "Someone from the church is organizing it."

"I don't want people to ruin their Christmases for us," I said with a groan. "Everyone's done enough. Plus it's too emotional for me."

"They just want to come caroling so you won't be so sad on Christmas," Isabelle said. "People care about you and Warren."

"I know they care," I said. "They feel sorry for us. I don't need to be reminded that we're the lonely freaks of Floral Park. While they're caroling, they'll be on the lawn thinking, 'Oh, those poor people,' and I'll be propped against the door wanting to die."

"I'll come over and be with you so you're not standing there alone," Isabelle promised. "Mark will come, too. I'll call Jeannine and Rob. Melissa and Brad. We'll all come."

"You'd better be here because I'm not opening the door myself," I said flatly.

On Christmas Eve, Warren and I hardly exchanged a word. The house stayed dark and quiet. We had no excited children waiting for Santa Claus, no presents to sneak out of the closets, no "'Twas the Night Before Christmas" to read aloud. We had presents for each other, but no stockings were hung by the chimney with care—because we doubted that St. Nicholas would ever be here again.

Christmas morning, I got up early and went down to the kitchen. If friends were coming to my house, I was determined that they be fed—especially on a holiday. By the time Isabelle and Mark and the other couples she'd called had arrived, I had a pretty breakfast spread laid out for them.

Jeannine's eyes welled with tears when she came in and saw the effort I'd made. "This is just what your house always used to be," she said, giving me a hug. "Huge spreads of food and everyone welcome. It's good to see."

"Don't think I'm back to cooking," I said grudgingly.

Jeannine just shrugged, not ready to point out to me that I was making hopeful choices every day, from taking a Thanksgiving run to making a Christmas breakfast. I thought I wanted to die, but the evidence showed that I hadn't completely given up on life.

Before long, the house was buzzing with friends in holiday sweaters, and I was secretly pleased when everyone piled food onto their plates. My homemade version of Egg McMuffins got raves, and the buffet of baked goods that I'd arranged prettily on platters inspired enough Martha Stewart jokes that even I had to smile.

Suddenly we heard voices raised in song outside. I looked anxiously at Isabelle, but she and Melissa marched me to the door and we flung it open.

A convivial group of men and women, probably forty or fifty strong, stood on our snowy lawn singing a cheerful Christmas carol. As they raised their voices, their warm breath turned to steam in the cold air, and some stomped their boots against the chill. I recognized some of the carolers, though not all. Seeing them gathered in bulky winter coats and colorful hats and scarves, I felt like I'd been transported into some

Hollywood version of a hometown Christmas, with kindly neighbors gathered to offer "tidings of comfort and joy."

To my great surprise, the carolers' good tidings did bring comfort. Joy wasn't yet an option, but comfort was certainly a start.

Most of them left after finishing their songs, but a few whom we knew well came in for hot chocolate or a muffin. Our friends left to get on with their own Christmas plans, but for much of the day, people drifted in and out, and we got through the day surprisingly easily.

"We're coming back for Christmas breakfast next year," Melissa said as she put on her coat to leave. "This was fun."

Christmas breakfast for twenty. A new tradition at my house.

Fifteen

People started telling me almost immediately that I should have more children. I hadn't yet hit forty, and the theory seemed to be that if my life had been brutally taken from me, I should just start another one.

Honestly, I thought they were nuts.

Children are not interchangeable. I loved Emma, Alyson, and Katie as individuals, and one could not replace another. I had three children and always would. I wanted to be *their* mother, not any mother.

Into the winter, I continued to wake up every morning furious that I was still in my house and not reunited with the girls in heaven. How could I survive a hurt this deep and an emptiness so vast? I realized that the same accident that took my children also destroyed my identity and my reason for being on this earth. For nearly a decade, I had devoted every bit of energy and emotion I possessed to being a mom, and now—like anyone else who loses a job she loves—I felt unmoored.

Emotionally, I couldn't begin to think about having more children. And practically, I didn't see how it could happen. The pregnancies had been difficult for me, and after Katie was born, I had my tubes tied. I had lobbied for the procedure after Alyson, but the obstetrician pointed out that at just thirty years old, I might not be done. And she was right.

The moment Alyson arrived in the world—with a smile on her face that never went away—I forgot about the miseries of the pregnancy and started talking about having another baby.

"No," Warren had said.

"No?" I asked. "You can't just say no. We're a couple. We have to talk about it."

"Nothing to talk about," he said, sounding like a stereotypical man. "Two is easy and three will be too much. I don't want more."

Not knowing how to countermand his unilateral decision, I took the stereotypical female route.

"Then I don't want to have sex anymore," I said.

We both wavered from our positions and in fact had plenty of sex. I hadn't gone back on the pill, which Warren knew, so maybe he had changed his mind. But we didn't discuss it, and when my period was late one month, I panicked and refused to think about it. Finally, Jeannine left an at-home pregnancy test in my mailbox.

"It turned pink," I said, calling her almost immediately.

"That's great!" she said. "What did Warren say?"

"I haven't told him."

Anxious about how he'd respond, I waited a few days, and then finally broke the news.

"We're going to have another baby," I told him one night after Emma and Alyson were asleep.

"I know," he said, kissing me.

"How do you know?"

"I could just tell."

The pregnancy with Katie turned out to be even tougher than the others, filled with anxiety and emotional swings, and Warren and I agreed that after this, we would count our blessings and not ask for more. Emma and Alyson had been born by Cesarean section and we anticipated Katie would be, too. The obstetrician said that three surgeries were usually the limit, and that having more could be a problem because of the amount of scar tissue. So, just before the delivery, the nurse gave me the papers to sign saying that I authorized "sterilization."

"Sterilization?" I asked her, slightly alarmed.

"That's what it is," she said. "Deciding to have your tubes tied sounds innocuous, but realize how dramatic it is. You don't have to do it."

"That's okay," I said, signing the paper. "Three's the charm."

I thought our family was perfect now—and complete.

A couple of months after the accident, I got a call from the obstetrician's office where I had gone with all three pregnancies.

"I hope you don't mind my calling," said the nurse. "But I want to pass along some advice." She had become something of a friend through all my visits, and now she gave me the name of a clinic where she thought I should go to get my eggs frozen.

"Why would I do that?" I asked.

"In case you ever want another baby," she said.

"I don't," I said quickly. Even mentioning the idea seemed like an affront. I'd had my three girls, and nothing could replace them.

But I also knew that I couldn't trust my own instincts anymore. I spent every day dazed and confused, and I didn't see any way to make sense of my new lot in life. Maybe the recommendation of a doctor or nurse could help.

I called a friend and went to the clinic. But I immediately found out I was too old to freeze my eggs. Apparently, you do that at age twenty-five or so, not thirty-seven. But the fertility doctor who broke the news had another plan.

"We can do in vitro fertilization," she explained. "We make the embryos and freeze those, which is more effective."

The doctor quickly described the procedure. It sounded like a lot of effort, but I was mulling over the idea and thinking "Why not?" when she dropped the kicker that answered that question.

"The cost for each cycle is about twenty thousand dollars," she said.

Twenty thousand dollars? Was she joking? We had just paid for a funeral for three children at enormous expense. I didn't have a job, and since Warren's real-estate appraisal business was tied to the scarily plummeting housing market, who knew what would happen for us financially?

"I can't afford that," I told her bluntly.

"Come back next week when we have the results from the exam and blood work," she said. "I'll check with Billing to see if there's any chance that your insurance covers the drugs." She handed me a huge stack of forms that I knew I would never fill out.

When I returned to her office for the follow-up, she looked worried and shooed away the friend who had come with me.

"I need to speak to Mrs. Hance alone," she said gravely.

It sounded like bad news, and I instantly inferred that they'd found something incurable in the blood work and I'd be dead in twenty-four hours. The thought made me unaccountably happy.

I had sunk so low that a devastating diagnosis promised to be a reprieve. *Hooray!* I thought idiotically. *I'm going to die and see the girls!*

But the physical results had been fine, and the doctor only wanted to inform me privately that my insurance would not pay anything. Well, that was that, there was nothing more to discuss. Between the cost and the paperwork, I decided I wouldn't think about it anymore. While the problem hadn't seemed very dramatic at the doctor's office, it took on enormous proportions when I told Jeannine the story a few days later. Warren was willing to do anything I wanted, and told me not to worry about the money. But the costs and procedure seemed overwhelming and I refused to put any more pressure on him.

"Why does everything have to be this way?" I wailed as I sat in Jeannine's kitchen. "Everything has been so hard since the accident. Why can't something good happen? Something should be easy."

By merest coincidence, Jeannine had a friend named Emily visiting who heard the conversation. And, by even greater coincidence, Emily's sister-in-law was an embryologist who worked for a fertility doctor in Manhattan. Overhearing our conversation, she offered to call her sister-in-law for advice.

The next day Jeannine called me excitedly.

"You have to call Wally," she said.

"Who's Wally?"

"She's Dr. Rosenwaks's assistant."

"Who's Dr. Rosenwaks?"

"The best fertility doctor in New York. Maybe in America or even the whole world. He got Celine Dion pregnant with twins. And a lot of other celebrities go to him, too," she said triumphantly. "Wally's expecting your call at nine a.m. tomorrow."

So the next morning, I picked up my phone, and as soon as I reached her and said my name, Wally started crying.

"Oh, Jackie, I'm so sorry. I know what you're going through," she said, as if we'd known each other forever. "My little nephew just died three weeks ago and my sister is inconsolable. But if you're still here and making it through, I know she's going to be okay."

We spent a long time on the phone, talking and crying. At the end, she told me to come in the following Wednesday.

"Tell your sister I'll pray for her son," I said as we hung up.

The next week, I tucked a picture of the girls in my wallet to give to Wally.

"Where are we going again?" Warren asked me as we got into his car to drive to Manhattan. "And who is this man?"

"Someone important," I said vaguely, wanting to think quietly on the drive.

Wally had said to have the receptionist call her when we arrived so we didn't have to linger out front. But, too embarrassed to request special attention, I just gave my name and sat down in the huge, modern waiting room, which was bursting with activity. Couples desperate to get pregnant came in and out, whispering to each other, going back to procedure rooms, and talking to nurses about blood tests and hormone levels. I'd never had to cope with infertility, and I sensed the tension in the air.

An hour went by. Then an hour and a half . . .

Finally, Wally came out and saw me.

"Jackie, what are you doing here?" she asked, having recognized the name on our chart. She beckoned us to come back through a side door. "Next time come through here and don't wait out front. You get VIP treatment."

We went into another glass-enclosed waiting room and watched as attractive, young nurses moved efficiently through the halls and exam rooms with pleasant smiles. Too intimidated to talk, we sat quietly until we finally got called to meet the famous Dr. Zev Rosenwaks.

Considering his credentials, I understood why people would wait any length of time to see him. In person, he was polite and respectful, with no airs at all. He did a thorough exam and checked Warren's sperm count. All good. Then we went to his office and he sat down at his desk.

"How do you want to proceed?" he asked, getting right to the point.

"I don't know. I don't want to get pregnant," I said, a comment that had probably never been made in that room before.

"Why are you here?" he asked.

"I just want to make embryos," I said, remembering what the doctor at the other clinic had advised.

He looked at me for a moment, as if about to ask what I wanted to do with the embryos if not get pregnant. I might have been announcing that I wanted to do a nice little project for a school biology class. But then he seemed to brush the comment away. *Of course she'll want to have a baby*, he seemed to be thinking. *She just doesn't know it yet.*

"Make an appointment with Wally and we'll get started," he said, standing up.

"Um, before that, where's the business office?" Warren asked. "We'll need to figure out the finances."

"It's taken care of," he said. And he walked out and shut the door.

In the sudden quiet of the office, Warren and I stared at each other, not sure what had just happened.

Finally I got up and opened the door a crack. I saw Wally standing nearby and gestured to her to come over.

"Wally? What does he mean it's taken care of?" I asked in a loud whisper.

"He wants to do this for you without charge."

"Why?" I asked.

She gave a little shrug and a big smile. "Why not?"

We started treatments in January. Couples going through the process often complain that in vitro fertilization is complicated and emotionally draining, but I had no emotion left to drain. I didn't mind the whole process, because it gave some structure to the otherwise oppressive expanses of empty time that had recently defined my life. There were daily injections and trips to the doctor's office every day to measure blood levels and the size of the eggs. Different friends drove me to Manhattan, and everyone at the office was incredibly nice to me. Wally regularly greeted me, and Hunter, the beautiful nurse assigned to my case, answered all my questions and called almost every evening with instructions. The head nurse, Jo, stopped by often to check on me, and Jenny, the medical assistant who took my blood, let me cry on her shoulder. But as nice as they all were, visiting this fertility clinic where—after three children—I would never have dreamed of being brought home my strange situation.

I'd think about where I had been before and where I was now and it just didn't add up. Could the person sitting in this cool, clean medical office having her eggs scanned really be the same one who used to romp in the backyard with three children? If that had been the real Jackie before, who was this woman now?

Even while moving forward with the in vitro, in the back of my mind I still figured that I wouldn't live beyond the year. I had never really let go of the thoughts of suicide that plagued me when the girls were first taken from me. A small voice in my head said that if God didn't get around to taking me soon, I could kill myself and all would be perfect: Warren could have the embryos and someone would gestate our baby. Everyone would have a piece of me, and I'd be in heaven with the girls.

Lying on the exam table one morning as the nurse scanned my belly to measure the eggs, I felt a little guilty. *Nobody realizes that I'm in no frame of mind to have a baby.*

After the first cycle, Dr. Rosenwaks retrieved eight eggs and five of them were successfully fertilized. He seemed pleased, and I—the perpetual people-pleaser—liked making him happy. At least I had accomplished something. Five embryos sounded like plenty to me, but he wanted to do another cycle so that we would have more than we needed.

In the next cycle, I made ten eggs, but something went wrong with the medication right before the retrieval and none of them was fertilized. Dr. Rosenwaks called me, disappointed.

"Let's do it one more time," he said.

"Oh no, no," I said. "I appreciate all you've done, but it's so much money. I wouldn't feel comfortable asking for even more."

"I insist."

I didn't really want to do another cycle, but I couldn't say no to him. His unwavering generosity moved me even more than the prospect of a baby.

On the third cycle, I made ten eggs and all ten were fertilized. I felt like the perfect student.

"Why don't we implant?" Dr. Rosenwaks suggested when he called me this time with the news. "Fresh is better."

"No, no, I'm not ready," I said, thinking, *I'll never be ready.*

"Well, you'll have fifteen embryos frozen," he said.

"Is that good?"

"It's very good."

"I'm so glad," I said. But at that moment, I didn't really mean it.

Part Two

2010

Sixteen

Having been raised a churchgoing Catholic, I couldn't shake the sense that I must have done something to cause the accident. God was punishing me. If my girls were gone in this senseless manner, it must be my fault.

"It has to be something we did," I told Warren, panicked one day. "God was mad at us."

"I didn't do anything," Warren said wearily. "I'm a good person."

"Go back to your childhood," I begged him. "Think. It has to be something."

"I won't, Jackie. We're not to blame."

"We must be," I insisted.

I took out a pad of paper and began writing a list of all the things I had done wrong in my life.

1. I stole a lipstick when I was 16.
2. I lied to my parents to go out with my friends.
3. I lied to Warren when I bought expensive clothes.
4. I made up a story about Emma's broken leg to get out of therapy.
5. Sometimes I'd let the girls eat a muffin in the grocery store while we shopped—and I wouldn't pay for it.

Even in my heightened emotional state, it seemed like a meager list. I went back to Warren.

"Don't you feel any guilt?" I asked him.

"No. I sent my kids away with my own sister, who I loved dearly, who was good to us and the children. I did everything in my power to prevent what happened from happening. I did nothing wrong."

"I know, but they're dead. We obviously did something wrong."

"Jackie, I did everything I could," Warren said wearily.

I had stopped going to mass because it seemed pointless, and a bad sermon from a priest could throw me into a funk. On the other hand, I had joined a women's prayer group—just in case. I was afraid not to.

"I come here out of superstition," I admitted to Kathy, the lovely woman who ran the group. "I'm afraid of what will happen if I don't."

"We're here to pray for you and your children," she said kindly.

We'd go around the room and tell our intentions and do a rosary. Everyone in the room asked for something nice. One woman needed a job, another prayed that the world would get safer. A few times I just prayed for Warren, because I understood that if he wasn't okay, I couldn't be, either. It was simple and straightforward, just hope and goodness without any overlays of guilt and confession.

My mom believed in the Rapture, a final resurrection when we would all be together again. She talked about heaven as a wonderful place.

"The girls never have to go through pain again," she said to me. "Doesn't that make you feel good?"

I had believed in heaven when my dad died at age fifty-six. And when my paternal grandmother followed a short time later, I was glad that they were together again. But now I had nagging doubts.

Is there a heaven? I wondered.

Who really knows? Maybe the girls were just in the cemetery, in the dirt.

Regardless, my hope that I would—and could—see the girls again persisted.

My childhood friend Cortney was the only one who was completely understanding. We'd known each other since we were four years old, and she loved me so much that she couldn't bear the thought of my suffering.

"Okay, I get it," she said. "If that's what you need to do, you should."

"You don't think I'm crazy?" I asked.

"No. You can't live in this pain. I know that."

Her affirmation had an oddly calming effect on me. I could be with the girls whenever I wanted—the timing just wasn't right yet. I always had something to get to first. I had to make it through Alyson's Communion. I could never let people's kindness go unnoticed, so I had to write thank-you notes to everyone who had given gifts and donations. And it wouldn't be fair to leave before I had celebrated Katie's birthday. I had to be here for Family Fun Day, of course. And then write more thank-you notes to all the volunteers. I might be suicidal, but I wasn't rude.

"I can't kill myself until after May," I told Dr. O'Brien during couples therapy one day.

"Why is that?" he asked calmly.

"I have to be here for Family Fun Day. It wouldn't be right for everyone who's working so hard if I weren't here."

"I think that's a good decision," he said.

"But after that . . . I don't know."

"Then just focus on May," he said. "After that, we can make another plan."

"I can't listen to her talk this way anymore!" Warren shouted, exploding in anger. "Every time I go out, I wonder if she'll still be here when I get home."

"She's here," Dr. O'Brien said, trying to provide some perspective.

"But she talks about killing herself all the time. You have to make her stop."

"Jackie needs that coin in her pocket, Warren. Don't take it away from her."

"I can't stand it," Warren persisted.

"You have to understand that it's helpful to Jackie to know she has a way out," Dr. O'Brien said reasonably. "But she hasn't taken it yet. And Jackie's a planner. If she has a date set in her mind that she has to get to, she'll get there."

But we all knew that May and Family Fun Day were still far away.

"Plan a trip together," Dr. O'Brien advised. "You both need some-thing closer to look forward to."

This time, Warren jumped in to help. He talked to Brad and Mark about where we could all go for a grown-up vacation. The guys settled on a long weekend in Key West—figuring there wouldn't be many children there. A nonfamily location was important. This would be a getaway for all of us.

"We have the tickets," I told Dr. O'Brien at the next therapy session. "We're going to Key West."

"That's great!" Dr. O'Brien said with huge enthusiasm.

"Why are you so happy?" I asked grumpily.

"The trip is another stepping-stone for you. You need those. We'll just keep jumping from one to the next."

"And when we get to the end I can kill myself," I said.

"But not until after Key West, right?" he asked. He knew how to make a deal.

"Well, we have the tickets. You know I can't kill myself now," I said.

The trip turned out to be ridiculously fun. With beautiful weather and delicious food to keep us going, we laughed for four days and left reality behind. At one point, the six of us walked into a shop in town filled with typical tourist paraphernalia. I started exclaiming over a little ceramic rooster that said "Key West" on it.

"I love this," I said. "I want it for my kitchen."

"Buy it," said Melissa.

I picked it up just as Brad spotted a huge light in the awkward (and ugly) shape of an octopus.

"Look at this!" he exclaimed, flicking it on and off. "An octopus light! Isn't it great? We've got to get it."

"Ugh," said Melissa. "Where would you possibly put it?"

"My man cave," he said with a wink. Given Melissa's household per-fectionism, Brad's "man cave" was the one room in the house that he was allowed to decorate as he liked. Melissa didn't get any say over it. But she tried a practical argument.

"We'd never be able to get that, uh, thing home on the plane," she pointed out.

"We ship anywhere," the shopkeeper chimed in helpfully.

"You do? That's great. We'll take it," said Brad. Then, turning to the rest of us, he said, "While we're shipping, we might as well get a lot of other stuff, too!"

"Oooh, good!" Melissa and I said.

On a vacation-induced high, we strolled around the store, picking out all the Key West crafts that we absolutely had to have—from wooden signs with silly sayings to a Santa on a surfboard.

"I'll get these," said Melissa, picking up salt and pepper shakers in the shape of Key West's most dreaded tourists—a heavyset man and woman in bathing suits.

We giggled and kept adding more items to our shipment. It reminded me of the shopping trips with Karen—just getting out of the house and indulging myself a little turned off the serious part of my brain.

Later, we wandered back into the sunshine, ate wonderful food, and sat by the ocean. Sitting in a lounge chair the next day with the sun beating on my face, I closed my eyes and thought about how sad I was. But as I tried to concentrate on my misery, I heard the gentle sounds of the waves on the shore and felt the warm breeze against my skin; bright sunshine hit my eyelids, making my interior life lighter.

I sighed and opened my eyes again.

"Here's a lesson," I said to whoever wanted to listen. "You can't be depressed on a beach. It just doesn't work."

Melissa laughed. "Well, then, maybe we should all move permanently to the beach."

If only. When the glorious getaway ended, my sun-induced high spirits fell.

Melissa and Isabelle had been sensitive enough not to talk about missing their kids while we were away, but as we sat on the plane home, I knew they could look forward to eager children greeting them at the door, telling them stories about what they'd done while their parents were away.

I sat on the plane, the window shade pulled. I'd lost the sunlight I'd had on the beach, the sun that forced my darkness away. The air-conditioning in the cabin was freezing, and a slight sunburn I'd gotten made the chill penetrate to my bones. My feet were so cold, I wished I'd worn socks and shoes instead of sandals. The murmur of the passengers faded away as I realized that all I could look forward to getting back to was crying in my bed. And the moment the plane landed, the guilt descended, too.

"That whole trip was so wrong," I said to Warren as we dragged our suitcases into our empty house. "We were laughing and pretending nothing had happened. It was terrible and disrespectful to the girls."

"We have to allow ourselves moments of being normal," Warren said calmly.

"We're not normal. I'd rather feel miserable all the time than have these ups and downs." My indignant words seemed to echo in the desolate room. "Why have fun if it's such a letdown to come home?"

"It's worth it. If you stay miserable all the time, you're not participating in life."

"Fine. I don't want to have to participate anymore. I'm done with having fun," I said adamantly.

"We have to keep trying."

"NO! That whole trip was wrong and makes everything worse!"

As I got more agitated, Warren did, too, and our conversation deteriorated into yet another argument. I should have learned from other experiences that any high would be followed by an even lower low, and in the following days, I sank deeper into depression. The pleasures I'd felt on the beach in Key West disappeared into buried memory—until Melissa called, a couple of weeks later.

"You'll never guess what arrived," she said, her voice deep with foreboding.

"What?"

"A huge box from Key West. I have the octopus light and all the other stuff right here. Should I bring yours over?"

I tried to revive the happy spirit of the vacation shopping spree, but it had long receded.

"I don't need any of that," I said. "What were we thinking?"

"We were thinking that we deserved to have fun," Melissa said gently. "Even you."

A few days later, she brought over the ceramic rooster. It sat in my living room for a long time, a vague reminder of being happy for a moment in my new world order. I would look at the rooster and a book of photos that Brad made from that weekend and be amazed at how carefree we had been.

How could I have felt so good? And will it ever happen again?

Seventeen

For our eleventh wedding anniversary at the beginning of April, I didn't expect any celebrating. I was too upset to recognize how much Warren wanted to make me happy. He liked to see my face light up, and he was growing worried that it never would again. I sometimes wondered if we were doing ourselves any favors by staying together. I had married Warren in part because he seemed so strong and solid, the man I could always rely on. When I was young, I was insecure enough that knowing a man could take care of me had an old-fashioned appeal. But now Warren's own inner resources had been so crushed that he couldn't possibly provide what I needed. Probably nobody could. I had become an empty shell, unable to give him the compliments, comforts, and caresses that he desperately desired. Just looking at each other caused pain.

A year earlier, Warren had marked our tenth anniversary by surprising me with lessons at a local dance studio—particularly amazing because he hated dancing. Whenever we went to a party, I begged him to join me on the dance floor, but he stood on the sidelines while I stepped out. So the lessons were the ultimate selfless gift and got me grinning immediately. He topped off the gift certificate for the lessons with a seductive dress that I could wear dancing and a full-day pass at a spa for hair, makeup, massage, and pre-dance indulgence. A perfect package.

"This is definitely worth another ten years together," I teased him. And I meant it. How could I not love a man so thoughtful?

But the accident happened before we got to learn a single dance step together. I ended up donating the lessons to the foundation for a raffle and sticking the dress in the back of a closet.

Most of the time, Warren didn't make a big deal of gifts. He'd often leave a package in the kitchen before he went to work, knowing I'd rip off the ribbon and open it myself. However, for our eleventh anniversary, Warren had a present that he knew I'd like. With an awkward smile, he handed me a prettily wrapped box and then stepped back, watching me closely as I opened it, probably hoping to see my face light up again.

"You bought it!" I said, opening the box and taking out a gorgeous diamond cross.

"The holy crap cross," he joked.

"I never thought you'd buy it," I said, holding it tenderly.

A few weeks earlier, I'd gone into the local jewelry store to thank the owners for the contributions they'd made to the foundation. Always friendly, they invited me to have fun and try on anything I wanted—and I got busy checking out pretty bracelets, fancy watches, and oversize cocktail rings. But my religious heart won out, and my eyes popped when I saw a big, sparkly necklace in one of the display cases.

"Holy crap, look at that cross!" I exclaimed, without thinking. "If I wore that cross, the girls could see me from heaven!"

When I went home and told Warren the story, he pointed out that I already had a cross.

"Not like that one. It would sparkle up to heaven," I said.

Now for our anniversary, Warren wanted the girls to see my cross from heaven. He clasped the heavy strand at my neck and I looked in the mirror.

"It's beautiful," I said. "I'm going to wear it all the time."

"I hope it gives you a little happiness," he said, his voice choked with tears.

We all need magic in the midst of misery, and that cross around my neck felt like a beacon of hope, connecting me to my girls in heaven. It also had earthly significance, as a gesture of love. Warren didn't believe that the diamond cross would let the girls see me. He didn't think we needed to spend money on jewelry right now. But he knew the cross might mean something to me, and that was enough. In the midst of all our fights and anger and hostility, I could pause now and then to touch the cross and feel a whisper of hope. Even if Warren didn't always know how to improve our situation or ease my anger, he kept trying.

The cross reminded me of another happy gift Warren had given me. A few days before my last birthday, I had overheard Emma on the phone with Warren.

"No, no, Daddy, you have to buy a pink bike," she had said, taking the portable phone out into the yard so I wouldn't listen. "It has to be pink."

I smiled to myself. The girls had been plotting a big birthday surprise for me, and they already told me that they wished I had a bike so I could go riding with them. I agreed.

"I can't find a pink bike," Warren told her. "What about a nice blue one?"

"No, pink."

"Find out if Mommy would like a blue bike."

Emma hung up and came back in. "Mommy, what's your favorite color?" she asked.

"You know my favorite color is fuchsia," I said, describing the deep pink that we all liked.

"Do you like blue?" she asked.

"I love blue, too."

"Oh, good!" she said, a smile lighting up her face.

On my birthday, I was out doing errands when the babysitter called to ask when I'd be home.

"Soon," I said, guessing why everyone was so eager.

A few minutes later, Emma called with the same question. I rushed to get home right away. As soon as I walked in the door, the girls began jumping up and down.

"SURPRISE!" they called out.

"Oooooh!" I said as they grabbed my arms and dragged me into the living room. The shiny blue bike stood in the middle of the room, and the girls had tied a big red bow on it.

"It's perfect!" I said, admiring the leather seat and handles and the big basket in front. They'd picked an old-fashioned beach bike, just what I needed to go riding with them.

After I admired the bike and hugged each of the girls at least twice, Emma suggested we go on my first spin around the block.

"Sure," I agreed.

Alyson wanted to come, too, but I hadn't been on a bike in ages, and I figured one girl at a time was all I could handle.

"I'll come back and get you," I promised Alyson.

Emma raced off to change from flip-flops to sneakers and to put on her helmet. We'd made safety rules long ago and they were inflexible.

"Where's your helmet?" Emma asked me when she came back ready to ride.

"I don't have one yet," I said, new to the game.

"Maybe you should wear your ski helmet," she suggested, ever careful. "And you should change your shoes, too. If I can't wear flip-flops, you shouldn't wear those."

"I'll be okay."

But I should have listened to Emma. White bell-bottom jeans and sandals with high wedges aren't proper garb for bike riding. We'd barely gotten around the block when my pants leg got caught in the chain and I fell over.

"Whoa!" I called as the bike tipped and I landed on the ground. I wasn't hurt, and when I started to laugh, Emma did, too. I came home with torn jeans, a dose of humility, and a promise to do better. After that, I bought more practical biking outfits and rode everywhere with the girls. In part, I wanted to supervise them and keep them safe. But I also just liked being outside with them and feeling like a kid again on my cushy leather seat.

Now I couldn't imagine that I would ever ride that bike again. I wanted to donate it to a charity, but Warren insisted I keep it.

"Why shouldn't I give it away?" I asked him.

"Maybe you'll ride it again," he said. "You never know."

I didn't know where he thought I'd ride the bike—or with whom. But I left it in the garage, a sad reminder of a happy time.

I'd always made sure that birthdays were a big deal in our house, but I couldn't imagine my birthday this year would be anything but misery. Turning thirty-nine, the famous Jack Benny age, didn't mean a thing to me. I decided not to observe the occasion in any way, not even the usual lunch or dinner with friends.

So it was completely unexpected when my friend Maria, the hospice nurse, came over that afternoon and gave me a birthday hug.

"There are some people here to see you," she said.

"What? What's going on?" I asked as about ten women suddenly filled my kitchen. They came from different parts of my life, and I couldn't imagine how they all knew each other—until I realized that since the accident, they had connected through me.

"A birthday gift. From all of us," Maria said, handing me a box. I opened it, and inside was a necklace with the letters EAK in diamonds.

For what felt like the first time in my life, I truly couldn't speak. All the exclamations of "Thank you!" and "That's so generous!" and "It's beautiful!" got caught in my throat. Overwhelmed, I just looked at my friends in wonderment.

"Happy birthday," Maria said.

The others joined in a chorus of good wishes, and then headed to the door.

"Wait, can I get you something to eat? Or drink?" I asked, trying to recall my manners.

But, not wanting to make me endure an extended emotional scene, they just waved and left. I stared at the EAK necklace and then plopped onto the sofa, thinking about the incredible kindness of my friends. Even in the midst of my despair, I recognized how lucky I was to be constantly buoyed by their compassion and goodwill. And their gift had extraordinary meaning. They knew I had EAK bracelets and beads and logos and T-shirts, and the initials were even in my email address. Now I could have this beautiful symbol of my girls around my neck, hanging close to my heart, every day. I spent the next several days writing each of them a thank-you note, expressing the gratitude I'd been too overcome to share.

With Warren's cross and my friends' EAK diamonds, I now had the two most beautiful—and meaningful—necklaces in the world.

I had a thoughtful husband and caring and attentive friends. Comfort and love wherever I turned. The support helped me get through every day, but how could anything fill the hole in my heart? What could possibly make up for what I had lost?

With the Hance Family Fun Day in May getting closer, everyone I knew seemed so busy with preparations that I worried that their jobs and kids and dinners were being given short shrift. I tried to participate because it was the right thing to do, but my heart wasn't in it.

Warren, on the other hand, threw himself into the planning. He and his friend John Power, the landscaper, led a major effort to clean up the Centennial Gardens in town. John brought his crew of some twenty gardeners to clean, weed, and to plant shrubs, and other volunteers joined in. We built a stage on one side of the gardens where bands could play at our event and at other occasions throughout the year.

"You should come help," Warren said eagerly, before one of the days of cleanup and flower planting.

"I don't want to come," I said, as always resisting his efforts to make me see the positive.

"But it's going to look great."

"I'm glad."

I stayed home, but throngs of people, including Boy Scouts and Girl Scouts, parents and children, and groups of teenagers, showed up to weed and clean.

"The gardens look amazing!" Warren told me excitedly that night. "In addition to everything else, we've given a great gift to the town."

I was glad that having a mission seemed to be helping Warren's mood. It wasn't doing as much for mine, but I knew I had to keep up a good front for everybody who was doing so much. My public persona was a lot better than what Warren got stuck with at home.

The week before Family Fun Day, Heather invited a big group of women to her house for a two-night party with a purpose. As always, I tried to keep a smile on my face. But mostly, I wandered around aim-lessly both nights while my artistic friends arranged raffle items decora-tively in big baskets, wrapped them with cellophane and colorful bows, labeled them, and made a booklet of what was for sale.

Despite all the sorting and wrapping and packing, everyone milling around Heather's basement seemed in high spirits. Maybe they felt the euphoria of doing something for a good cause, the satisfaction of creat-ing hope from horror, meaning from misery.

"You brought everyone together," one of my friends said as she sorted through a pile of donated stuffed animals. "People are making new friends and working together. Everyone's having fun. It's so great."

Great, I thought. My girls were dead, but people had made new friends. Was that supposed to be a silver lining? I looked around at all the women working hard and I tried to remember that they were doing this for Emma, Alyson, and Katie. But the noisy chatter in the basement pounded in my ears and the cheerful voices grated.

I tried to ignore the screaming voices in my head telling me to run away. I couldn't do that. I had to stay and participate. I would honor the feelings of the people who were trying so hard to do something good.

By the time we finished, we had 120 baskets. It had been a lot of work, but it also meant a lot of money we could raise.

"How are you doing?" my friend Deana asked, coming over as I stood staring at the booklet where I was supposed to be writing down basket numbers. So far, I hadn't written a thing.

"Just fine," I lied.

"Are you sure?" Deana asked. Deana's children were the same ages as my girls and she had thrown herself into the planning. "This is probably harder for you than you realize."

"No, it's fine. I'm okay." I felt my smile wavering. "I guess I'm just getting tired."

I tried to look enthusiastic. It was all so nice and generous and good. But even a million baskets wouldn't bring back my girls.

Please get me out of here . . .

• • •

There was no way I could get out of May 22. That I survived the whole day without collapsing, screaming, or sobbing in public is a testament to strong will and modern medicine. I had already learned how to make myself go numb in order to get through any ordeal. And with thousands of people expected to show up for the festivities, "getting through" was the best I could hope for.

The morning was all about the races, and the sheer number of people who showed up—more than 1,200—was overwhelming. We started with a Peewee Race for children under seven, who ran over a bridge and got medals and cupcakes when they finished. Even I had to admit it was cute—most of them walked away holding their award in one hand and a cupcake in the other. Next was a one-mile Fun Run called "Emma's Mile" that attracted loads of kids, from ten-year-olds to teenagers. Then a 5K race with close to a thousand runners and walkers, cheered on by live music from a teen band.

After the medals (lots of them) were given out, we regrouped for the afternoon, and for the first Hance Family Foundation Fun Day.

We had 250 volunteers, and around 3,000 people showed up at the now-beautiful Centennial Gardens. I wandered around saying hello to the girls' friends and classmates, their teachers and camp counselors, neighbors and storekeepers and people I knew from around town. This whole community of friends and family had mourned together in the face of our tragedy. Now, in the place where the girls had lived their short lives, people who had been so deeply affected by their loss wanted to find hope again, and they rallied around out of goodwill and genuine feeling. However much pain I felt, as I looked at all the familiar faces, full of kindness and purpose, I recognized the triumph of a town that could make such an effort to memorialize the girls.

There was so much going on that I couldn't take it all in. We had live music and games, face painting and mini-manicures. The New York Islanders hockey team had sent their mascot and arranged for games like slap shot. Children played on the "bouncies" that had been donated and took pictures with teens who had dressed up as fairy-tale characters. They made pictures in "Aly's Art Gallery" and hung them on a line with clothespins for everyone to see, then got costumes in "Katie's Corner" for dress-up games.

"Emma's spirit, Alyson's joy and Katie's innocence shone through on every face in the crowd," Bernadette wrote later on the foundation website.

By every measure it was a smashing success.

And yet I couldn't have been happier when it was over.

Eighteen

July. A whole year since the accident.

People gathered protectively around me as the day approached, but, oddly, it was the ordinary days that were harder to get through.

I wrote a letter to my friends on July 21:

"People often ask me if I feel better than I did a year ago. The answer, simply stated, is 'no.' My mind is much clearer, but with clarity comes a lot of heartache and anguish. I have cried every single day since the accident. Holding it in would be much worse, so I always allow myself to cry. I know what it is like to see life go on around you and not be able to get out of the quicksand that you feel you are drowning in."

For the previous twelve months, I had started many sentences with "Last year I went with the girls . . ." or "Remember last year when the girls and I . . ." Now I couldn't say that anymore, and I couldn't believe how much time had gone by since I had seen my girls. Instead of the passing time healing the wounds, it just cut them deeper. I missed Katie's hugs and Emma's wisdom and Aly's smiles. When we still had our normal, daily routines together, I counted our time apart in minutes and hours, not weeks and months. And even those minutes had sometimes seemed like forever.

Katie will be in kindergarten all morning, I used to think. *What will I do with all that time?*

Now I had to reorient myself and think in terms of years.

Years without my girls.

I went to one meeting of a grief-counseling group for parents who had lost children. The mothers there were supportive and full of hope. But their devotion unnerved me.

"Your children stay with you forever," said one woman, who described a lovely ritual she had enjoyed that year on Mother's Day.

"How long since your daughter died?" I asked her.

"Twenty-two years next month," she said.

I felt my heart sink.

Twenty-two years?

I couldn't imagine two decades of living in pain without my girls. I wanted to run screaming from the room. Looking around at the mothers whose children had died ten, twenty, or thirty years ago, I felt myself gripped by fright. They seemed placid and peaceful—but they still attended this grief group.

Maybe it never gets better.

Warren wanted me to believe that our lives could get better, and after the lesson of Key West, he suggested we spend some of the summer by the ocean.

"You can't be depressed on a beach," he said hopefully, remembering my comment.

Melissa had decided she could never return to the beach club where we had been last summer, and she rented a house in the Hamptons. Warren and I stayed there for a while and then shared a house with Isabelle and Mark on Long Beach Island. Coddled again by the sound of waves and water and warmed by the sunshine, we made it through.

While we were at the beach, my mother stayed at the house in Floral Park, ostensibly to dog-sit our old wheaten terrier, Oliver. Mom had been depressed and struggling this year, so devastated at losing her grandchildren that I couldn't expect her to be able to comfort me, her daughter.

Looking after the dog gave her a purpose, and she eagerly offered to stay at the house when we escaped to the beach. Maybe being surrounded by the girls' familiar things gave her the comfort that it sometimes did me.

Early in the week, she called me at the beach to check in and see how we were doing.

"I guess you're okay with the swing set coming down," she said, just a slight edge of anxiety in her voice.

"What?" I asked, my voice rising in a shriek.

"Oh, um, you didn't know? I assumed you did. Your friend is here taking down the swing set. He said Warren wants it down."

I hung up and ran hysterically over to Warren.

"The girls loved that swing set!" I screamed, remembering when he had bought it for Emma's first birthday. "And we still have kids coming over to the house who play on it!"

"We have to take it down," Warren said. "It's getting old and could be dangerous. We can't risk someone playing on it and getting hurt."

I couldn't decide if "dangerous" was just an excuse for Warren to get rid of a memory he found painful to see every day. But he was insistent, so I let it go.

My mom's call prepared me, so when we got back from the beach, I braced myself to face a gaping hole in the yard. But our landscaper friend John hadn't just taken down the swing set—he had started a beautiful rock garden and waterfall to replace it. I immediately thought of the little Japanese rock gardens you put on your desk to help you relax. In the same spirit, this natural memorial exuded a sense of peace. For the next several weeks, John and Warren worked on the project together. When it was done, I still missed the swing set, but the tranquil garden created a corner for contemplation and calm.

As Year Two got under way, my once-wonderful life seemed to recede farther into the past. Birthdays, first day of school—we'd been through this cycle once, and everyone expected the second go-round would be easier. But it wasn't. It was like being adrift at sea in a rowboat—steady waves pulled me farther and farther away from the beautiful shore I had left behind, and I couldn't yet see any safe ground on the other side.

Psychiatric manuals give people a year to recover from grief. My year was up with no recovery in sight. No protective scars had formed over the raw grief, and if anything, each day got harder and harder.

Whoever writes those manuals doesn't have a clue.

Even Oliver seemed to be having a hard time. He was getting old, which meant that soon I'd be losing him, too. Warren had bought him for me as a surprise shortly after my dad died—so he was like our first baby. When Emma joined the family several months later, Oliver seemed mildly offended. At Aly's arrival, he looked at me like, *What? Another one?* But he seemed to get used to having the girls around, and Emma adored him. Once when Aly was about four years old, she reached into his mouth to take away food that he'd gotten from the garbage—and he snapped.

"You have to put down a dog who bites," the vet said after Aly got stitches.

But Emma wouldn't hear of it. Protective of all living creatures, she locked herself in her room with Oliver.

"If he goes, I'm going," she announced dramatically.

Preferring to keep both of them, we hired a dog trainer to come to the house instead.

"The dog needs to know that the hierarchy in the house is you and Warren, the girls, and then him," the trainer told us. "Right now he's treated like a king and thinks he's top of the heap."

A king? Well, maybe I did cook special meals for Oliver. So we took the trainer's advice and set new rules. Once we established a different pecking order in the family, Oliver's behavior improved dramatically. He was never aggressive again.

But he stayed spoiled.

After the girls were gone, I cooked for him and nobody else. Our sad old dog seemed as lost and lonely in the empty house as I did. Then one day, a year after the accident, Warren surprised me by bringing home a new dog.

"What am I supposed to do with him?" I asked, unable to imagine rousing myself to take care of a new dog.

"Oliver needs a friend," Warren said.

The little puff of white fur he'd brought home was a Havanese who already had a name tag on his collar that read JAKE W. HANCE.

"You named him already?" I asked Warren.

"Not just any name," Warren said triumphantly. "J-A-K-E—Jackie-Alyson-Katie-Emma. *W* for Warren. The dog is named for all of us."

Oliver did perk up in Jake's presence. But however thoughtful his name, I didn't want a new dog.

I refused to love him.

"I'll take good care of him," I told Warren, "but that's it. I don't have any love left to give."

Frisky Jake did everything he could to win me over. He curled up in my lap when I sat crying alone. He ate store-bought dog food instead of insisting on homemade. He scurried onto the windowsill and peeked between the venetian blinds to watch me when I went outside.

But caring about a dog who had never met Emma, Alyson, and Katie seemed like a betrayal, just like enjoying a garden where they'd never sit held very little joy. I felt hollow inside. Like the Tin Man, I was missing my heart.

Nineteen

Life had stopped for me. I couldn't expect that it would stop for other people, too, but in many ways it had. Friends had put their own activities on hold to sleep at our house and bring us meals and be available at all hours. Now, more than a year later, they needed to let their families return to normal. They still came by all the time, called, and surrounded me with help and support. But the shock had lessened and everybody wanted to move ahead with their own lives.

Many of our friends' children were seeing therapists for anxiety disorders that had cropped up after the accident. The psychologists urged the parents to do whatever they could to provide an atmosphere of stability and constancy. Nobody abandoned me or kept their children from me, but I would have understood if they did. I was the monster-under-the-bed personified, the epitome of everyone's worst fears: a mother who couldn't keep her children safe.

Even though I understood others' need for normalcy, I found it hard to stomach any efforts at life-as-usual. Each seemed another step toward forgetting my girls and abandoning their memories.

Jeannine sent out invitations for her annual Halloween party, which she had canceled the previous October. It hit me hard. All the anger I normally aimed at Warren got redirected at one of my very best friends. How could Jeannine do this to me?

"Who's going?" I asked Isabelle as the day got closer.

"Just about everybody," she admitted.

"Are you?"

"No, I'll stay home with you. I'd much rather do that than put on a costume."

I felt deeply grateful but didn't admit it. However much I hurt, I didn't want to inconvenience anybody.

"You can go if you want," I said with a shrug.

"I'm not really into Halloween," Isabelle said loyally. "I used to go because everyone else did. This is a great excuse to stay home."

Isabelle is kind and sweet and funny, and with her gentle charm turned on full force, I made it through the evening of the party. But after Isabelle left, my mood turned black. I stayed up all night, unable to control my fury.

At about 3 a.m., needing to vent, I sent a text message to Jeannine:

"I have to get this off my chest. I don't understand how you could have a Halloween party where you're laughing and having fun with all our friends. It breaks my heart. Birthdays and Christmas we all try to celebrate, but you didn't have to do Halloween. It's not necessary. I know this is wrong of me and I'm being irrational and selfish. But it's what I'm feeling."

By 7 a.m., Jeannine had texted me back. She apologized for hurting me and said that was the last thing in the world she wanted. But she needed to have the party for her family. She and Rob had been hosting Halloween parties since before the children were born, and not celebrating was weird for them. The children had been upset.

"The kids wanted to have Halloween again," she wrote. *"We could explain not having the party last year, but now their lives have to get a little bit back to normal. I apologize again for how you feel but it's what we had to do."*

I realized she was right. Jeannine is so competent and steady that I rely on her judgment to lead the way. And maybe that's why the party, which she always held the weekend before Halloween, stung so deeply. Whatever Jeannine did was carefully thought through and considered. She had four children of her own to think about, and she understood that people needed to keep going with their lives. She wanted me to keep going, too.

But I couldn't do that yet.

• • •

"What are your plans today?" Warren asked one morning as he got dressed for work and saw that I had crawled back under the covers. "Who are you going to see?"

"I don't want to see anybody."

"It's Thursday," Warren said, persisting. "You should go to your bowling league."

"I don't feel like bowling today," I said testily.

"You have to go bowling."

"Really, Warren? My kids are dead and you think it's important that I go bowling?" I glared at him across the room. "I have the right to do whatever I want."

"We all have to do things," Warren said, standing his ground. "I have to live with this pain, too. I don't have a choice. As miserable and sad as I am, I have to keep going. What if I didn't go to work?"

"I wouldn't care."

"You'd care. We wouldn't be able to pay the bills, and we need a roof over our heads."

I pulled the covers over my head. "Leave me alone," I said, my voice muffled by the blankets. However strong my muscles might be from running, I was too emotionally tapped out to move.

"Listen to me!" Warren ordered, shouting like a marine sergeant at basic training. "If I need to go to work, then you need to get out of bed," he said angrily.

"Why? I have no kids to take care of and nothing to do. I want to stay in bed today."

In the back of my mind, I knew that Warren was right, and he wanted only what was best for me. Finding something to keep me busy was better than staying home by myself to wallow in my misery. Warren realized that, and I did, too. And though he wouldn't admit it, he was scared for me to be alone.

Since Warren's office is near our house, I used to call him sometimes when the kids were little, asking him to dash home briefly so I could run to CVS or do an errand.

"What if I worked far away?" he'd ask.

"But you don't!" I'd say cheerfully.

Now, without children to take care of, I no longer had any reason to ask him. But he appeared often during the day to check on me, anyway. Finding me in bed invariably led to another fight. So sometimes when I didn't want to face either Warren or the world, I'd show up at Isabelle's doorstep.

"Can I lie in your bed?" I'd ask plaintively when she answered the bell.

She'd hug me and let me in, and I'd nest for an hour or two (or three) on her soft sheets, safe and alone. Maybe it was a little weird, but what in my life wasn't weird? Other times, I'd go to Laura's house across the street to take a nap. But rather than just walk directly over, I'd drive around the corner and park the car where Warren couldn't see it. If he stopped home, he'd think I'd gone out. Like a teenager sneaking off for a smoke, I snuck away to sleep.

After the holidays, something clicked in me. Other people were moving on with their lives, but my life was essentially over. Every parent on earth could understand my not wanting to go on—I felt extreme guilt for not having protected the children and the extraordinary loneliness of being here without them.

Standing in the living room after Warren left for work one morning, I made a conscious decision to kill myself. Being reunited with my daughters in heaven had always been a theoretical coin in my pocket, as Dr. O'Brien had said. Now I wanted to make it real.

Late that night, I began searching the Internet for the best ways to end my life. I'd never owned a gun and didn't like violence, so that was out. Hanging would be grotesque.

Pills seemed an obvious solution. Always thinking ahead, I'd been hiding away a few pills from every prescription, and I had plenty that I could swallow at once. I'd be glad to take them, but you get no guarantees with pills.

I read about other methods of ending my life, amazed by how much specific information about suicide and death is available online. Antifreeze, which is odorless, colorless, and has a sweet taste, had a certain appeal. So I had my answer: antifreeze and pills. I felt a certain elation at finding a solution to my pain. I'd do it at the Floral Park Motel, so Warren wouldn't have to find me in the house. He should get to keep living in his own home without feeling it might be haunted. I'd leave my car in the motel parking lot so everyone would know where to find me.

With the plan fully settled in my mind, I went to bed calmer than I'd been in a long time. I fell asleep immediately and had the most vivid dream I'd ever experienced. I saw myself standing at the entrance to heaven. Just beyond the gates, I could see Emma, Alyson, and Katie, smiling and sweet and close enough to touch.

"Mommy, Mommy, you're here!" they called excitedly.

I started to rush toward them, but God didn't let me inside the gates.

"You didn't do everything you could on earth," he said.

"I did," I whined. "I've prayed, I've written every thank-you note. I'm suffering so much."

"The doctor gave you a gift. Why haven't you used it?" God asked.

"I want to be with my girls," I pleaded.

"You have to take the gift and at least try to use it. And then you can come back."

I woke up with my heart pounding.

Try . . . and then you can come back.

The words had been so clear I didn't know if the conversation had happened in real life or a dream. I lay in bed for a long time, repeating every word over and over.

That afternoon, I was driving to do some errands when I pulled into a parking lot and began crying. For sixteen months I had stayed stuck in the same moment, with no dreams or aims or goals. I couldn't think about a future because I wanted only to retrieve the past. Some part of me understood that what had been lost couldn't be found again. Heaven may be the pipe dream we cling to when this world is too agonizing, but as long as we are alive, we need hope. Nobody can live without hope. And for the last sixteen months, I had none.

Sitting alone in that parking lot and trying to control my sobs, I pulled out my cell phone and called Jo in Dr. Rosenwaks's office. "I can't live like this anymore," I told her. "Everyone is moving on but me."

"I'm glad you called," she said without hesitation. "I'll talk to Dr. Rosenwaks and get right back to you."

I hung up, relieved. I figured there was no way I'd actually get pregnant, but at least I was doing what I'd been told to in the dream. Trying to accept the gift of the frozen embryos.

Twenty

tried not to think too much about any plan for pregnancy until the next week, when Warren and I got in the car to drive to our appointment. Traffic getting into Manhattan that morning was even more backed up than usual, and as we inched along behind a huge exhaust-puffing truck and maneuvered into the Midtown Tunnel, we looked at each other uncertainly.

"So, why are we going to this appointment?" Warren asked, his hands clutching the wheel. "Does this mean you want a baby now?"

"I don't know," I said. I hadn't told him about the dream—and I wouldn't for a very long time. "I don't think I want a baby. Not now. Do you?"

"We're going to the office," Warren said. "We must have a reason. We have those frozen embryos."

"But I don't think I want a baby," I said again. "What are we going to say when we get there?"

"Let's just find out about the process," Warren said.

When we got to the office, Dr. Rosenwaks didn't ask why we had come—he just assumed we wanted a baby. By taking control and giving us a plan, he made it very simple. For starters, I had to go off antidepressants for a couple of months, and since I didn't otherwise have fertility problems, he'd do the implantation on a natural cycle, without drugs.

When you are confused and uncertain, it helps to have someone who seems to know exactly what you should do—and the doctor's certitude was a relief. He was taking care of everything for us, and that's exactly what we needed. I looked over at Warren as Dr. Rosenwaks spoke, and our eyes locked. Something clicked in both of us. Since the accident, we had no next steps to look forward to, no future to plan. Now we might. We would try to implant the embryos.

That evening, I looked longingly at the bottles of antidepressants, sleeping pills, and antianxiety medication that had been lining my kitchen cabinets for the past year and firmly shut the door. I'd stop right now. Now that I'd decided, I wanted to get this process under way.

But I worried that I might become totally unhinged once I'd given up the medication. At our next session with Dr. O'Brien, I warned Warren that I'd be even tougher to deal with in the coming months.

"Warren, how are we going to do this?" I asked. "I'm crazy now with medication. How's it going to be without it?" The very thought scared me, and I couldn't imagine how my husband would handle it.

"It'll be fine," Warren said, as he always did. Why do men always pretend everything will be fine?

Dr. O'Brien was more realistic. "Warren, it's going to be a challenge. Are you up for it?"

"Of course I'm up for it," Warren said.

And so we started.

One day shortly after, we woke up to a blizzard that had whipped up overnight. The whole town had shut down from the high winds and hard-driving snow, and Warren and I knew we'd be stuck in the house together all day. With schools closed for the weather and all our friends at home with their children, the only distraction I had was the occasional snowplow grumbling by. Trapped in the memory-filled house, I felt my anxiety begin to rise. As usual, Warren and I started to fight. We had no particular reason—maybe an argument was the only entertainment we could imagine today.

With no other outlet for my tension, I raced down to the basement, my mind spinning and my heart pounding through my chest. Barely able to breathe, I walked erratically in circles, talking like a crazy person, wondering why I had agreed to Dr. Rosenwaks's plan.

"What am I doing, what am I doing?" I said to nobody in particular. "I can't do this. The whole idea is nuts. Why do I want to get pregnant, anyway? I can't just start my life all over again."

Warren came downstairs and tried to calm me down—which only made it worse. I continued pacing, arms flailing, mind and words racing at a hundred miles an hour.

"This is crazy, this is crazy!" I ranted. "What are we doing? This was such a stupid idea. Why do I listen to people? I'm not doing this, Warren. I want my girls. I want to see my girls. Screw this, anyway."

Normally, Warren would leave and go outside when my hysteria got too much for him, but with the blizzard outside, there was no escape.

"I can't take this, Jackie," he said, clutching his hands to his head.

"Oh really, Warren? You promised Dr. O'Brien you could do this. You promised me you could handle it. Now you're changing your mind?"

"I didn't know you were going to be a lunatic," he said.

"I've got to get out of this house," I said, looking out the window at the raging snowstorm.

"You're not going anywhere," Warren said impatiently. "There's three feet of snow outside."

"I'm taking a walk," I insisted.

"You're crazy!" he shouted.

"I know. I already told you that."

I rushed upstairs and called Bernadette.

"Sure, let's go for a walk. Great idea," she said, always upbeat. "But how are we going to meet? We can't take the cars out."

"We'll meet halfway," I suggested.

I bundled up in ski pants and boots and headed out into the storm. The plows had barely made a path through the middle of the road and huge piles of snow were everywhere. I climbed over the snow, a ten-minute walk that took four times as long. When I finally arrived, Bernadette was rosy-cheeked and smiling as the snow fell on her white knit hat.

"You made it!" she said.

We walked for nearly three hours, climbing the snow mountains, talking, and finally laughing.

"Jackie, you're doing the right thing with the in vitro and the embryos," Bernadette said, always calm and reassuring. "You have to try this. Nothing's easy right now, but you can do it."

We went to her house and relaxed over hot cocoa. I felt the warmth oozing through me. She was right. If I could climb over snow mountains, I could cope without my medications.

A few days later, when the weather had improved and Karen and I had gone off on one of our Tuesday excursions, she mentioned that she knew an acupuncturist who might be able to help with my tension.

"Acupuncture?" I asked dubiously. "You must be kidding."

"It's worth a try," she said.

On a lark, we drove over there and I met the acupuncturist, a lovely woman named Michelle. Karen told her my story and she offered her services for free. The next thing I knew, I was lying on a table with needles stuck in my ears, nose, and forehead.

"To help you get rid of the crazy thoughts and calm your mind," she said, painlessly slipping another needle into my forehead. She added a few needles to my outstretched hands, then looked at me with satisfaction.

"I'm going to leave the room now," she said. "Just lie there for about half an hour and relax and clear your mind."

Relax? Me? She must be joking. The minute she left, I jumped off the table and got a mirror out of my pocketbook to see what I looked like. I started to giggle. The thin needles jutting out everywhere looked silly beyond words. But they didn't hurt. And what the heck? Walks in the snow, giving up antidepressants, trying to get pregnant—like the slim needles currently sticking out of my head, none of it could hurt. At this point, taking new paths was the only chance I had of finding a reason to go on.

Over the next few weeks, Warren sensed that attempting to get pregnant was my last-ditch effort. I had decided that if it didn't work, nothing more could be expected of me. I could bow out of this life knowing I had made every effort to find a purpose for myself. Reasonably enough, he worried about what would happen if the implantation didn't work. As the weeks went by and we waited to do the first implant, he got increasingly nervous.

"You know you're not likely to get pregnant the first time," he said. "You can't get upset if it doesn't take right away."

"That's fine," I said airily. I didn't add that I hardly expected to get pregnant. I didn't really care, either. I'd take advantage of the gift, and when it failed, I'd be free to do what I really wanted.

"We'll try it three times, okay?" Warren asked. "Three cycles. And promise me that you won't get upset if it doesn't work right away."

Upset? I'd more likely be pissed if I *did* get pregnant.

Three attempts at implanting the embryos would, with various delays, bring us to June. So now I had a real date I could point to, an endgame for my pain.

By June, I'd be pregnant. Or I'd be with Emma, Alyson, and Katie.

I had the first implantation in February. I felt unbearably awkward lying virtually upside-down on a tipped-back table, fully exposed to the nurses, doctors, and techs who crowded around my bare bottom, their attention riveted on what looked like a high-tech turkey baster.

What am I doing here? I thought as I stared at the ceiling and tried not to feel humiliated.

The night before, fifteen of my friends stopped by for a surprise Getting Pregnant party. They gave me little pink and blue presents—candles, Hershey's kisses, and colorful frosted cupcakes.

They might have been more excited than I was. As I lay on the table, clutching so tightly to the sides that my knuckles turned white, I wondered if I was the only woman in my (uncomfortable) position who didn't care what happened. I'd always been a good girl and a high achiever and more competitive than I realized, so I wanted the procedure to work. But deep inside I was ambivalent.

After the turkey-baster team left the room, I lay perfectly still for a couple of hours, as they suggested, then made my way home carefully. I stayed on bed rest for the next two days. Women have been getting pregnant for a long time, and the folklore about what works goes on forever. My friends had ideas—and I tried them all. I ate a whole bowl of pineapple because someone told me that it helps the embryos stick, and then I chowed down on a bag of walnuts because I heard they have embryo-sticking advantages, too. I stayed off my feet for a full week. I didn't go running at all.

I told myself that I was just trying to convince people that getting pregnant was what I wanted. I told myself that I already had three children and I didn't want to betray them by thinking for one minute about having another child. But if I truly didn't want it, why do all those things? Why pineapple and walnuts and bed rest? My mixture of guilt and pain and excitement and hope was a complex stew that I didn't fully understand.

Still, I couldn't help but secretly hope I was pregnant. The greatest joy I had felt in my life was my three girls, and a grain of optimism hidden deep inside me said that maybe I could find some hint of that joy again. I mourned the loss of the girls so deeply at least in part because life is a gift, and it was so unfair that it was taken away from them. With a new baby, maybe I could begin to appreciate the gift again.

Every night since the accident, I had prayed to the girls in heaven, asking that I be able to join them very soon. But the night before the implantation was the last night I said that prayer, asking not to wake up the next morning. Once the embryos were implanted, my nightly prayer to Emma, Alyson, and Katie changed.

Please make Mommy pregnant.

My girls listened. They always listened.

Dr. Rosenwaks had warned me not to take any store-bought pregnancy tests, because they could be unreliable with in vitro. I just had to sit tight (and eat pineapple) until my appointment for a blood test.

But a week before the appointment, Denine and Laura showed up at my house for our usual Monday TV night, and before *The Bachelor* even started, they pulled a home pregnancy test out of a bag.

"Come on, it can't hurt," Denine said, brandishing the box. "I just want to see what happens."

I took it to the bathroom, peed on the stick, and then stared hard, watching for something to change. A minute or two passed. I could barely see a shadow. But maybe, just maybe.

I ran upstairs and woke up Warren, who had gone right upstairs after work to avoid the girls' night in the living room.

"Is that a line?" I asked.

"I don't see it," he said, rubbing his eyes.

"It's here, look."

"Yeah, maybe that's a line," he said. "But don't get excited yet."

Too late for that. I felt an unexpected thrill tingling through me.

The next day, I took another test, and the line seemed a little darker. I'm not very good at keeping things to myself, so the news eked out, and my friends reacted with bubbling enthusiasm. We might have been high school kids talking about sparkly prom dresses and fragrant corsages rather than grown-ups considering the possibility of a real baby. Every night that I had friends over, someone brought me a new pregnancy test.

"Try it for me! I want to see it, too!" Jeannine insisted when she popped in on Tuesday.

"Oooh, let us see!" said the women in the knitting group I had joined, a couple of nights later. Melissa and Isabelle each demanded their own proof. By the end of the week, I had taken twenty-seven pregnancy tests. I numbered them all and lined them up and took a picture. Sure enough, the lines got progressively darker.

But even with all that, I felt as nervous as any first-time mother-to-be when I went to Dr. Rosenwaks's office for the blood test. I didn't mention my previews, and he promised to call quickly with official results.

The next day, I decided not to go bowling—that seemed risky at this stage—but looking to be sociable, I joined the team for lunch afterward. We had just settled down at the table when my cell phone rang and I saw Dr. Rosenwaks's number. I grabbed Isabelle and practically yanked her out of her chair. "It's him!" I whispered loudly as we both ran out of the room.

"Jackie, everything looks good," Dr. Rosenwaks said as Isabelle leaned close, trying to hear. "You're pregnant. We'll keep following it closely, and do more blood tests, but the numbers are strong."

"Oh wow, really?" I looked at Isabelle, as stunned as if I had never seen any one of those twenty-seven sticks. Then, turning back to the phone, I asked the doctor, "Are you happy?"

He laughed. "Yes, I'm very happy. Are you happy?"

"Yes," I said, surprised that I truly meant it. "Thank you so much for everything."

I hung up and Isabelle and I began dancing around and giggling like teenagers. I felt like a great success.

We went back to the restaurant, and I knew I couldn't possibly chit-chat right now. "I'm so sorry," I told them, "but I have to leave."

"Are you okay?" one of the women asked.

"Yes, I'm pregnant," I admitted. "Please don't tell anyone. I mean it—don't tell anybody at all. Even my husband doesn't know yet."

They cheered and offered congratulations and one woman got up and gave me a peck on the cheek. Some of these women I hadn't known long and I certainly didn't know them well. But circles of support are formed in the most unexpected ways, and since we rolled bowling balls together down shiny alleys, they ended up being among the first to know my secret.

I called Warren immediately, and by the time I got home, he had rushed home, too. He shouldn't have been shocked—we'd been previewing the idea for days—but having Dr. Rosenwaks's confirmation suddenly changed our well-spun fantasy into incontrovertible fact. I found him slumped on the sofa, an emotional mess.

A normal couple would have hugged and kissed in delight, but, gobsmacked by our new situation, Warren and I just stared at each other and hardly said a word. I sank down on the sofa next to him. The elation I had felt with the bowling group now wobbled as shakily as a gutter ball in the tenth string.

When Warren finally said something, it wasn't what I'd expected.

"I'm exhausted," he said, standing up. "I have to go to bed."

Though it was still the middle of the afternoon, Warren had hit emotional overload. He wanted a baby and had supported me every inch of the way, but the reality was just too much to take in.

So there I was, sitting all alone with my news. I called my mom and her reaction was a noncommittal "Uh-huh." Maybe she was trying to gauge my feelings before reacting too strongly, or she sensed immediately what a weird situation it might be.

"You're pregnant," she said slowly. "That's good?"

"Mom, I don't know."

"How many babies?" she asked.

"I think just one," I said. "I mean, it better be just one."

Dr. Rosenwaks usually implanted three embryos in a woman my age, hoping one would survive. But I had argued for just one. I couldn't cope with more than one baby. He insisted that he never implanted a single embryo—the odds were too low—so we settled on implanting two. In the next week or so, my hormonal levels were so high that we all began to suspect twins. But no—we quickly discovered that I had one healthy baby growing.

After the first shock passed, Warren and I began to talk again, almost unwilling to admit how we were feeling.

"Where will we put the baby?" I asked him one afternoon. "How will we work it out?"

"We have time to think about this," he said matter-of-factly. "We're going to be okay."

"Do you think I can do this again?" I asked.

"Of course. It will be fine," he said. He had become preternaturally calm and even-tempered.

We both felt a little hope. A lot of anxiety. A bit of excitement. And extraordinary gratitude for what Dr. Rosenwaks had done for us. *"You are one of the reasons that Warren and I are still here on this earth,"* I wrote to him a couple of weeks later. *"The day we found out we were pregnant . . . Warren and I felt joy. It was strange. We had not had joy in our life for over a year and a half."*

Even as I wrote the words, I wondered if we had truly felt joy—or if that was just what I thought we should feel. But the elation I'd experienced during that call at the bowling alley had been real. Joy and uncertainty can coexist, I told myself.

"We actually peeked into the future," I continued. *"We had not spoken about the future since the accident because we did not want a future without our beautiful girls. I think that was the best part of this—for the first time Warren and I had hope. Hope that maybe we could have a future. You gave us that hope."*

Telling friends and family the news turned out to be even more satisfying than hearing it ourselves. After nineteen long, sad months, I began to feel that the black cloud had shifted. Maybe not lifted—but shifted. Instead of seeing pain and sadness reflected in other people's eyes, I suddenly got to see hope and happiness and perhaps relief. For all these months, people had naturally wanted to whisper words of optimism—but none came to mind. How could anyone promise hope when the future had been wiped out? Now the miraculous news took away some of the pain everyone had carried.

Emily Dickinson's famous poem "Hope" begins:

Hope is the thing with feathers,
That perches in the soul,
And sings the tune without the words,
And never stops at all.

Our new hope perched precariously on my shoulder—or maybe in my belly. But I still sensed that, like Dickinson's metaphoric bird, it could fly away at any moment.

Part Three

2011

Twenty-one

After the initial euphoria passed, unreality set in.

Pregnancy is always a long road, and since we'd frozen the embryos almost a year earlier, this one had already been longer than most.

Warren and I still had no idea how to feel about our new situation. Handling grief had been hard enough; trying to handle grief with this overlay of rejoicing seemed almost impossible. As usual, we took our emotional mayhem out on each other. Our fights intensified. Now the future wasn't just an empty void, it was filled with haze and uncertainty. Could we really be parents again?

Dr. O'Brien tried every technique he knew to convince us that we had been good parents—and could be again. Warren seemed to accept that. While I theoretically understood the premise, I couldn't accept the idea in my heart. I hadn't protected Emma, Alyson, and Katie, so how could I dream of being responsible for another life?

Good mothers don't let three children die.

My life and expectations had spun so completely out of control that I couldn't really believe that I would have another child. I had been cautious during my first three pregnancies, making sure that everything proceeded as expected, but now I expected only disaster. Every time I went for a sonogram or check-up with my obstetrician, I anticipated bad news.

"A nice strong heartbeat and everything looks fine," the doctor said at one visit early on, looking at the sonogram on the screen.

I turned in great surprise to the image. "Really? The baby is still alive?"

"Yes, of course," she said with a smile.

Of course? I had assumed the opposite. Since the accident, I had come to believe that anything good I got in life would be snatched away. Surely the pregnancy was just another form of divine taunting.

Early in my second trimester, my anxiety and confusion seemed to deepen. Though on one level I wanted a baby, on another, I couldn't bear the thought of being disloyal to my three girls by loving someone other than them. Warren no doubt had his own fears, but he refused to discuss them. And he didn't want to hear the details of my jittery dread, which I insisted on sharing with him morning and night. He shut me out, not wanting to be made more miserable by my endless angst.

"You're so mean!" I yelled at him one Friday night. "How can you sit there and watch TV when I'm in such pain?"

He had walked away from me in the middle of a sentence, unwilling to listen to me wonder whether we had the right to bring a new baby into our unhappy house. Emma, Alyson, and Katie had been so joyous, but now Warren and I were always so sad. A black cloud hung over us, and I shuddered to think of exposing an innocent baby to our misery.

"I can't hear this anymore," Warren called out, not moving from in front of the TV.

"You have to!" I shouted.

Our argument intensified that night and only got worse the next day. We spent all weekend in pitched battle. We screamed and cried, and our stress rose to levels that we knew couldn't be good for any of us.

"We're acting terribly," Warren said disgustedly at the end of the weekend. "We don't deserve this baby."

The fighting had left me ragged. I didn't eat or drink—all I could do was cry. I wasn't trying to undermine the pregnancy, but I just couldn't pay much attention to it, either.

"You have to take care of yourself," Warren said angrily as he left for work on Monday. "We weren't responsible for the accident or what happened to Emma, Aly, and Katie. But if this baby isn't born, we are responsible."

"I'm not doing anything bad," I said halfheartedly.

"If something goes wrong, I won't be able to live with myself," Warren said as he slammed the door and left.

I tried to take a few sips of water, but nausea overwhelmed me. I'd never had morning sickness, so the nausea had a more emotional source. For nearly two years, I'd thought of the future only as a date for when my life would end. Now the future loomed large and real and frightening. Warren's words resounded in my head.

If this baby isn't born . . . we are responsible . . . won't be able to live with myself . . .

I remembered all the care I'd taken in previous pregnancies and thought about how carelessly I was behaving now. I started to panic that after the weekend we'd just been through, something horrible must have happened to the baby.

I called Laura. "The baby is dead," I told her tonelessly. "I know it. Can you take me to the ER?"

Laura didn't ask a lot of questions. She raced over and bundled me into her car. We drove to North Shore Hospital, and the next thing I knew I was stumbling to the front desk and beginning to cry.

"I need a sonogram immediately because my baby is dead," I said to the nurse in the emergency room.

Or at least that's what I thought I said. I intended to sound polite and rational, but apparently, I began blathering and sobbing and making no sense at all.

"I've been crying all weekend and not eating or drinking and now I killed another baby and I'm completely devastated. Someone please help me, I need a sonogram."

The triage nurse looked at Laura, who filled her in on who I was in quick whispered sentences.

Soon I was sitting alone in a completely bare room. A nurse had taken away my jacket, purse, and cell phone, and I had nothing to do but sit and stare. Through a glass panel in the front, I could see that a man was stationed outside the room, keeping watch. It slowly dawned on me that this probably wasn't the place to get a sonogram.

Laura must have made some calls for help, because Isabelle, Jeannine, and Melissa showed up very quickly.

"We have to get you out of here," Melissa said, all business.

"Why? What's going on?" I asked.

"They're doing a psychiatric evaluation," Jeannine explained. "They're worried about suicide. They want to admit you to a psych ward."

I closed my eyes. This hospital didn't seem so bad. After the weekend I'd been through, maybe it would be fine to stay here for a while and rest.

"I just want some quiet," I said. "It's okay. I'll stay."

But my friends had other ideas.

"We'll get you out of here and take care of you," Jeannine said firmly. "Tell them you're fine and need to go home. You were worried about the baby and just wanted to check the heartbeat."

Two psychiatric residents appeared and asked to speak to me alone. Jeannine and Melissa looked worried as they left, and Isabelle squeezed my hand. But the medical residents were both nice women, and I was happy to talk to them. I didn't care if they made me stay. I didn't really want to go home.

But when they stepped out of the room, my friends called Dr. O'Brien. As soon as they could, they came back in and handed the phone to me.

"Snap out of it, Jackie," Dr. O'Brien said, without too many preliminaries. "Do whatever you need to get out of there."

"Why can't I stay?" I asked.

"They're going to put you in a psychiatric facility where you don't want to be. If you need an in-patient residence, we'll find one. But I repeat: Do whatever it takes to get yourself out. Now."

I hung up the phone and sighed. A temporary escape from home would be nice, but he sounded urgent and it seemed out of my hands. Melissa and Jeannine and Isabelle were bustling around, talking to the psychiatric residents and giving assurances that I wouldn't be left alone. They had me out the door and back in Floral Park before I knew what had happened.

By the next day, I was feeling a little better. But thinking about what Dr. O'Brien had mentioned, I started researching private retreats. The problem was that with their mountain backdrops, infinity pools, and "holistic rehabilitation," they were wildly expensive—more for Hollywood celebrities than for me.

"If you really need to go, I'll get the money together somehow," Warren said.

"The places sound so nice," I said dreamily. "Do you think I should?"

"Not really," he admitted.

In general, Warren worried that if I went away, I would never come home again.

A few days later, I confronted Warren with a new idea.

"Let's move," I suggested. "Get a new house and a fresh start for the baby."

"I don't think it's a good idea right now," he said flatly. "Let's have the baby first. There's been enough change. You might want to stay here."

"Is it fair to bring a baby into a house with all these memories?" I asked anxiously.

"They were happy memories," he said. "I don't want to lose those."

He looked out the window and I suddenly saw again the summer evenings when we had family barbecues, Warren standing by the grill while Emma carefully came out holding a tray of hamburgers and hot dogs for him to cook, and Alyson and Katie watched him flip them onto the fire. After we ate, the girls would run around the backyard and I could still see Warren carrying Katie into the house when she got tired, snuggled in his arms, a look of contentment on both their faces.

His resistance to moving irritated me, but I didn't argue further because in truth, I still got some peace from being in the girls' rooms. Many days, I would lie down on each of their beds, one after another, and cry. But now I couldn't just worry about me, I had to think about this baby. Was it fair to bring her into a home where every corner was already imbued with memories of lost sisters? And why wouldn't my husband ever see another point of view?

Before the accident, Isabelle and I had talked about expanding our small houses for our growing families. We both considered moving elsewhere, but our neighbor-friendship was so special that renovations seemed like a better idea. The close connections between our children gave everyone so much joy that any house problems seemed irrelevant.

"I'd give up my house in a minute to have a neighbor like Isabelle," said my friend Kathy, who lived in a huge, exquisite house that made everyone's eyes pop.

"It's a deal!" I joked. "You get Isabelle and I'll take your house." But even as we laughed, I understood what she meant. Friendship trumped room size any day.

Isabelle is like the sister I never had and always wanted—funny and sweet and up for anything. Our husbands referred to us as Lucy and Ethel. We used to come up with crazy schemes together and in the days when our children played together regularly, Isabelle and I did, too. She was easygoing and laid-back and made everyone laugh.

As moms, Isabelle and I were usually running around with the kids, shopping or carpooling or making plans. But one spring when Katie was about four, Warren happened to pop home several days at the exact time that Isabelle was over. And each time he came in, he managed to catch Isabelle and me in a rare moment of relaxing.

"Where are the kids?" he asked one day when he raced in to pick up some papers and found us drinking coffee in the kitchen.

"In the yard playing," I said.

"No they're not," said Warren, looking out the window.

"Then they're in my yard playing," said Isabelle, stepping into the doorway and waving.

Warren just shook his head and muttered about the easy lives we had.

"How does he always come home in the five minutes we're not doing anything?" Isabelle asked, mystified. "It's like he has some magic radar."

The next time it happened, I jumped up from the table. "Pick up a sponge! Pick up a broom!" I called out to her. "Make it look like we're doing something!"

When Warren came in, Isabelle had her coffee in one hand and was idly holding a broom in the other. Warren looked at her strangely but this time didn't comment.

We weren't off the hook yet. A few days later when the kids were playing, Isabelle came up to my bedroom to see a big pile of clothes I'd just bought.

"Try them on, I want to see!" she urged.

So I stripped down and pulled on a new outfit. After getting Isabelle's approval, I took it off and reached for another one just as we heard Warren's car pulling up.

"Oh no, not again," I said, standing in my underwear and feeling very exposed.

"I can't believe it!" Isabelle said. "The radar again. He's going to make fun of us for goofing off."

"I don't want him to catch me trying on clothes," I said, scooping up my purchases and throwing them into the closet. "What should we do?"

"Get into bed!" Isabelle said. "Under the covers, quick."

Giggling, we both jumped into the bed—Isabelle fully clothed and me not so much—and pulled the quilt over us.

We heard Warren's footsteps on the stairs. A moment later, he stood in the doorway and looked at us, baffled.

"What are you two doing?" he asked.

"Watching TV," I said brightly.

"In bed?" he asked. "In the middle of the day?"

"We just felt like it."

He stepped into the room—and, of course, the TV wasn't on.

"We turned it off when we heard you coming up," Isabelle volunteered.

Warren looked at us oddly. He grabbed what he'd come in for and fled.

Isabelle and I tried to wait until he had gone back outside to burst into hysterical laughter, but we didn't succeed very well.

Now that I was pregnant again, Isabelle and I still laughed together all the time, and she regularly came over to visit. But beyond that, the gate between our houses stayed mostly closed. With their best friends gone, her children stayed in their own yard, traumatized by loss and not wanting to experience the pain of coming over. A therapist Isabelle consulted suggested that it might be helpful for Kailey and Ryan if they didn't have to stare into the empty bedrooms across the way anymore. But Isabelle wouldn't hear of it.

"I'm not moving away from you," Isabelle insisted loyally. "Don't even think about it."

She hired an architect who drew up plans to double the size of her house. Eight thousand dollars later, we studied the plans together.

"This is silly," I told her. "You'll have this giant mansion on a block that doesn't have anything like it. You'll never get your money back when you sell."

"Then I won't sell," she said. "I'll live here forever. I'm not leaving you, Jackie. I wouldn't do that."

Her loyalty moved me, but how could I ask her to make that kind of sacrifice? I'd already learned how a life plan can fall apart. "Maybe you should think about moving," I said. "It's okay. I don't know how I'll feel once the baby is born. What if you build this big house and then I want to move?"

But Warren wasn't planning to move, and he felt adamantly that Isabelle and Mark should stay. He and Isabelle talked about how our baby-to-be would make everything just like it used to be. The two yards would be filled with happy children again.

"You two are unrealistic," I told Warren. "What Kailey, Ryan, and the girls had isn't going to happen again. It's never going to be like it was."

"Why not?" he asked. He wanted to recapture the past, but it wouldn't happen. The kids wouldn't be anywhere near the same age.

"Ryan will be eleven when the baby is born. Maybe he'll babysit, but he won't be her best friend. And the baby's not walking through the gate to Isabelle's house anytime soon."

For once I was the rational one in the crowd, able to see clearly what they didn't want to admit.

"Warren doesn't want me to move," Isabelle said one morning when she came over to talk about her expansion plans.

"Then Warren's being selfish," I said. "Anyway, have you looked at the house for sale on Adams Street? It looks pretty online. It's the right size for you. And it's only a mile away."

Isabelle shook her head. "I don't want to look."

"You should," I insisted.

Some days later, Warren called me from work and he was crying. Even before I heard his voice on the phone, I heard a loud, gulping sob.

"What's wrong?" I asked him.

"I told Isabelle she could move," he said. "She liked the house you told her about. I think she's going to make a bid."

I called Isabelle and she was crying, too. "How will I get breakfast if I move?" she asked, only half joking.

Leave it to Isabelle to find the sweet spot of our friendship. Her husband, Mark, and I were early risers, and on weekend mornings, one of us would go out to pick up bagels for everyone. We both have excessive energy, while Isabelle and Warren like to sleep in. We always joked that if Mark and I were married, we'd have a big clean house and be doing projects all the time.

"The bigger question is what Warren is going to do for junk food if you move," I teased back. Given that our own cabinets were either barren or stocked with healthy food, Warren often called Isabelle asking if she had any Ring Dings or Doritos to spare.

The day the moving van pulled up to Isabelle and Mark's house, I felt lower than I expected. Her move to Adams Street signaled a fresh start, and though my pregnancy should have signaled the same, I didn't feel it yet. I wanted my old life back. I wanted my children. I wanted my children playing with Isabelle's children between our backyards.

That night, I showed up at Isabelle's new house with dinner.

"You came!" she said happily, flinging open the door.

"Don't get too excited. It's just takeout," I said, putting dinner down on top of an unpacked box.

She giggled and brought me inside. Despite the boxes, I could see how happy she was in her new house. We both would have liked the gate between our backyards to swing forever, and for our houses to ring with the happy voices of Kailey, Ryan, Emma, Alyson, and Katie all playing together. But that was gone and something else had replaced it. I understood for maybe the first time that change didn't have to destroy me.

"I'm happy for Isabelle," I told Warren when I got home. "I guess this is what people mean when they tell us we have to move on."

"We'll never move on, Jackie," he said. "What happened will stay with us forever. But we do have to try to move. Just keep moving, a step at a time. That's the best we can do."

He was right. Getting on to the next phase of my life would happen slowly. I looked at my belly, which protruded slightly under my shirt. One small step at a time.

Twenty-two

Once when Alyson was very young, we were talking in her room, and I asked her if she wanted to be famous.

"Nooo, Mommy, I don't want to be famous," she had said, shaking her head.

"You don't?" I asked, surprised. "Why don't you want to be famous? I'd looove to be famous." I stood up and struck a movie star pose.

Aly giggled. "I'm happy just the way I am," she said. Outgoing and comfortable in life, she didn't need to imagine a spotlight shining. "But you should be famous, Mommy. You are famous!"

Sometimes those words came back to haunt me.

Because of the accident, I knew what it was like to have photographers snap my picture when I least expected it, or to have store clerks' eyes widen when they saw the name on my credit card. Interest in what the tabloids had dubbed the "Taconic Tragedy" seemed to linger, though Warren and I did nothing to encourage it. We didn't speak to the reporters who continued to knock on our door, and while I became email friends with at least one well-known network TV reporter, I let her know from the beginning that I didn't plan to do an on-air interview. What would be the point? Except for the written statement we gave early on, we tried to stay out of sight, maintaining a public dignity.

My brother-in-law Danny had no such instincts.

Maybe Danny's desire to clear Diane's name overrode everything else—including his better judgment. From the beginning, Warren and I distrusted Dominic Barbara, the sleazy lawyer who used Danny to whip

up a media storm right after the accident. In February, the courts found
Barbara guilty of various misdeeds and suspended him from practicing
law for eighteen months. He promptly retired. But plenty of other people were still turning Danny's head. In late winter, we heard that HBO
planned to run a documentary on the crash, produced by a filmmaker
named Liz Garbus. Danny signed a deal with her.

"Why is he doing this?" I asked Jay, Danny's sister-in-law and his
media sidekick. Since Danny didn't speak to Warren and me anymore, I
got all my information through her.

"I guess we're all still looking for answers," Jay said.

And maybe Danny wanted money. *The Washington Post* reported rumors that "Daniel Schuler was paid $100,000 to participate in the film."
(The film's publicist said it was much less—and it probably was.) When
Warren and I got a call from the filmmakers, we immediately declined
any offer to be interviewed. No discussion. We doubted the documentary would make HBO proud. Filmmaker Garbus seemed to be continuing on the path Barbara had set of finding a medical explanation for the
accident, something that would shed light on why nondrinker Diane had
been drinking. I didn't object to her skepticism, and I shared the view
that something must have happened that none of us really understood.
But the idea of making a public spectacle of it was too much.

"What do you think the movie is going to say?" I asked Warren one
night. "Is there any way we can stop it?"

We couldn't stop it, of course. A free and open press is great—until
you become its victims. Thinking about the documentary made my
stomach churn. Why bring the story up again? In our 24/7 news culture,
shouldn't something else be front and center by now?

Warren received a letter from the producers, asking for permission
to exhume Diane's body. Since we owned the cemetery plot, he would
have to agree before anything could happen. It seemed sordid and horrifying, but Warren and I decided that if Danny needed answers, we didn't
want to stand in his way.

Much as I wanted to stay out of the spotlight, I also wanted people
to remember our daughters. It drove me crazy when reporters talking

about the accident said that the victims had included Diane, her daughter, Erin, and "her three nieces in the backseat."

I am the mother of those three beautiful girls! I wanted to scream. *Emma, Alyson, and Katie are not just anonymous "nieces."*

Meantime, talk of lawsuits continued to swirl. We had lost three children, and now we could lose everything we owned, too. According to the convoluted laws of insurance and legal responsibility, Warren could be sued because Diane was driving his car. Really? You sue a car, not the person driving it? Apparently we could have a round robin of suing: I could sue Diane's estate on behalf of the girls. Danny could sue Warren on behalf of Bryan, because it was his car. And so on. The press jumped in, having a field day with stories of family-turning-against-family, which infuriated me all over again. Maybe we weren't in Norman Rockwell bliss at the moment, but all anyone wanted was to get whatever was due from the insurance companies. Though it was a complicated way to divide a very small insurance pot, the lawyers insisted it was necessary.

Warren simply wanted it over. He told the Bastardis, the family of the men killed in the SUV that hit the Windstar, that we would give up any money that we might deserve from the insurance if we could just settle quickly. Through their lawyer, they said no. I certainly understood that people in mourning after a tragic accident can get caught in a tortured cycle of anger and recrimination. But this might have been the ultimate example of blaming the victims.

My nerves were already frayed by the pregnancy, and now we were dealing with lawyers and lawsuits and the ridiculous possibility of our being sued for big sums of money. Knowing that the whole horrible story would be a TV show that people watched for casual entertainment drove me completely wild.

Just when everything was as grim as could be, it got grimmer. HBO announced that the title of its documentary would be *There's Something Wrong with Aunt Diane.* Emma's last words to me.

"Oh my God, how could they do that to us?" I wailed. "That's horrible! It's cruel! Do they even have the right to use that title?"

How could a person with any normal human sympathy exploit

Emma's last words as a TV catchphrase? Maybe producers and network executives were as heartless as the Hollywood stereotype. I called HBO, begging them to change the title. For almost two years now, I had replayed the words from my last conversation with Emma over and over in my head. I heard her every inflection, thought about what she must have been thinking and might have been feeling. Ours had been a private conversation, a private exchange between mother and child. Now it would be nothing more than a catchy title to get ratings.

In late April, our foundation had received a $30,000 check from HBO with a lovely note:

"Please accept this donation on behalf of HBO Documentary Films. We're so sorry for your loss. Emma, Alyson and Katie live on through the good work you're doing with the Hance Family Foundation."

I had jumped up and down shrieking in delight. All the good we could do with that money! The network hadn't asked for anything in return. Warren was more distrustful.

"Don't cash it yet," he had said. "Let's see what's in the movie first."

"Oh, you're killing me!" I said, joking, as I clutched the check. "The movie's already made. Let's cash it and do something positive with it."

But Warren had convinced me to wait, and now I was glad. "You were right. No way can we accept this," I told Warren as soon as we learned the movie's title. We wrote a note to HBO explaining that the foundation was sending the check back. We suggested that if they really cared about doing good, they should make a contribution in the girls' names to one of the other charities that the foundation supported.

As far as I know, they never did.

I had tried to be understanding about Danny's eagerness to cooperate with HBO. If he wanted answers or absolution (or both), that was fine. But now he'd crossed the line. He could sell his own soul, but what right did he have to take advantage of my daughters?

"I bet he didn't have approval of the title," Jeannine said, trying to calm me down and offer some perspective. "He probably didn't have much control at all."

"Then he shouldn't have signed the contract!" I said. "Doesn't he think of anything?"

When I complained about the title, the people at HBO were sympathetic in the same way that customer service reps from your credit card company tend to be when you've been overcharged—they murmured how sorry they were, said they'd look into it, and then didn't do anything at all. They probably figured that if the title got me this riled, it would stimulate ratings, too.

Very early one morning, my mind was racing a million miles an hour and my pent-up anger at Danny felt like it would explode my heart. I didn't begrudge him whatever money he got for participating in the documentary—he needed it—but I badly wanted an apology. Diane couldn't talk for herself, and Danny needed to say I'm sorry on her behalf. He also needed to recognize how his actions affected other people.

I grabbed my phone and began tapping out a text:

"Do you ever consider Warren and me in any decisions you make? Warren spoke lovely words about Diane and Erin and Bryan at the funeral. Did you ever thank him? He got the burial plots and took care of everything. Doesn't that count with you?"

People warn against making phone calls to ex-lovers when you're drunk. How about not texting a brother-in-law when you're tired and angry? On the other hand, I don't think I said anything unreasonable. I thought I was being helpful and giving him the advice nobody else would offer.

"It doesn't matter how the accident happened," I went on, *"eight people are dead and they need an apology. Diane's not here to speak for herself and you need to apologize for her. It's like when a child does something wrong— you stand by her, but you still apologize."*

I didn't hate Danny and I even had some sympathy for him. He needed to take care of Bryan all by himself, and he didn't have a lot of resources to do it. While Warren and I were surrounded by loving friends, Danny seemed adrift, with nobody to give him good advice. All I wanted to do was point out how hurtful his behavior had been in the hope that it might change. I didn't believe in turning your back on people. I still had faith that hearing from me would give Danny a new perspective, and we could all hug and be friends again.

I read the text over. I thought about it.

I hit Send.

A few minutes later, he texted back his reply:

"You're crazy. Go get help."

I stared at my phone and began hyperventilating. After all these months of pain, is this where we had ended up—pointless name calling? We were still family and needed to support each other in our time of need. How did we get to this place of no communication? Maybe Danny's stonewalling meant he really did know something—something bad—that he wanted to hide. We had all been devastated by the same event, and I wanted to talk and get answers, too. I cared about my nephew and wanted to see him again.

Needing to restore some sanity after that nasty one-line text, I grabbed my cell phone again. No texting Danny this time—I'd call him. I didn't really expect him to answer, but suddenly he was on the line. He wasn't nice—and then neither was I. We started screaming at each other, months of no communication ending in a burst of emotional attacks and accusations.

I hung up and began crying uncontrollably. Suddenly I couldn't breathe. I began clawing at the sofa, gasping for air, trying to get myself under control. I couldn't get any air into my lungs. I rushed downstairs to the basement, where Warren's brother David was sleeping, and told him the story.

"You can't tell Warren!" I insisted. "He'll be so mad. But help me! I can't breathe."

"Calm down, calm down. Think of the baby," David said. He led me upstairs, to get a paper bag I could breathe into. Just then, Warren appeared.

"What's going on?" Warren asked.

"Nothing," I gasped. "I'm just . . . it's okay . . . I can't breathe."

But David ignored my warning. "She texted Danny," David told him. "And then she called him."

"Why did you do that?" Warren moaned. "Why did you contact him?"

"I'm so sorry," I said, sobbing. "I wanted to make things better. But it only gets worse."

"You're not going to get what you need from him," Warren said. "Why do you keep trying?"

"I want him to apologize. I don't understand any of this. We were all so close. How can we not be in each other's lives?"

"He won't apologize," Warren said. "Stop. Just stop."

I sputtered out the whole story, and I watched Warren's face slowly turn to a frozen mask. The anger seemed to seep from his pores, and if we had been in a movie, flames would have begun shooting from his eyes.

"I'm done," he said. "This is it. I've bitten my tongue long enough."

He started heading out the door and I ran after him, tugging at his arm.

"Where are you going?"

"To Danny's. This is enough. I can't take much more," Warren said, clutching his car keys.

"Please stay," I begged. "Remember our rule? No driving when you're angry."

"I don't care. I can't hold back anymore," he bellowed.

The intensity of his rage scared me. "Stay here," I said, sobbing and clinging to him. "I'm sorry. I shouldn't have called him. I just had things I wanted to say. He should understand what he's doing."

"I'll kill him," Warren said. The threat reverberated as he slammed the car door and revved the motor.

I tried to run out to the driveway, thinking I would stand behind the car so he couldn't go anywhere, but he was faster and pulled out while I stood there sobbing, watching him go.

I don't know where Warren ended up that morning, but he didn't go to Danny's and like so many other upheavals, we both let it drift away. Warren's ferocity reminded me that while he usually kept his emotions in check, he still felt them as deeply as I did. I had my fabulous friends to talk to almost every day, but who was there to support Warren when he and I resorted to attacking each other rather than leaning on each other? He had a lot of close friends, but they were at work all day. If Warren felt overcome by a wave of sadness at three o'clock in the afternoon, he was unlikely to interrupt Brad at the investment bank where he worked or Doug at his office to get some bucking-up or emotional support. Thank goodness a couple of his friends popped in a few evenings a week to sit on our couch. Nothing monumental was ever said, it was just important that they were there.

Our neighbor Laura, who had known Mr. Hance since childhood, called him one day when she saw Warren desolate. She figured having his dad to talk to might help.

"Warren isn't doing well, he's having a hard time," she said to Mr. Hance.

"Why is he having a hard time?" Mr. Hance asked, looking for something specific.

Did she really have to explain? Laura didn't know what to say. Mr. Hance had lost four grandchildren and his only daughter in the accident, but his response was to remain stoic.

When Laura told me the story, I called Warren's dad myself.

"Your son is falling apart," I told him. "You need to help him."

"What should I do?" he asked.

"Just come be with him. You don't have to talk. Just sit and watch a baseball game with him on TV."

Both my mother and Warren's father were struggling with their roles vis-à-vis Warren and me. My mother had been a wonderful babysitter for the girls, close and loving and always ready to rush over when we planned an evening out. She was a rock star in their eyes. When she arrived, they always shouted "Nanny!" and ran to the door in delight, their faces glowing at the prospect of the unconditional love that only a grandmother can give.

After the accident, she felt as unmoored as I did. She had lost her three granddaughters—and in her eyes, she had lost her daughter, too. I was different, empty. I had always been relaxed when she came over, never looking over her shoulder or giving instructions on how to babysit. Now I was tense and cold and didn't have much to say.

Mr. Hance had also been a great babysitter for the girls, and they loved him just as much. But now he didn't feel comfortable coming over, either. And maybe I didn't help. One day when Mr. Hance showed up unannounced and tried to talk to me, I gave him a cold, what-are-you-doing-here look. I wasn't feeling very friendly, and I suppose he sensed it. Part of me wanted him there to commiserate with Warren, but part of me recoiled. I sometimes felt like I was drowning in Hances. With Warren, his brother David, and the ghost of Diane always in our house, I had to control myself from lashing out.

Warren's role in our marriage was still to take care of me—despite my resentment that he wasn't always up to the task anymore.

"You have to get Jackie through her pregnancy," friends whispered to Warren every time we went out. "Her hormones are wild right now. Be understanding."

What Warren understood was that I could get away with anything—and he had to put up with it. I wasn't taking any pills for anxiety or depression, and I had a baby growing inside me, and I'd been through a lot to get to this point. On days when I felt particularly cranky, I wondered why women have to take on all the burdens. So I let myself be melodramatic and tempestuous.

"Just a few more months," those same friends promised Warren when I abruptly left a party pleading exhaustion, then lay in bed for a full day crying.

"Does anybody worry about how I feel?" he asked as Isabelle and Jeannine and a host of others came in and out of the house to make sure I was okay.

"No," I said bluntly. "Not right now. You're not the one who's pregnant."

I could handle the physical burdens of being pregnant (and pregnancy hormones, like PMS or menopause, can become just a good excuse for bad behavior), but the whole process felt overwhelming. Even though I had asked Warren about moving and getting a fresh start, I realized I didn't want to start again. I wanted to live in the house where I could still hear my daughters' laughter. If we moved, my life with my daughters might fade even more.

Almost nothing in the house had changed since the day of the accident. Their beds were practically shrines for me. I still went into the girls' bedrooms and fluffed their pillows and made sure their slippers were lined up. I lay down on the comfy mattresses and thought about them. I had insisted that the girls make their beds every morning because I didn't like the thought of them getting into unmade beds at night—it just didn't feel as good. Once I explained, they agreed, and carefully straightened the covers and pulled up the comforters every day before school.

Such good girls.

Someone gave me a book about a woman who had lost her beloved husband in a tragedy, and she described how she immediately packed up all his clothes and belongings and got them out of her home. A few months later, she renovated and repainted so she wouldn't have to live with the memories. I wanted to live with memories. They would help keep the girls with me forever.

But now we had to get ready for the baby, and figuring out how to arrange the house was complicated. The room Emma and Alyson shared—which we still called "the girls' room"—would get a crib for the baby, replacing Emma's bed. And we would turn Katie's tiny bedroom into the walk-in closet that the girls always wanted. Sometimes on vacations the three of them shared a room, and they talked about doing the same at home and making Katie's room a dressing room for all of us. Now it would happen.

One Saturday in June, I went shopping with Melissa, and I really wasn't thinking about cribs and closets and bassinets when I walked into the house and went upstairs to put down my packages. I couldn't believe my eyes. Katie's room was empty—the bed and dresser gone. All the clothes and personal items that had been in the drawers were thrown helter-skelter into Emma and Alyson's room.

"Oh my God! What happened? Where's Katie's bed?" I yelled, freaking out. "What happened to all her things? Warren! What's going on?"

I raced frantically around from room to room, shocked at the sight of my children's rooms in such disarray.

Warren came trudging up the stairs, his face pale and sweat beading at his brow.

"We said we were going to do this," he reminded me. "I wanted to get the room done and everything moved while David is still here." After staying with us almost every weekend since the accident, his brother was being reassigned by the air force and heading off to Turkey in August.

"But look at this room!" I cried. "This is not how you treat Katie's stuff! How could you do this? Everything is just thrown around! You can't do this! What were you thinking?"

"I had to do this quickly. I couldn't sit and fold clothes!" he yelled back. "We took the dresser to the basement to refinish. And we gave Jonathan the bed for Maddie. She's just getting out of her training bed and can use it."

I began to howl. I liked our neighbors Jonathan and Desi, and I enjoyed watching their little daughter Maddie zip around the street on Katie's bike. Warren had shined it up and put on a bell and tassels before giving it to her months ago, and it was cute as could be.

But to have Katie's bed across the street? To look out the window and know that Katie's bed was over there, so close but no longer mine? I guess I knew we had to give her precious bed away to make the dressing room, but I hadn't really thought it through.

"I want it back!" I screamed.

"Jackie, it's Maddie's bed now," Warren said.

"I want it back. Put the bed back, put the dresser back. I don't need the closet and I want everything as it was."

"No, that's it," Warren said adamantly. "It's done."

"It doesn't make any sense!" I yelled. I went to the open window and began screaming so everyone outside could hear. "I want my bed back! I want Katie's bed back!"

Warren tried to drag me away, but I was screaming and crying and out of my mind. I went to Emma and Alyson's room and threw myself on their beds, clutching at Katie's clothes, which had been thrown everywhere. I cried hysterically, unable to stop. Warren gave up trying to calm me down and finally left me alone.

After close to an hour, my sobs slowed down. But I still lay there, my head on the sodden pillow and my body trembling. From outside, I heard Desi's voice. She had come over and was standing on our front lawn, talking to Warren.

"Should I bring the bed back?" she asked.

"No," Warren said. "Please don't worry. Just go in your house and let it sit."

A few minutes later, Laura came over. She talked to Warren outside for a little while, and then I heard her tread on the stairs. I managed to sit up. She stood in the doorway of Emma and Alyson's room and looked around.

"Let's get this room cleaned up," she said.

"Can you believe what Warren did?" I asked.

Laura shook her head. "He was trying to do the right thing. It wasn't easy for him, either, Jackie. David told me that when they were carrying the bed down the stairs, Warren threw up."

I closed my eyes briefly. Funny how our bodies respond to stress. I couldn't eat. Warren threw up. It happened often now. I heard him in the bathroom gagging, as if his body wanted to reject everything and somehow purify itself. Life without his girls just made him want to vomit.

I got off the bed. "He didn't plan this very well. I would have packed up their things."

I had already bought some pink bins for the girls' things, and now Laura and I folded everything carefully and tucked pictures and pants and pajamas into the bins. I left out a few things to hang in the closet Warren would build.

Much later, Warren came back.

"What are you doing?" he asked.

"Packing. Everything can go in the attic over the garage," I said, reasonable at last.

He stared at a pink pillow I had shoved into one of the bins. It was in the shape of a crown and said *Princess* on it. He leaned over and pulled it out, clutching it close.

"The Princess pillow doesn't go in the attic," he said. "It has to stay out."

He put the silky pillow that he had once bought as a gift for Emma against his own scruffy cheek, and tears filled his eyes.

I looked away. "Okay," I said. "The pillow stays."

We packed together that whole night.

The next day, Desi called to ask if I wanted the bed back, and I felt a bit of relief when I told her she should keep it.

Now that I had gone off all my medications for the sake of the pregnancy, I felt scared—I had taken them for so long. I believed in the drugs, and whether it was a placebo effect or real chemical action, I worried about being without them, so I continued to take Ambien to help me sleep. Instructions for a drug like Ambien are very specific: take the pill and then lie down and let it work. If I stayed awake on Ambien, I ended up crazy and hyper. Once I found myself furiously sweeping the garage in the middle of the night. Another time, I raced around frantically, sorting through all the girls' pictures and tossing them all over the floor.

Now that I was pregnant, I often got up to go to the bathroom during the night, and once I was awake, with drugs in my system, my mind roared a million miles an hour and my adrenaline felt out of control. One night at 4 a.m., I got an urge to make homemade brownies. I pulled out half the pans in the kitchen and dragged out every bit of chocolate and flour I could find. Instead of making batter, I made a mess.

The next morning, I decided to stop taking sleeping pills—partly to protect the baby, and partly to protect me.

Warren's experiences with sleeping pills seemed even worse.

"You have to let it work," I reminded him when he took a pill, then went off to do something other than curl up in bed.

But he hadn't learned the lesson. One night when he took an Ambien and didn't sleep, he went downstairs and completely destroyed the basement. I don't know what he thought he was doing, but he pulled every picture off the wall and every sports trophy off the shelves, and threw all the girls' toys and puzzles and games into a giant pile. He never mentioned it in the morning. Maybe he didn't even remember. When he went off to work, I saw the disaster downstairs and knew exactly what had happened in the middle of the night. I called my friend Denine to come help me clean up the mess, and we spent the whole day filling three huge garbage bags with broken remnants of the girls' playthings.

Were we really all just bubbling cauldrons of hormones and chemicals and neurotransmitters? For once, I couldn't really be angry with Warren, because I didn't think what he'd done had anything to do with the real him. And, come to think of it, had either of us been "the real Warren" or "the real Jackie" since the accident? It was as if our essential core as good, happy, and reasonable human beings had been wiped out by the accident. Neither of us quite understood ourselves anymore.

"All finished," Denine said as she closed the last garbage bag.

"Thanks," I said. "But can we keep this between us? I don't want to make Warren feel any worse."

"Sure," she said. "That's nice of you."

But how could I keep from discussing it with Warren when the overflowing garbage bags on the driveway would be indisputable evidence? I didn't want to rub his face in actions that had been undertaken by some alternate pod-Warren.

"I can take the garbage bags to my house," Denine offered. "The garbagemen can pick them up there."

"Ooh, would you? Thanks."

I helped her load the garbage into her trunk. It's funny how much I wanted to protect Warren this time. I felt my heart soften toward my husband as I thought about all that he was struggling with, too. He must already have been suffering a psychic hangover from his rampage the night before, and he didn't need to suffer more.

After the debacle of moving Katie's bed, I decided to take control of the situation a few weeks later, when we were ready to move Emma's bed out to make room for the crib. Another set of neighbors, Gina and Sal, wanted the bed for their guest room and I quickly agreed.

"I'd be happy to know you have it," I said.

Their then-preteen daughter Erica used to babysit the girls. I'd call her during the day if I had an errand to do, and she'd always run over on short notice. She had a sweet relationship with the girls, but she'd been away at summer camp when the accident happened. Coming home to find the girls gone and the funeral done and over, she was very upset. For a long time, she couldn't even look me in the eye. I liked the idea of having Emma's bed in her house. Erica could watch over it with the same gentle kindness she had shown the girls.

Moving the bed wouldn't be easy. Emma had a captain's bed with drawers underneath for storage, and it was oversize, so it wouldn't go around the corner of the staircase in our house. To get it into her room, we'd had to arrange a rope-and-pulley system outside the house, hoist it to the second floor, then squeeze it in through her window. Now we planned the reverse. I made arrangements with our neighbors Sal and Jonathan to come over to help Warren. They'd take the bed out the window and onto the roof, then shimmy it down the side of the house.

I took off the sheets. I folded up the covers. I lay on the bed for the last time. I wouldn't let this move be as awful as the last. The guys were coming over on Sunday to undertake the project, and I'd just quietly leave the house until they were finished.

"I'm prepared," I told Warren.

But I wasn't prepared for what happened on Tuesday night, five days before the bed was to be moved.

At about 2 a.m., I woke up from a sound sleep, hearing strange noises above me. I lay very still, trying to imagine what could be happening. I didn't think burglars were trying to get in, and if they were, I didn't care. (*Take anything you want. Everything I care about is gone.*) But the sounds were too rhythmic and persistent for a burglary. Finally realizing where the racket was coming from, I got up and went into the girls' room.

In the moonlight, I saw Warren, his back to me, panting and moaning as he shoved Emma's bed out the window and onto the roof.

"What are you doing?" I asked, flicking on the light. "You can't move the bed alone."

"Why not?" He looked at me, his eyes wild, as he continued ramming the bed through the open window with superhuman effort.

"Stop, Warren. You can't get the bed off the roof in the middle of the night."

"I'll do it in the morning."

"So you're going to leave Emma's bed outside all night?" I asked, feeling my own panic rising.

"I checked the weather. It will be fine," he said.

"Oh my God." I covered my face with my hands. "You can't be doing this."

"What's wrong? Why are you upset?" he asked, as if not aware that his bizarre behavior was answer enough to the question.

"You're supposed to be doing this on Sunday with the guys," I said.

"I couldn't wait until Sunday," Warren said, talking too fast, his voice on the edge of frantic. "I'm feeling too anxious. I might as well take care of it myself."

I went back into bed and lay there, my eyes wide open. Warren had sounded crazy, but it had to be his medication talking. Why else would he be wound up, overwrought, and bursting with energy at 2 a.m.? Given his other post–sleeping pill rampage, I guess hoisting a bed out a window wasn't that strange.

But understanding what had happened didn't make it any better. I lay under my own covers, staring at the ceiling, feeling the emotional weight of Emma's bed pressing down on me from the roof. Emma's bed, perched precariously outside, defenseless against the night air. An innocent object—like an innocent child—left exposed and vulnerable. The image of the solid wood frame teetering on the roof seemed a metaphor for my deepest, darkest sense of shame. I hadn't protected the girls. Hadn't kept them safe.

Perhaps the connection seemed remote, but as the hours ticked away—3 a.m., 4 a.m.—I could think of nothing else. In his agitated state, Warren thought the night air wouldn't harm Emma's bed. But in my mind, the least we could do now was protect everything connected to the girls—to their memory, to their lives.

I didn't sleep for one moment. At about 4:30, I texted my running friends:

"Can't go this morning. Warren had a bad night."

I got up anyway, done with lying there sleeplessly. Too tired to run, I could at least take our dog Jake for a walk. An hour later, I was outside strolling in front of our house with Jake when Una came by—a one-woman running group this morning.

"Hey, you're up," she said, slowing down. "What's going on?"

"Look," I said, pointing up. "There's a bed on my roof."

Una cocked her head upward and came to a dead stop. "Oh, wow. Do you need Doug to come over?"

"No. It was so stupid of Warren. But he's going to have to figure out how to get it down today himself."

Luck, in the form of our extended circle of family and friends, bailed him out. Warren stayed home from work, not feeling well after the long night, and by coincidence, my brother Mark came over that day just to hang out. Our neighbor Jonathan was working from home, and he came over, too.

"Good news, Warren, come here," I called out as soon as they arrived. "You're getting that bed off the roof now!"

The three men got a rope around the heavy wooden form and shimmied it down the side of the house. By two in the afternoon, twelve hours after Warren had started the project, Emma's oversize captain's bed was on the ground.

But even that wasn't the end.

After all the huffing and puffing going down, the guys realized that the bed wouldn't fit up the staircase at Gina and Sal's house. Nobody was in the mood to suggest additional adventures that involved more roofs, ropes, and windows.

"What should we do?" Warren asked.

Everyone who had been involved in the bed-moving escapade was now standing on the sidewalk, staring at Emma's bed. I made it clear that I didn't want it back. I looked at Jonathan and had an immediate idea. When something is right, I know it.

"Could you use it?" I asked him. "It matches the other bed. And you have two children."

He looked at me anxiously, remembering the hysteria that resulted the last time he agreed to take a bed. But I was smiling, so he nodded.

"Well, sure," Jonathan said. Then mentioning his son, he added, "Colton is getting old enough for a bed. He'd love it."

Was it a twist of fate? Coincidence? Destiny? A sweet joke from my angels in heaven? One way or another, Emma's bed and Katie's bed ended up in the same house again, in children's rooms right next door to each other.

As with so much else, it wasn't easy, but we had gotten there.

Twenty-three

Everybody I knew seemed thrilled about my having a new baby, and why shouldn't they be? I'd gone through a lot to make it happen. I kept reminding myself that I'd made a decision. But had I made the right decision? With Emma, Alyson, and Katie, I had been so proud to have a happy house and happy family. Children deserved no less. But if happiness wasn't in my repertoire anymore, maybe I couldn't give this baby the good life she deserved.

I kept flashing back to a day shortly before the accident, when Warren and I had a disagreement, and since we had a pact never to argue in front of the girls, we sent Katie and Alyson outside to play. Our quarrel didn't amount to much, but when it ended, I raced down to the basement with hurt feelings and burst into tears.

Alyson must have spotted me from where she was playing in the yard because she stopped what she was doing and came over, pressing her face against the basement window.

"Mommy, don't cry," she had said.

She looked unbearably sad, and her sorrowful expression cut to my heart. Seeing me weepy had drained away all her normal cheer. I couldn't do that to her. I immediately wiped away my tears and gave her a big smile.

Now that I was halfway through my pregnancy, I kept remembering how I felt seeing Alyson's sad face and knowing that I had caused her sorrow.

I'd been able to change my mood very quickly for Alyson, and she easily returned to her usual good spirits. But what would life be like for the new baby, coming into a house imbued with pain? Would gloominess be her standard mode?

"I'm thinking about putting the baby up for adoption," I told Melissa one day in my second trimester.

"You're not putting the baby up for adoption," Melissa said. "We're all going to be here to help you. That baby will be as loved as anyone on earth."

Her words resonated. Even in the darkest times, I felt loved and sustained by my friends, and their generous spirits would be equally nurturing to the baby. In fact, taking care of her would be a piece of cake in comparison to putting up with me. I immediately decided that the baby would have three godmothers—Melissa, Isabelle, and Jeannine.

If my crazy thoughts now focused on adoption, at least I no longer thought about suicide. I couldn't. I had a responsibility to this pregnancy and something to worry about more important than myself.

"You were such a good mom with the girls," Isabelle said sweetly, "and you're going to be a good mom again." She looked at me with her big doe eyes, and I couldn't help smiling. Even when she was being sincere, Isabelle brought out my sillier side.

"How about the time I couldn't stand the noise in the house? Remember? I sent Katie over to you, then locked myself in the bathroom," I said.

"Which of us hasn't done that?" Isabelle asked with a laugh.

I had yearned every day since the accident to hear the girls giggling and laughing, or even squabbling and whining. How could I have ever wanted to escape happy pandemonium? I would give anything to have the sounds of normal family commotion again. To me a new baby crying wouldn't be noise, it would be a return to the music of our lives, an end to the eerie quiet.

Isabelle was right. Even in my pregnant, insecure state, I knew in my heart that I'd been a devoted mom to Emma, Alyson, and Katie. They reveled in the comfort of my affection and were growing up confident and strong. Each day before school, I gave them a hug and a kiss and nobody ever walked out of the house without a smile.

Except one morning, when Emma was in third grade. She had gotten the day off to a bad start by refusing to let Aly borrow her coat. After I insisted she share, she went into theatrics about how unfair I was and began to cry. I tried to get her to stop, but she began ranting because she didn't like the way her hair looked.

"You're behaving like a brat," I had told her, which made her cry even harder.

Why was my nice girl behaving this way? As she left for school, she looked back at me, but I looked straight ahead and didn't do a thing—no hug, no kiss, no "Have a nice day."

As soon as the door closed, the whole surly scene began eating me up. I felt awful. How could I let Emma go to school unhappy? Maybe she hadn't behaved well, but she was an eight-year-old girl who needed reassurance, not reprimands. As the adult, I should remedy the situation and make her feel better. I pulled out a pad of paper and quickly wrote a note apologizing for the bad morning and telling Emma I loved her. I sealed it in an envelope and drove to her school.

"Could you get this note to Emma as soon as possible?" I asked the secretary in the front office.

"Sure, Mrs. Hance," she said. "Is anything wrong?"

"Not after she gets the note," I said, relieved.

Making sure children are happy and loved and secure. My job. I'd done it well once and maybe—with the love and support of my friends—I could do it again.

The cliché when you're pregnant is to say you don't care if it's a boy or girl as long as you have a healthy baby. I wanted a healthy baby. I also wanted a girl. Some fertility clinics will check the DNA of an embryo before implanting, but Dr. Rosenwaks liked to interfere as little as possible, so he didn't screen for sex. Meanwhile, I told everyone I was sure it was a boy—and I meant it.

At the twenty-week sonogram, the technician said the baby would be sufficiently developed that I could find out the sex.

"I don't want to know," I said firmly.

The emotional strains of this pregnancy had practically brought me to the brink, and I figured the next months would be even harder if I knew the baby wasn't the gender I secretly wanted. Or maybe not so secretly. Everyone understood that I desperately hoped this baby would restore some of the joy I had felt with my three girls.

"Really?" asked the technician, whom I hadn't met before. "Are you sure you don't want to know?"

I lay very still on the table for a moment. I had to accept sometime that I would be bringing up a boy. "Okay, let's find out," I said.

She took another minute to verify, not wanting to make a mistake. "You're having a girl," she said finally.

I started crying. Bawling. Tears rolled down my cheeks and my whole body shook. The technician had no idea what she had said wrong and nervously left the room. Outside, someone filled her in on who I was, and she came back smiling.

"Are you sure it's a girl? Are you sure?" I asked her.

"I'm sure," she said.

"It's really a girl? And it's alive?"

"Look at her heartbeat."

Her.

Heartbeat.

My own heart was fluttering wildly.

The moment I knew the baby would be a girl, I also knew her name.

Kasey Rose.

I'd picked Kasey a month before the implantation even occurred, while I idly watched the Miss America Pageant on TV one night. I only half paid attention as the contestants stepped forward at the start of the show to introduce themselves. One of the contestants announced herself as Kasey—I never caught the last name—and when I looked at the chyron on the screen, I saw Kasey with a *K*.

I gasped. I'd always loved the name Casey, but I'd never seen it with a *K* before. I literally jumped off the sofa, as excited as if I'd won the lottery. This was it! A beautiful name that included an E-A-K for Emma, Aly, and Katie. I felt as if the Miss America contestant were talking directly to me.

After I got pregnant, I thought about how I could ever thank Dr. Rosenwaks for his extraordinary gift. I had already written him a long note of gratitude, but any present I thought of seemed inadequate. A box of fancy chocolates? A bottle of expensive champagne? A gorgeous bouquet of flowers? Wait, I could do better than that. If I named the baby Rose in his honor, the flower would never lose its bloom.

Warren and I weren't fighting now so much as we were overwhelmed and uninvolved with each other. Even at this point, two years on, Warren kept most of his dark thoughts to himself. His way of coping with grief involved physical labor—building, moving, growing. Maybe that is typical for a guy. He took comfort from building the rock garden and waterfall in our backyard where the swing set used to be, and he spent hours at the Centennial Gardens planting and pruning and cleaning for our Family Fun Day. It took me awhile to notice another physical action he took on behalf of his daughters.

Tattoos.

About two months after the accident, Warren had a cross tattooed on his chest over his heart. For the design, he chose the same green cross we had used on the mass cards at the girls' wake.

I didn't say anything.

A few months after that, I noticed something missing from Emma's room. A picture she had made with a peace sign and the word *peace* written across it in her pretty handwriting had disappeared from her wall.

"Do you know where Emma's picture went?" I asked Warren the night I noticed it was gone.

"Which picture?" he asked. But from the expression on his face, I knew that he knew exactly which picture I meant.

And he knew that I knew.

"The peace sign," I said.

"I'll show it to you later," he said.

"Show it to me now."

Warren slowly unbuttoned his shirt and pushed away the sleeve, and I saw Emma's handwriting. He had taken the picture to a tattoo artist and had it imposed on his arm.

The last drawing Emma ever did would now be part of him forever.

I was stunned. And that wasn't the last of his body art.

Warren spent a lot of time sitting in the rock garden he had helped build in the backyard to memorialize the girls, and he told me that he always saw a red cardinal there. He thought of the cardinal as a sign that the girls hovered near.

A few months later, the cardinal landed in a tattoo on his other arm—with branches that held the letters E, A, K.

"Do you like it?" he asked, showing off his cardinal.

"I do," I said. "But I think you've got to stop with the tattoos."

One Friday evening Warren came home from working in the city unexpectedly late. The next morning, he came downstairs without a shirt and walked around the kitchen, as if trying to get me to notice him. Warren rarely strutted around shirtless, but I must have been too absorbed in worrying about my own expanding baby tummy to pay attention to him. He bumped into me a few times, and when I still didn't say anything, he came very close and thrust his biceps in my direction.

"Are you ever going to notice?" he asked.

"What?" I asked.

He pointed to the cardinal tattoo. It had now sprouted a new branch with a *K* on it for Kasey. And on the other arm was a brand-new tattoo: *Emily, Alyson, Katie,* and *Kasey* were all written in cursive script, with a peace sign.

I touched the *K* and all four girls' names gently. Never once in all the years I'd known him had Warren talked about a tattoo, yet now he couldn't stop. "Are you going to be one of those guys with tattoos all over your body?" I asked, teasing him gently.

"Maybe," he said.

The body art gave me a new insight into my husband. Sometimes I didn't think he thought about the girls or the tragedy or the changed circumstances of our life. But then he did something like emblazon their names across his body, and I realized that he was as desperate to hold on to them as I was.

Twenty-four

On Emma's eleventh birthday, two years after she was gone, I went to the cemetery to deliver the gifts I had bought for her. I sat down by the stone and told my eldest daughter about Kasey Rose, her baby sister who would be coming soon. I explained that I hoped to love Kasey unreservedly, but that didn't mean I would ever love her any less. Love is not a finite product that you need to carefully allocate and divide. Just like when Alyson had joined our family and then Katie, the love I had to give would simply grow and expand.

What I said made perfect sense, and Emma, always a smart girl, would surely understand. The bigger question remained whether or not I could convince myself. Right now, Kasey seemed a lot less real than Emma, Alyson, and Katie.

After coming back from the cemetery, I fell apart. Yes, I was pregnant and everyone was happy for me—but when would we all acknowledge the elephant in the room? I was having this baby only because three other children were dead.

As often happened when grief overwhelmed me, Warren and I began fighting. Even as we fought that weekend, I could see that I was wearing him out.

"I'm having a panic attack," I said at one point in the middle of the night. "I can hardly breathe."

Our months of therapy paid off as he tried to offer some empathy. "Jackie, if I were feeling the way you are, what would you tell me to do?"

"I'd tell you to take a Xanax and an Ambien and go to sleep," I snapped. "But I'm pregnant, so I can't take either."

"Then what else can I do for you?" he asked.

I looked at him, tears rolling down my face. For so long now, I had wanted my husband to take care of me again, yearned for the man who wasn't himself broken by grief and pain. I needed him to hold me and let his strength seep through my pores and revive me. I didn't need a husband—I needed Superman.

"What can I do for you right now?" Warren asked again, practically.

"I don't know," I said. "Maybe a hug."

"A hug?" Warren looked at me with some combination of surprise and contempt. "A hug? Really, Jackie? I've been asking you to hug me for a year. And now that's what you want?"

I kept sobbing, and Warren left the room. He was right. He had been asking me to hug him for months and months, but my heart was too cold and broken to do it. Now that I finally wanted his embrace, could it be that his heart had grown too cold? I had been hurtful for so long that maybe neither of us could get what we wanted.

A few minutes later, I heard footsteps on the stairs, and Laura came in.

"What are you doing here?" I asked.

"Warren called me to come over and help," she said.

"It's the middle of the night and I don't want him to call you," I said. "I want him to take care of me."

"You haven't let him do that in a long time," Laura said reasonably.

"I asked him to hug me," I said.

Laura gave a little smile. "Well, maybe that's a start. You both just have to learn how to do that again."

With each of my previous pregnancies, I had gained forty or fifty pounds and delighted in my round, fecund shape. But as I moved into the last trimester with Kasey, I had gained only fifteen pounds. I never felt hungry, and having a hard time accepting the pregnancy, maybe I resisted letting my body grow. I tried to eat healthy foods and kept exercising, but

I never called the doctor to ask any questions. Why worry when I didn't believe this baby would ever be real? It seemed too much to hope that she was growing and healthy.

Wherever I went, people came up to me with big smiles on their faces to offer congratulations.

"Oh, I'm so happy for you!" a woman I barely knew said when she saw me in a store one day.

"Thank you," I said, uncertainly.

"A new baby is just what you deserve!" she said eagerly. "Are you feeling good?"

"Yes, fine," I said with a wary smile as I walked quickly away. I felt the usual stabs of guilt. Is this what would happen now? Would everyone forget about Emma, Alyson, and Katie and want to talk only about the new baby?

Warren anticipated the end of the pregnancy with great hope and expectation, and he started talking about a baby shower for me.

"I don't want a shower," I said. "The girls can't have a party, so why should the baby?"

"Everyone wants to congratulate you. You might as well get it all over with at once."

Warren made plans for a ladies' lunch. I figured it would be like a birthday dinner they'd had for me—a small group of women gathered to celebrate quietly, which had been perfect. For the shower, Warren would pay for the food, and we would use Melissa's house.

But as the party got closer, I started to balk. I didn't feel deserving of a party and I didn't want friends doing anything more for me. People had done too much already. I told Melissa and Isabelle I wanted to cancel.

"We can't really do that," Isabelle admitted.

"Why not? We'll save Melissa a lot of trouble."

Reluctantly, she admitted that Warren hadn't planned a small gathering, after all. He had rented a catering hall—the same one where we'd had Alyson's Communion party—and more than a hundred people had been invited.

"Are you kidding?" I asked.

"It's too late to get out of it," Isabelle said. "It's a luncheon. Everyone's looking forward to it. Don't worry. It's going to be fine."

He had invited everybody.

I felt nothing but anxiety at the thought of a party, and late at night, I wondered, *Why can't he do what I want?*

I tried not to get angry at Warren. Deep in my heart, I knew that his motives were good. He wanted to feel as buoyant and eager as any father-to-be. Throwing a baby shower for his wife, he could feel normal. We had always liked parties and celebrations, and this was his way of saying that the baby was worth celebrating. He hoped the baby would bring the end of sadness, and he was announcing that the world could stop feeling sorry for us—we had embarked on a good and happy time. The party was his promise to every friend who had suffered through our sadness that glimmers of sunshine were again peeking through the clouds.

But, of course, he didn't say any of that.

The day before the party, I got my hair blown out and Isabelle came over to help me decide what to wear. I pulled out a sparkly minidress I had bought a few months earlier. I'd probably bought it in too large a size, and I'd never worn it, because it had just hung on me.

"This one makes me look like a circus tent," I said, holding it up.

"Try it," she said.

I pulled it on and with my slightly bigger belly, the dress swung gracefully. Isabelle grinned. "That's the one. Wear it."

So I did my makeup carefully and put on the sparkly minidress and a pair of stiletto heels.

"You look really good," Warren said, smiling at me with a twinkle in his eye when I came downstairs.

"I'm eight months pregnant."

"And you look really good," he repeated.

I smiled. The genuine compliment from my husband made me feel unexpectedly good. However much I had trampled on our marriage since the accident, the love and deep connection were still there.

Warren drove me over to the hall and promised that he would come to the women-only luncheon only at the very end. I gave him a kiss and went inside. The room was filled with women I knew from every part of my life—neighbors and close friends, women from my prayer group and my bowling group, relatives from both sides of the family, even some of the nurses from Dr. Rosenwaks's office. I introduced people to one another and the conversation never stopped. Everyone sipped colorful drinks and ate hors d'oeuvres, and the pile of beautiful gifts on a side table grew higher.

"You look radiant," said the mother of a friend. "It's so good to see you smiling."

"Don't worry, the smile is fake," I said with a laugh.

But with all the people around, I giggled and talked and accepted compliments. At one point, I glanced at my watch. I'd made it through the first hour. I slipped out to the ladies' room. Fortunately, it was empty, and I closed the door of a stall, sat down, and cried for five minutes.

I cried for Emma, Alyson, and Katie, and for the life with them that I had lost. Even in the midst of a party, I couldn't forsake them. I wondered if everybody in the room understood the subtext of the party. Probably. But it is hard to be sad and hopeful at the same time, so everyone but me would be trying hard to put the girls out of their minds.

I dried my eyes, fixed my makeup in the mirror, and went back to the party. All these people had come to celebrate with me, and I wouldn't ruin the mood. The room swirled with good spirits and goodwill that I wanted to appreciate. A group of women gathered around me and I heard myself laughing happily with them, faking it to make it through.

At the end of the party, Isabelle, Jeannine, and Melissa came back to the house, bringing all the gifts with them. It was overwhelming. On the invitation, Warren had asked that everyone bring presents unwrapped so that I didn't have to cope with opening packages. He knew that would be painful. People had been generous and creative, putting baby gifts in beautiful baskets with clear plastic and colorful ribbons. Now, as my friends untied the bows, I couldn't bring myself to ooh and aah at the darling pink outfits that fluttered forth, or at the crocheted blankets and knit sweaters and tulle-skirted dresses that would make any baby (and mom) happy. Melissa took all the clothes to wash, and all the bigger items that we didn't need right now we put in the garage.

Exhausted by the draining day, I went off to lie down, and when I came back, the three of them were still opening and organizing and arranging. Unexpectedly, Warren's mother, Eileen, appeared at the house.

What are you doing here? I thought as she puttered around, trying to be helpful.

I'd been shocked that Warren had invited her to the shower, given that they hadn't had a relationship in years. When I asked him why he'd been so generous and welcoming, he looked pensive.

"I don't want to hurt anybody," he said. "There's enough hurt going on around here. I can't be the cause of any more."

I was in awe that he been able to forgive the mother who had walked out of his life when he was a young teenager. Now, seeing his mother in our house—ironically, the house where she had grown up—I wondered if she'd watched the HBO documentary over the summer, or heard the interviews with the executive producer who theorized about the psychological damage that Diane might have suffered when her mother left the family. The anger had percolated in Warren for so long that I marveled at his ability to be so forgiving now. Diane, the youngest, had probably been hit even harder. We would never know if Eileen's decision to walk away from her family as a young mother had indelibly harmed Diane— and led to our pain.

Jeannine, Isabelle, and Melissa tried to keep Warren's mother occupied as I walked out of the room. Seeing the presents being opened was making me sad. I'm a big proponent of thank-you notes, and I'd written a generic one that was already printed up. But the three of them kept careful lists so I could add personal thanks to each one.

The after-party lasted longer than the party, and I tried to be as forgiving as Warren had been to his mother.

Later that week, Warren sent an email to Isabelle, Jeannine, and Melissa:

Thank you for everything last Sunday. Your complete unself-ishness was special. I see the sadness, joy, and hope in all of your eyes as you start this journey right alongside of us. Jackie and I could not do it without you.

I was always amazed how Emma, Aly, and Katie could be so different when they all came from the same place. You three and Jackie are different women from completely different places get-ting along like sisters—loving, hating, fighting, and making up. Sunday had it all. But mostly it had what I miss the most—the feeling and sounds you can only get in a family. So no matter what life gives us, I hope the four of you never forget the sisterly bond you have. Always remember what's important in life . . . friends, family, and friends who are family.

He was right.
I would remember.

Twenty-five

Just when I thought the coast was clear, the paparazzi showed up again. In mid-September, a couple of mornings after the shower, friends started calling and texting to make sure I wasn't upset by the picture in the newspaper.

"What picture?" I asked.

I frantically went online to the *New York Post* website. Print newspapers may only be good for wrapping fish (as the old saying goes), but their websites last forever. And there it was—an article headlined "Taconic Mom's Baby Joy," with a photo of me walking across my lawn.

"She has gone from bearing an unspeakable burden to bearing a brand-new life," the article began.

In the picture, I had on pajama bottoms, my hair was pulled up in a ponytail, and my hand rested on my belly. I knew exactly when the picture must have been taken, when I walked over to see a neighbor the previous week. I seemed to have a smile on my face, which fit into the theme of the story. But if anybody had asked, I could have explained that at that particular moment, the look on my face was really a grimace of pain, which also explained why I was holding my side.

"Jackie Hance . . . was spotted outside her Long Island home last week, noticeably pregnant as she smiled and chatted with a neighbor. Hance declined to comment."

Declined to comment? Actually, nobody had asked me a thing. No reporter had approached me and, most disturbing, I hadn't even seen the photographer on the street. If I had known someone was stalking me, I wouldn't have been outside in pajamas.

The article quoted an unnamed "pal" as saying, "We're all there for Jackie right now. It's such a special time. We just want this to turn out OK . . . They deserve some joy."

Nice sentiment, but once again, I'd have bet my baby's first bottle that the comment was a figment of some reporter's imagination.

Everyone thought it was sweet and positive, but oddly enough, the idea of people thinking I was happy infuriated me. It took nerve for a reporter to suggest that I could be happy when my kids weren't here. And the headline made me equally furious.

"I'm not the Taconic Mom," I said to Warren. "Your sister is the Taconic Mom. Not me."

I resented it deeply whenever I heard that label, but for once, I decided to let it all go. There was nothing I could do and I wasn't going to let a tabloid drive me crazy.

A few days later, I was out with Karen and Isabelle at the mall when I started getting terrible pains.

"Are you okay?" Karen asked.

"I'm fine, I'm fine," I said. "I just need to sit down." But I must have looked terrible, because Karen insisted we leave.

I knew I wasn't in labor because those pains are intermittent and this pain was constant. When we got back to Floral Park, Isabelle wanted to stay with me or take me to the hospital, but I insisted she leave.

"I just need to lie down," I said.

But the moment Isabelle left, I called the doctor and described my symptoms.

"Sounds like it may be kidney stones," the doctor said. "Get yourself over to the hospital."

I decided I could handle this myself and not bother anyone, so I punched in the number for a cab. Warren pulled up before it arrived. "Get in the car," he said, shaking his head at my decision to be self-sufficient at a time like this. "I'll drive you."

When we got to the hospital admitting desk, the nurse couldn't find my name in the system. We eventually figured out that the obstetrician had been trying to preserve my privacy and protect us from prying reporters. In my hospital room, a lovely nurse named Rachel appeared to take care of me. She suggested that I should register under an alias.

"Any idea what name you'd like to use?" she asked.

I shrugged and, changing the subject, complimented her on her beautiful necklace.

"The gold is so pretty," I said effusively. "I don't wear much gold but that's beautiful. I love it."

We talked for a few minutes and then she repeated that I needed that alias.

"You pick it," I said, collapsing onto my pillow. I certainly didn't feel like myself—but I didn't have a name for whoever was lying in this bed.

"Well, let's see, my first name is Rachel, and you like the gold, so how about if we put those together? Rachel Gold." She smiled and stroked my head again. "You can be Rachel Gold. Does that work for you?"

"Sure." Rachel Gold. I felt an odd mix of confusion and amazement at how easy it was to assume a new identity.

Doctors coming in and out the rest of the day all looked at their clipboards and said cheerfully, "Hi, Rachel, how do you feel?" Sometimes I forgot to respond and Nurse Rachel would gently nudge me.

The diagnosis turned out to be a gallstone attack, and after two nights in the hospital, I went home. But I knew that when I came back to the hospital to have my baby, I would once again be Rachel Gold. It seemed right: Jackie Hance had been the mother of three wonderful girls. When they died, part of her died, too. She had become a different person.

Jackie and Rachel. My life had changed so dramatically that it shouldn't have surprised me to have a different name. I had to get used to being myself and someone else at the same time.

We were getting close to the finish line of this pregnancy, but Warren wasn't sure that we'd ever cross it.

Going out with friends usually worked as a good pick-me-up for Warren and me. But one weekend in September, we hit an all-time low when even that didn't work. We had joined a few couples at a nearby restaurant, and as the conversation swirled, Warren seemed far away. He didn't pay any attention as Brad chatted about possibly buying a vacation home and Mark reported how happy he and Isabelle were in their new home.

"I always want to have a dream," Mark said. "That's what keeps me going."

The comment made me stop. How nice it would be to have dreams for the future again. I looked over at Warren, who pushed his food around on his plate but didn't bother to eat. Or even to look up.

"What are your dreams, Warren?" I asked, trying to get him into the spirit.

"I dream about getting through the day," Warren said. "That's about all."

"That's so depressing," I said.

Warren put down his fork and dropped his head into his hands. "I'm exhausted," he said. "I think I need to go home."

Brad sighed. "You two are just so sad tonight."

Warren got up from the table and as I followed, Brad reached for my hand. "Let him just go to sleep tonight, Jackie," he whispered. "He's completely worn down."

Warren and I drove home in silence, and following Brad's advice, I let him go upstairs without another word. I was beginning to understand that my high energy and roller-coaster emotions could wear people down. I could generally keep fighting and talking and talking and fighting all night, but right now, that would be counterproductive. Warren needed to get his reserves back.

"Last night at dinner was the first time I felt that I didn't even fit in with my friends anymore," I said to Warren the next morning.

"Why not?" he asked.

"Maybe because they were talking about dreams for the future," I said. "We need to have dreams again, too, Warren. To dream is to hope. We've got to keep dreaming in order to live."

I hoped he'd feel the uplift of the moment, but instead he shook his head. "I'm so broken inside," he said shakily. "All my reserves are gone. I can't dream. I can barely get through a day of work."

Warren's own grieving process hadn't been as loud as mine, but it had been just as tortured. It hurt to see him sinking lower and lower under the burdens of sadness and lawsuits and anxiety about the future. And I didn't make it any easier for him. "How do I get my husband back?" I asked. "The one who took care of everything."

A profound sadness washed over Warren's face. "I don't know how to give you what you need," he said. "I realize you don't like me to call your friends when you're upset. You want me to take care of you. But I don't feel like I can. I can't even make my wife happy anymore."

I looked at him, stunned. His moment of vulnerability now stopped me cold. I never thought Warren heard me before when I said I wanted him, not my friends, to comfort me in my darkest moments. The other night when I was crying and he called Laura, I assumed he just didn't want to deal with my hysterics. But standing with him now, I suddenly had a new perspective. He wanted to be my white knight, my emotional savior. How mortifying for him to feel that he didn't have the strength to be the hero on the horse, riding in to save the day. The world had different expectations for how Warren and I would handle our tragedy.

I, the shattered mother, was allowed to fall apart, scream in pain, rage at the unfairness of fate. Warren, the heartbroken father, was expected to go to work and prop me up.

I stepped a little closer to him now.

"Remember what I said that night? I need a hug from my husband."

He looked at me distrustfully. The flip side of not getting what I wanted from Warren was that I hadn't offered the love, comfort, and support he needed, either. I had resisted any physical affection for a long time. Our discussing it the other day hadn't gotten us anywhere.

"Can we at least try it?" I asked.

Awkwardly, standing in the kitchen, we put our arms around each other. My belly got in the way and we smiled and readjusted. The hug didn't last long, but it was a start.

Two broken people, looking for the glue that would help us mend, and daring to hope we could each find it in the other. Maybe that was the best kind of dream of all.

Twenty-six

My anxiety had only been getting worse as the pregnancy progressed, and I couldn't sleep and wasn't eating much. I had still gained only fifteen pounds. The baby seemed healthy, but the doctor didn't want to take any chances. Though my due date was still some weeks off, she scheduled a Cesarean section for October 6.

"That's Warren's birthday!" I told her delightedly. "You picked a perfect day!"

I'm always looking for omens, and this seemed like a good one. I wasn't sure what the coincidence of the date signified, but somehow it felt lucky.

My doctor, Randi Rothstein, explained that she would do an amniocentesis before the delivery to make sure the baby's lungs were sufficiently mature. Only once the baby passed that test would I come in for the C-section.

I marked October 6 on my calendar with a big red star. At least I was off the hook for buying Warren a birthday present. The baby would be his gift, all wrapped up in one of the soft pink blankets and pretty satin hair bows I had received at the shower.

But at the next doctor's visit, Dr. Rothstein had changed the plan. "Hospital policy doesn't allow an amnio to check the lungs until thirty-eight weeks," she explained. "So we'll push your date back to October eleventh."

"You can't do that," I said, feeling like a little kid who's just had a lollipop taken away.

"It's only a week," she said consolingly.

I started to explain about the lucky day, but then stopped. She didn't seem like the superstitious type.

I called all my friends to tell them about the date change, and I kept moaning that this must mean the good omen had turned bad. Most told me not to be silly, or echoed Dr. Rothstein's comment that it was only seven days. But Warren, used to my looking for portents and prophecies, had a better way to save the situation. He had just come home from work and was opening and closing kitchen cabinets, looking for something to eat. But he saw my crestfallen face and immediately sat down at the kitchen table with me.

"October eleventh," he said thoughtfully. He doodled on a piece of paper for a minute, and then grinned. "Thank goodness she changed it, because October eleventh is the perfect date. Numerology. It couldn't be better."

"What are you talking about?" I asked.

"It's 10/11/11. Look." He slid the paper over to me and I saw: 101111.

"So what?" I asked.

"So, ones for girls and zeroes for boys. I'm the 'zero' in the lineup. You're the 'one' to one side of me. And my four daughters are on the other side."

I looked at the numbers again, which seemed to swim in front of my eyes. "Show me again."

"That's Jackie," he said, pointing to the first 1. He slid his finger over to the 0. "That's Warren." Then the next lineup of 1s: "Emma, Alyson, Katie, Kasey. So it's Warren surrounded by his five ladies."

101111.

I got it.

"That's kind of amazing," I said, suddenly smiling.

"And I don't even mind being the big fat zero," he joked.

Maybe you can make anything seem like a good sign if you try hard enough. A lineup of numbers can signify a date on the calendar, or it can be the stand-in for a loving and growing family. It's just a question of being positive in how you interpret numbers—and life.

• • •

On October 10, my doctor took my amnio to find out if I could deliver the next day. The results would come back in two parts—a "rapid test" took six hours, and the fuller test took twelve.

The rapid report wasn't encouraging. "It looks like you're going to have to wait another week," the doctor said when she called me.

"Oh no," I said, sighing heavily into the phone.

"I'll call you about nine p.m. when we get the other test back and let you know definitely," she said.

Since it was Monday night, Denine came over to watch TV as she always did, and Karen joined us, too. My mom had come from New Jersey because she thought we'd have the baby the next day, and she hadn't been convinced to stay home by the earlier call. We all sat in the living room, watching TV and eating ice cream. Warren popped in and out several times, asking if the doctor had called yet.

"It's not going to happen," I told him. "I won't be at the hospital. Plan on a regular workday tomorrow."

When the first TV show was over, Karen said, "It's nine o'clock. Call her, Jackie. Maybe she forgot to call you."

I picked up the phone to call, then put it right back down. Forgot? How likely was that? I still had my hand on the receiver when it rang.

"Hello?"

"Pack your bags," the doctor said. "You're going to the hospital tomorrow to have your baby."

"You're kidding. Oh my God." I dropped the bowl of ice cream and watched it spill all over the floor. I shook all over.

"I thought it would be next week."

"The twelve-hour test came back fine. Tomorrow it is."

I suddenly felt nothing but sheer terror. The doctor had warned that the C-section would be difficult, and I couldn't face physical pain. I also worried what my reaction to the baby might be. What if, instead of a burst of maternal love for the daughter who had just come into my life, I started crying for the daughters I had already lost?

While I stared at the puddle of ice cream spreading across the kitchen floor, all the anxiety and guilt and uncertainty of this pregnancy came to a head. When Warren came over, I grabbed his arm.

"Please don't make me do this," I said in a hoarse voice.

"You're going to be okay," he said as he put an arm around me.

"I don't want to be cut open again."

"You'll be fine," he said soothingly. "You've done this before."

My friends told me that everything would be fine, cleaned up the messy kitchen, and offered kisses and good wishes. They left and my mother, overcome by her own emotions, disappeared to the basement guest room to go to sleep.

Warren put his hand on my back, a gentle hoist as we headed up the stairs to bed. We crawled under the covers and as he held me, I trembled in his arms. I couldn't stop my spiraling thoughts. I would go to the hospital in the morning, and who knew what would actually happen? In the scenario everyone else expected, the next time I returned home and got into this bed, my baby would be here with me. After all I had been through, that still seemed too unreal to imagine.

Kasey Rose Hance came into the world at 10:20 a.m. on October 11, 2011, weighing 6 pounds 13 ounces. She was perfectly healthy, with rosebud lips and long eyelashes that she blinked endearingly for her first look at the world.

I'd had an epidural, so I couldn't feel most parts of my body. I moaned groggily from whatever sedatives the doctors had given me.

I saw Warren holding her.

"Look, Jackie. Isn't she great?" He held the pretty baby out to me, but I could hardly take her in. The moment was too overwhelming.

A nurse came in then and took the baby to get cleaned up, and Warren left the operating room with her. Someone wheeled me into the recovery room and people began coming in and out—Jeannine and Isabelle and Melissa were all there, and so were Cortney and Kara from New Jersey, and Laura and Bob from down the street, and Warren's dad and my mother and I don't know who else.

I tried to focus but, disoriented from all the pain medication being pumped into me, I couldn't recognize faces or remember details of why I was in the hospital. My grasp on reality started slipping away.

"Is someone taking care of Oliver?" I asked, forgetting that our dog Oliver had died many months ago. I didn't ask about our new dog, Jake. Maybe the blur of analgesics had transported me back a few years.

"How is Emma doing?" I asked. "Is Emma okay?"

"Emma's not here, Jackie. You know that," Warren said, stunned by the flash of amnesia.

"Wasn't Emma just born? How is Emma?"

Warren started getting upset, worried about a return of the memory loss I'd suffered after the accident. The nurses promised him that it was just the drugs speaking, and they turned out to be right; an hour later my awareness returned.

I went to a private room and a nurse brought in Kasey. I tried breast-feeding and she took to it immediately. Then the nurse insisted on try-ing a technique called skin-to-skin, where she placed the naked baby on my exposed chest and wrapped us both together in a blanket. I lay there feeling awkward and uncomfortable as Warren and our friends snapped pictures. But there must have been something to it, because the baby, feeling my body warmth and heartbeat, immediately stopped crying.

As the afternoon wore on, the postsurgical pain became so awful that I clenched my fists in anguish. The nurses administered more drugs through the IV, but nothing seemed to work. In desperation, Warren called the nurse from the delivery who had been generous and gentle and offered to help however she could.

"Someone forgot to unclamp the intravenous, so nothing was get-ting through," she said when she came to the room. Warren turned beet-red, furious that I had suffered when it could have been averted.

"This should help," the nurse said, fixing the line.

But twenty minutes later, I still didn't feel any relief.

"You shouldn't be in this much pain," Warren insisted. He called the pain management team, but they must have had a lot of pain to manage that day, because more than an hour passed before anyone arrived. As we waited, Warren could barely control his anger. Finally at my bedside, the pain team quickly discovered the problem—the epidural needle had fallen out hours earlier. Instead of any medicine going into me, it was collecting in a puddle on my back.

"Everything went wrong?" Warren asked, in disbelief. "The intravenous line wasn't opened and the epidural had fallen out? How could that be?"

"It's okay, Warren," I said as I saw him getting more and more infuriated. "Just be nice to everyone. They're trying."

"This shouldn't have happened! How stupid! You didn't deserve that!" he roared, wanting to take care of me.

"Relax, I'm okay now," I promised him.

He wanted to stay the night, but I insisted he go home and get some sleep to relieve his tension. I put the baby in the nursery and tried to do the same. The next few days in the hospital passed smoothly, though we laughed that Warren never stayed a night. One day, he went with the Floral Park fifth-graders to the foundation's "Grow With Me" event at the Centennial Gardens. It had become Warren's favorite program in memory of the girls, but he looked so exhausted when he stumbled into the hospital afterward that I sent him home again. Friday night, when he arrived after work, he seemed to be getting sick, and I insisted he leave one more time.

"I need you healthy when I get home," I told him.

I felt comfortable in the hospital, well cared for and in control. Several of my friends asked if they should plan to stay over with me when I got home, but I insisted I'd be fine. My mother would be there if I needed backup, and we'd cope. I could handle one little baby.

But the moment we left the hospital on Saturday, I started to panic. Warren came to get me, and a flock of neighbors thronged the house when we arrived. I just wanted to lie down.

"Go rest," Warren said chivalrously. "I'll take care of Kasey."

I went upstairs and started crying, laid low by some combination of postpartum depression and the devastating realization that I had gained one baby only because I had lost three. I'd experienced depression after Katie was born and remembered calling my mother to tell her that I couldn't possibly handle a third child. But the intensity of my emotion this time was off the charts. I lay in bed, sobbing. I felt both sickened and sickly. I couldn't function, and my hormones were spiraling out of control. I stared at Kasey Rose and sometimes she looked exactly like Emma as a newborn, sometimes like Katie. Either way, she was here because they weren't.

By nighttime, Warren finally passed out in fatigue, and I took Kasey with me to another room. As often happens with newborns, she cried regularly during the night, and we stayed up together, both of us inconsolable. I tried breast-feeding her, just to calm her down, but nothing seemed to help. Her cries ripped through me, giving me chills of terror and despair.

I had expected that the sounds of a baby in the house would be a welcome relief after the defining silence of the last two years, but my subconscious mind began playing strange tricks. The new noise of Kasey crying in her crib echoed the haunting sound I still heard of Emma crying in Diane's car.

Kasey and Emma. Both crying. I couldn't stop either of them. In my tired, hurting, befuddled postpartum state, I didn't even know which of my children I was hearing. The first cries of Kasey seemed as poignant and terrible as the last cries of Emma.

On that first night home, Kasey slept several hours at a stretch, but I stayed up, wanting to be at her side if she woke and started whimpering again. By the next morning, I was exhausted and shaken to the core.

"Why did we do this?" I asked Warren as I sat cross-legged on the bed and rocked back and forth. "What were we thinking bringing this baby into the world? We were fine before."

"We weren't fine before, Jackie."

"Yes, we were."

"We were getting through each day, but we weren't dealing with life. Kasey is going to make us start living again."

"Is that good?"

"I think so," Warrren said, though his voice faltered with uncertainty.

Quite possibly, the very concept of living again had us both paralyzed with fear. Kasey was like a spotlight shining on all we had lost. Before this, we—and particularly Warren—had been able to sustain days of denial, putting the misery aside and just going about daily life. Work, eat, watch TV, go to bed. Don't think, don't feel. But now Warren had to come home from work and help me take care of the baby. He had to be a father in real life, not just in memory.

For the last two years, I had been a mother to three girls who weren't here. I would never stop being their mother. But now I had another daughter whose needs were more urgent.

Warren called Isabelle to say that he didn't know what we had been thinking, but we really did need help, after all. Just as she had after the accident, she made a schedule for people to sleep over so I could get some rest and support. During the day, the house was already packed with people stopping by. I had no confidence in myself and was almost scared to touch my baby. I watched other people take care of her and love her.

I can't do that, I thought. *Let them do it.*

Kasey's fussy time seemed to be in the evening, between six and eight o'clock, when she was tired but not yet ready to go to sleep. She'd cry unless someone held her. Gina and Sal from across the street came by one evening, and when Sal held her, she immediately calmed down. Maybe that's what Kasey needed—a strong, confident cop to hold her, rather than a tremulous mother. I stood back and watched as my friends kissed her and hugged her and handled her effortlessly. Would that ever be me? Being a mom had seemed so natural to me once, and now I could barely remember what to do. I felt awkward around the baby, stiff and unsure of how to behave.

For three days straight, I didn't eat or sleep, and I sobbed far more than Kasey did. By Tuesday, I looked gray and could barely move. I'd never felt worse in my life. I'd lost the fifteen pounds I'd gained in pregnancy plus another seven or so on top of that. I couldn't swallow, and even I could see that I was thin as a rail. Warren kept urging me to eat, but I felt like my throat had closed up and nothing could possibly get through. Karen came to take me back to the doctor.

"This must be what death feels like," I told her, almost too exhausted to get to the car.

Dr. Rothstein ran some tests and quickly discovered that I was anemic, which could partly explain why I felt so bad. She gave me a prescription to treat the iron deficiency, along with a warning: "If you don't start eating, I'm going to have to put you in the hospital," she said, after examining me.

She sent me to my psychiatrist, who put me on Prozac and clonazepam and said it wasn't a surprise that postpartum depression had hit me hard. I felt like I had been plummeted right back to the weeks after the accident, that nightmarish time when I felt total devastation twenty-four hours a day. Although I hadn't realized it, I had gotten so much better since then, being back in that condition was a shock. As had happened the very first night at home, hearing Kasey cry plunged me into some anomalous form of post-traumatic stress disorder. Like a soldier coming home from war who hears a car backfire and experiences the horrors of war all over again, I heard Kasey whimper and relived again and again the last conversation I ever had with Emma.

I found myself afraid to be alone with the baby. I imagined getting so unnerved by her cries that I would just walk out the front door and leave her. It didn't require Sigmund Freud to interpret that as an emotional metaphor for the guilt I felt about Emma, Alyson, and Katie. I had abandoned them when they needed me. I hadn't taken care of them. Nothing could relieve me of my secret shame. If I stopped to think about it, I understood that the car accident was an inexplicable incident, a one-in-a-million or -billion or -trillion occurrence that nobody could have foreseen. How different for Kasey, whose little cries foretold only that she needed a simple diaper change, a bottle, or to be gently and lovingly rocked.

I could do all that. I just didn't know it yet.

"Why can't God make this easy?" I asked Isabelle.

"What do you want God to do?"

"Make her a good baby."

"She is a good baby!" Isabelle exclaimed.

In fact, after that first long night, Kasey fussed less than most babies, and everyone marveled at her pretty features and easy temperament. Instead of feeling maternal pride, I shuddered at my disloyalty to her sisters.

Alyson was a happy baby, too. Has everyone forgotten her? Is it only about Kasey now?

After seeing Dr. Rothstein, I tried to get myself to eat, but I had less success with sleep. Each night I stayed awake, wandering around my room, wondering what I had done. Even if friends had stayed in the house to help, I listened for every peep from Kasey and rushed in. Sleep deprivation can cause confusion, hallucinations, and depression, and while international courts have disagreed on whether it's a form of torture, all agree that it is cruel and degrading.

And I was doing it to myself. This was way beyond the normal weariness any new mom feels, which I had experienced three times before. Unlike when the girls were infants, with Kasey, I didn't sleep when she slept. I didn't sleep at all.

At the end of the week after I saw the doctor, a miracle happened. Kasey slept for five hours one night, and I did, too.

I woke up the next morning feeling like a new person. I looked at my baby in the morning light and touched her soft sweet cheek.

I picked her up from her crib, and even as I held her, I felt a strange sense of dislocation. Was my previous life a dream? This baby was real, a tangible, sweet-smelling presence in my arms. But how did she get here? How did I end up in this spot? Trying to put the pieces of my life together was like attempting to solve a jigsaw puzzle that had extra pieces in the box.

A sad mother whose three daughters have died.

A hopeful mother who has a new baby.

Could both of those women be me?

In some ways, it had been easier to be sad every day and let myself think only of a tomorrow when I would see Emma, Alyson, and Katie again. Warren was right—I hadn't been living, I had just been biding time. Now I had to be here—in the moment—for Kasey.

As I started to get some physical strength back, I felt stupid having people sleep over and ended Isabelle's schedule. I could take care of Kasey. But my mental picture of desertion continued to terrify me. One night Warren stayed at a Jets game that went very late and I roamed alone through our dark and quiet house. Kasey slept comfortably in her crib. I suddenly had visions that I would walk out the door and abandon her, leave and not come back. Frightened of my own thoughts, I called Denine to come and be with me.

The escape fantasy scared me—until I started mentioning it aloud. And then nearly every woman who heard it gave me a knowing smile.

"Come on, Jackie, stop thinking you're so special," teased one of my friends, a devoted mother of three. "There are times we'd all like to walk out of our own lives and start again."

I looked at her in shock. "Really?"

"Really," she said. "I think it's part of being a parent. Or maybe just part of being married."

Her nonchalance gave me a new perspective. I thought of Warren's mom, who hadn't just thought about leaving her children—she'd actually done it. Maybe when life got too hard, it was easier to run than stick it out. But there was something heroic about facing down difficulty and pain and uncertainty and standing firm, no matter what.

"I'm going to be here for you," I whispered to Kasey. "I'm not going anywhere. But you know that you have three sisters, don't you?"

I sat down in her room, where all four girls' names were written on the wall. I rocked Kasey and looked at the pictures of her sisters.

Maybe we didn't have too many pieces of the jigsaw puzzle. For the first time I realized that maybe we had the right number—and I could figure out how to put them together for a beautiful picture after all.

Twenty-seven

At my six-week checkup, the doctor said she'd clear me to start running again the next time I saw her. I whooped with delight. Running meant getting back to life. After that, everything else would fall into place. It had to. Her news gave me a greater surge of excitement than any Prozac prescription could possibly provide.

My next appointment with her was scheduled for a Monday, but patience has never been one of my virtues. On Saturday, I called Bernadette to ask if she'd come for a first run with me.

"Aren't you supposed to wait?" she asked.

"The doctor's going to give me a clean bill of health in two days," I said cavalierly. "Let's go today."

For the first time in months, I put on my black running pants, black-and-purple jacket, and a purple knit cap. Bernadette came by in an almost matching outfit, but sporting a white knit cap against the late November chill. We grinned and took off down the street. I felt a little shakier than usual and after about a mile, Berne called out, "Jackie, are you okay? Should we stop?"

I shook my head and kept going. With every step, I was starting to feel better. We went for about three miles, and I got home feeling like the world was good again. If I could run, I could take care of Kasey. I could clear my head and move forward.

Now that I was running and feeling healthier, my spirits started recovering, too. One Sunday night, I turned on the TV to *Oprah's Lifeclass*. I've always been a sucker for inspirational uplift, and as Oprah talked about overcoming adversity, I sat bolt upright. Over the last couple of years, I had come to understand that tragedy—of all kinds—struck more people than I could have imagined. The absolute aloneness I felt after that July day, the sense that I was the only one whose life had slid off a cozy path, had disappeared.

While I was pregnant with Kasey, I got the courage to write a magazine article about the girls and the accident. As soon as it appeared, I started getting letters and emails from people all over the country who wanted to share their own anguish with me—sickness, death, loss. The old adage that "misery loves company" sounds cynical, but maybe it's about the natural instinct to share experiences and find comfort in those who have survived worse than you.

There is so much pain in the world; maybe one thing I could do was to help people know they weren't alone. When I heard about a terrible car accident on the nearby Meadowbrook Parkway that killed three college-age kids, I understood the devastation the parents must be feeling. I wanted to tell them the pain would get better, even if they couldn't possibly believe it. I brought flowers to the parents who lost a son and went to the wake of the two girls also taken in that accident. All three were killed driving together to their summer jobs as counselors at a camp for the disabled.

Great kids, just like mine.

Meaningless loss, just like mine.

As I listened to Oprah, I understood that everyone grapples with their own demons. Misfortune, devastation, and sadness are, unfortunately, more the norm than the exception. Whatever the degree of loss, you have to fight back, find your own happiness despite it all.

At least I was taking baby steps in the right direction. No longer did I wake up every morning angry to be alive. For the last two years, I had told myself every day that my only purpose was to be with my daughters, and if they were gone, I should die, too. Now, with Kasey, I made a new choice. To live.

Kasey deserved the same happy childhood that I had tried to give her sisters. When they were little, I consciously put aside my own problems—anxiety, bulimia, uncertainty—to be the joyous, confident, giving mother they deserved. Now my problems felt a lot more dramatic. But the conclusion was the same.

If I was going to live, I might as well make the most of it. For all of us.

Before the accident, living a comfy life in a nice town surrounded by happy friends and family, I thought that "disaster" meant Emma's not getting the part she wanted in a play. Looking back, I don't understand why I ever wasted one single moment being unhappy or depressed.

The unyielding despair I had experienced since the accident was understandable, of course—but what purpose did it serve anyone? Though I had managed to crawl out of the caverns of complete misery, I could still feel gloom emanating from my soul.

I listened to Oprah for a while more, then called Jeannine, knowing she wouldn't hem and haw if I posed a direct question.

"Is it hard being my friend?" I asked her. "Do I project negative energy?"

"You're dark a lot," she admitted.

Dark. Well, I couldn't disagree with that. But I didn't want to be dark anymore. I wanted to be a force of light instead. I wanted Kasey to feel only positive energy from her mother.

"Am I one of those people who sucks all the energy out of a room?" I asked, using Oprah's lingo.

"No," Jeanne said without hesitating. "You've had a very bad time. But we still feel the positive person there underneath."

"Oprah says we should get rid of the people in our lives who suck out the positive energy," I reported.

"I'm not getting rid of you," Jeannine said with a little laugh.

"Well, I'm going to try to get rid of the negativity in myself," I promised her.

A few mornings later, I put my new attitude to the test. Warren came into the kitchen while I was feeding the baby, and I could tell immediately that something was wrong. Maybe he hadn't slept well or he'd had one of those middle-of-the-night attacks of grief that struck like lightning and burned just as deep.

As often happened, his despair came out as belligerence.

"You're starting to look anorectic," he said, standing over me with arms crossed in front of his chest.

"I'm fine," I said, trying not to be put off by his stern demeanor. "I'm feeling good."

"You promised that once you started running again you'd eat more."

"I have plenty of power bars and yogurt to sustain me," I said.

"That's not enough," he said fervently.

"Oh no? How did you become the expert?" I asked, starting to get irritated. "Maybe you should be eating better and exercising more yourself."

"You need strength to take care of the baby," he said, trying to provoke me. And it worked. Despite my plan to be a source of positivity and light, it was hard to break old habits.

"I am taking care of her. In fact, I'm the only one of us taking care of her," I said. Our back-and-forth continued, and in a pattern we had repeated too many times now, the silly tiff blew up into a full-fledged fight.

At some point, I walked out to put Kasey down in her baby seat. I didn't want her—even at two months old—to hear us fighting.

"Let's end this argument," Warren said when I came back into the room.

"Fine," I said, giving positivity my first conscious try.

"Fine?" He looked at me incredulously. He often asked to "end it" when our fights got out of control, and I never agreed. I usually had at least one more thing I had to say. But not this time.

"Yes. Let's end it," I said.

"That's it?" he asked, sounding surprised—or disappointed.

"Yup. You want to end it, let's end it."

Warren went off to work, and instead of calling him as I often did after we fought to cry, complain, or attack, I just put the disagreement aside and went about my day. I had a babysitter coming for part of the morning, which meant I had two hours free, just for me. I wanted to use the time to feel good, not waste it in anger and arguments.

Warren must have been stunned not to hear from me because as I roamed through Target, contentedly shopping, my cell phone rang.

"I want to talk about this morning," Warren said.

"What about it?" I asked, pushing my cart through the housewares aisle and wondering what we might need.

"Why did you end the fight?" he asked.

"You said you wanted to end it, so we did."

"But you never agree. So what happened this time?"

I sighed, slightly exasperated. "Warren, you must be joking. I'm in Target. Are you really calling me here to ask why we're not fighting?"

"I just want to know what was different about this morning," he said.

"I have two hours without the baby. Some rare free time for myself. I'm trying to use it productively. Fighting isn't productive."

I could hear his incredulity through the phone. "So that's it?"

"That's it," I said. "And I love you."

The truth is that I couldn't really explain what had made today different. Maybe just thinking about positive energy had given me some. Letting go of anger felt a lot better than holding on to it.

Sometimes our marriage felt like a seesaw—when one of us was up, the other was down. We never seemed to be in the same place at the same time. And maybe that was good. When I hit bottom, Warren had stayed strong to pull me off the ground. But now that I seemed tougher and more determined, Warren could give in to his own disquiet.

Friends still stopped by regularly, and our house was often packed with people when Warren came home from work. He usually slipped quickly through the living room, often giving Kasey a quick kiss, before disappearing for the night. One night, Warren got home and barely said hello. A few minutes later, he sent me a text: "Can you bring Kasey upstairs without anyone noticing?"

Without asking him why, I gently took the baby from the neighbor who was rocking her and headed to our bedroom.

"What's wrong?" I asked Warren.

"There were so many people, and I didn't feel like talking," he said. "But I wanted to see her."

I put Kasey on the bed next to him and lay down, too. The three of us stretched side by side—a small and slightly awkward family gathering on a big comfy bed. Kasey's sparkly dress shone in the light, and she looked irresistible.

Warren cooed and cuddled for a few minutes, then handed her back to me. "Okay, thanks," he said. "I'm exhausted. I'm going to sleep."

"That's not fair," I said. "You can't just get home from work and go to bed anymore. The day's not over. We have a baby who needs us. You have to spend time with her."

"You don't really need me," he said. "There's always someone to take care of her."

"But you're her father," I said. "I don't want to do this alone."

Warren looked despairing. "I know, Jackie. I'm going to try, I really am. I just can't do it tonight."

I shook my head. How could I ask Warren to share my timetable for recovery? He had coped with my abject misery, and now I should be respectful of his need to adjust. But it was tough. For two years, I had cried and screamed and raged and stared down my hopelessness. Now with Kasey, I wanted to inch forward to the future. But Warren had spent that same time trying to be stoic and denying the pain. He closed down at the end of the workday and tried to keep grief from edging its way into his consciousness.

I suppose he thought if he could shut out the memories, he wouldn't hurt so much.

But he couldn't shut out Kasey.

Looking at his little baby girl, he saw again in full living color the faces of her sisters, and he wasn't prepared for the deluge of emotions that holding her raised. Along with the affection and love and need to protect came the agony, grief, wretchedness, and torment that he had been trying to avoid.

"There's dinner in the kitchen," I said, thinking that practical matters provided the safest ground.

"Did you cook?" he asked hopefully.

"Don't press your luck," I said with a laugh to lighten the mood. Neighbors continued to drop off home-cooked meals and take-out extravaganzas. My amazing support network was stepping forward in every way possible to help us raise a happy and healthy baby—and to make sure that Warren didn't go hungry. But cooking had always been both a favorite hobby and a way I showed love. Kasey would be ready for solid food soon, and even if I couldn't whip up cakes and soufflés just yet, I needed to do better than power bars and diet soda.

A few days later, feeling particularly brave, I put Kasey into a cute outfit and bundled her up to go outside. As we stepped out the door, Warren called on my cell phone just to check in. Isabelle often teased that despite our fights, Warren and I remained as close as high school sweethearts joined at the hip.

"What are you doing?" Warren asked, not expecting any ground-breaking answer.

"I'm going to the grocery store," I said casually, as if going to the local grocery store were as much a nonevent for me as it would be for most moms. "We need bread and milk."

"The grocery store?" Warren asked. He sounded so shocked that I might as well have said I was heading to a strip club to learn pole dancing. "Are you ready for that?"

"Yup!" I said. "It's like ripping off a Band-Aid. Better to do it fast and get it over with."

The visit to the store was uneventful. I popped bread and milk and a few other things into my cart and headed to the checkout. I still recognized the ladies at the registers, and they knew me, too. They clucked and cooed over my pretty baby, did the transaction, and that was that.

No big deal.

A few days later, I took Kasey to the big supermarket and emerged equally fine—grocery bags in hand and emotions unscathed. One dark place gone from my life.

I reminded myself regularly that all I could do was try my best and make myself overcome other uncertainties. As with the grocery store, I worried about taking Kasey for a walk by myself. Being seen in public with my baby unnerved me. What would people say? It was time to find out. I put Kasey in her stroller and ventured outside, just the two of us, walking through town. By now, most people in Floral Park recognized me and many stopped to talk.

One woman I'd never met came up and introduced herself, gushed over Kasey, and then took my hand. "I'm so glad you have a new baby," she said simply. "But I want you to know that I still pray for Emma, Alyson, and Katie."

"Thank you," I said, tears of gratitude filling my eyes. What could be better? She admired my pretty baby but saw Kasey as one part of a larger family of sisters, all equally beloved. This stranger had struck the magic formula.

I continued the walk and realized I felt fine strolling with my baby.

Just like any mom.

I made little faces at Kasey as we walked, acting as silly as every new mother who gets thoroughly entranced trying to make her baby smile. Kasey looked so sweet and she deserved a happy life.

When we got back home, I called Isabelle. "I think I may like her," I said.

"Like who?" she asked.

"Kasey."

Isabelle laughed. "That's good to hear."

"No, I mean it. I don't love her yet, but I'm starting to like her." I paused, even that admission causing a tinge of guilt.

"I still miss Katie's hugs," I added quickly. "I wish Kasey could hug me like Katie did or smile at me like Aly."

"She will," said Isabelle. "Give her time."

One day, I stood with Kasey and contemplated the pictures of Emma, Alyson, and Katie on the wall.

The girls had been real, my flesh and blood, my beloveds. But now they had vanished, and Kasey would have things they never did. Emma had yearned to go to Disneyland, and I promised her a family trip when she turned ten and Katie would be old enough to enjoy it, too. But putting it off meant none of them ever got to go. I wouldn't wait to take Kasey to the Magic Kingdom. Carpe diem. But would taking her be a way to honor the girls' memory—or seem simply unfair?

Holding Kasey as I walked around the room, I rocked back on my heels in confusion.

BA—Before the Accident—my life had been happy and busy and filled with children and love. AA—After the Accident—had been sad and miserable and lonely. Now I had unwittingly stumbled into a third stage, which included parts of each and memories of both. I struggled to understand the jumbled mix of BA happiness and AA sorrow that I now experienced every day. In this new stage—AAA? After After the Accident?—the disparate pieces of my life started to merge into a coherent whole.

A couple of days later, a friend came over and wanted to see Kasey.

"She's in the girls' room," I said, gesturing toward the upstairs. And I realized that the whole was beginning to form. Kasey's crib and toys and clothes graced the bedroom that Emma and Alyson had shared, once and always "the girls' room." Many of Emma's and Alyson's favorite belongings remained there, and their old treasures mingled easily with Kasey's new ones. Instead of being eerie, the combination seemed just right. The "girls' room"—maybe now more than ever. Kasey was one of the girls. Instead of thinking I shouldn't delight in my new baby, I needed to incorporate her experiences with those of her sisters, and vice versa.

In the first weeks, while other people had coddled and kissed Kasey, I had cared for her quietly. I hadn't talked to her on the changing table. I had fed her dutifully. But now we chatted all the time, and I told her about her sisters. One day, as I changed her diaper, I started singing a little song. I thought I made it up as I went along, but the words must have been in my heart since the day she was born.

K is for Katie
A is Aly
S is for Sisters
E is for Emma
Y is for YOU!

I sang the little tune, and Kasey gurgled happily. Before long, that became our special song. I sang it as she lay looking up at me on the changing table, or when I rocked her in my arms to put her to sleep. The song became a magic ditty that soothed her from any distress. Or maybe the words calmed me down, and Kasey felt that ease. Whatever the case, the song said that Kasey fit into a whole family and a bigger story. She had sisters who loved her even if they couldn't hold her. But she was more than an addendum to a tragic tale. She gleamed as a precious girl on her own, a little bundle of hope and possibility who existed both as part of a continuum and as a distinctive soul. Her sisters contributed to her name and identity, but the Y—the You!—had to be allowed to shine as brightly and boldly as the other letters.

Twenty-eight

bonded to Kasey and liked taking care of her, but guilt still hung over me like a black cloak. I tried to push it aside. I needed to love this baby. In TV commercials and sappy family movies, the mother looks into her baby's eyes, the music rises, and her face softens in a haze of tenderness. Joy and happily-ever-after are sure to follow.

Or maybe real life, with all its heartbreak and tragedy, would follow instead. I feared giving my heart to a baby, knowing the risk of having it broken. So many other friends and family members already loved Kasey unconditionally. Why couldn't I? I kept remembering the exact moments when I fell in love with each of the other girls, and I wondered when—or if—that would happen with Kasey.

With Emma, I had gone back to work after two months. Having found a wonderful babysitter in Salvina, I didn't worry about being away from her. Little did I know. The first day back on my job seemed to last forever, and as I raced home to pick up Emma, I was almost hysterical to see her again. I rang Salvina's door impatiently. The moment she opened it, I rushed into the house and scooped Emma into my arms, a rush of devotion surging through me.

Wow, I really love this baby, I had thought.

I smiled at Salvina, who touched my cheek, reading the ardor in my eyes. "You love your little bambino," she had said.

With Alyson, I had the love epiphany at seven weeks, when she smiled at me. Alyson had a big, fat smile that embraced the whole world.

The first time she flashed it at me, I knew I would do anything for her. And that feeling never went away.

Katie was just six weeks old when I took her for a regular checkup and the doctor thought she might have a problem that required a neurosurgeon. I couldn't get an appointment for a couple of weeks. Beside myself with worry, I spent the time reading everything I could find about cranial stenosis, a condition where the soft spot closes too fast and there is no room for the brain to grow. The surgeon has to cut the skull open, and after surgery the vulnerable baby wears a helmet as protection. For two weeks, I had a lump in my throat. The thought of my baby needing surgery was overwhelming because I loved her so much. Katie turned out to be perfectly healthy, and my fears slipped away, but the love never left. Neither did the desire to protect her and keep her from suffering.

Three girls. Three moments of falling in love.

And now Kasey, my fourth girl.

Early on, infants have endless needs, and all they give back in exchange for a mother's exhausted efforts is an aura of helplessness and a fragrant smell of baby powder, warm milk, and purity. Eventually, that changes.

One day when she was nine weeks old, Kasey slept all the way through the night. I got up at 4:30 a.m. for my usual run, and when I peeked at her, she was off in some happy dreamland. I left, knowing Warren was home, and when I came back an hour or so later, Kasey hadn't stirred. Feeling my usual postrun energy high, I wanted to feed her and change her and get the day started, so I nudged her gently in her crib to wake her up. She opened her eyes as I picked her up—and she smiled at me.

I felt my heart melt.

"Seriously? You're smiling?" I asked, starting to laugh. "I just woke you up! What kind of perfect baby are you, anyway?"

She smiled again.

I smiled back at her.

I felt the rush of baby-love that I remembered so well, the stirrings of deep affection rousing my heart. I fed Kasey and played with her for a while, and then I realized she was still tired. No early-morning runs for this baby! I put her back down in her crib and she fell asleep. I stood there for a long time watching her, feeling an odd mix of pride and satisfaction and relief. I knew my baby. I knew what she wanted and needed. As I pulled a blanket over her, I realized my glow was coming from more than a renewed sense of competence.

I love her. I feel like her mom, I thought. *I love her.*

For a moment, I wanted to stop myself and tell Emma, Alyson, and Katie that I still loved them, too. But I didn't need to. They knew.

Everyone asked what I would do for Kasey's first Christmas, and my answer was—nothing. A three-month-old doesn't need Santa, and however far I had come, I wasn't quite ready to celebrate. Jeannine and Isabelle offered to make holiday cards for me with a family picture but I declined. I didn't need them to help me with cards or gifts or decorations—I liked all that stuff. And I'd do it next year.

But once again, our friends wouldn't let the holiday pass unnoticed. The previous year, our friend John had placed a graceful white fir tree on our front lawn and Isabelle and company left a basket of ornaments on a table with a notebook, a pen, and a picture of the girls. Friends, neighbors, and people passing by stopped at our house to tie a decoration on the tree and leave their good wishes. It looked so pretty that I couldn't help feeling some holiday cheer. Isabelle had put a note on the door asking people to respect our privacy, but I took it down, horrified. How could I not welcome well-wishers inside? The house was filled with people and noise and laughter—and, as happened so often, the silence crushed me when they left.

That wouldn't happen this year. With Kasey, the curse of quietude had ended. Silence no longer choked us.

On Christmas morning, our friends came over for my now-traditional (three years running!) holiday breakfast spread. John had left another tree outside that the neighborhood children could decorate.

Warren and I took Kasey outside and watched together as the children draped ribbons and ornaments on the green branches. People stayed longer than we'd expected, eating and talking and enjoying the good feeling. When they finally left, a different kind of panic descended. I had too much to do. I wanted to visit the girls at the cemetery, and I needed to fit that in fast because we were planning to drive out to New Jersey for Christmas dinner with my brother Stephen and his family. I hadn't been to Stephen's house since before the accident, and I had steeled myself to restart the tradition that the girls had loved. Families should be together, and Stephen's three children had been hurt by our absence.

"The kids miss their aunt Jackie," my brother had said to me one day.

"Their aunt Jackie's not here anymore," I had said sadly. The carefree, fun-loving person who adored nieces Isabelle and Marguerite and nephew Spencer seemed to be gone for good.

But maybe Aunt Jackie could come back to the fold. With Kasey, I finally felt strong enough to handle being part of the family again. I eagerly anticipated introducing Kasey to her cousins.

The only problem: time was not on my side.

"I'm not dressed and the baby's not dressed and we still have to get to the cemetery!" I shouted at Warren. "Tell my brother we can't come! We have to visit the girls!"

Warren checked his watch. Sure enough, we didn't have time for everything. But with my extended family waiting for us in New Jersey, and a Christmas ham ready to slice, he had a different list of priorities.

"Let's skip the cemetery and get to your brother's," Warren suggested. "We'll visit the cemetery another day."

"Are you kidding? How could I not see the girls on Christmas?"

"Jackie, you don't have to go there to see them. They know," he said.

"We have to fit everything in," I persisted. "We can't leave the girls out and we can't leave out Kasey. Let's see, you go to the cemetery and I'll go to my brother's with the baby. Or, no, I'll go to the cemetery and you go to my brother's. Or maybe—"

"Calm down," Warren said, interrupting my tirade.

I glared at him, my mind spinning plans.

"Jackie, we have to live in the present," Warren said firmly. "And that means all of us going to your brother's together and celebrating Christmas. The girls are with us wherever we go."

I'm not sure why his good sense penetrated this time, but it did. I put Kasey in her special red plaid taffeta Christmas dress and pulled myself together faster than usual. We got to New Jersey, and I walked into my brother's house, still shaken, but holding the baby in my arms. Some relatives who hadn't seen Kasey yet gathered around, and my cousin Michele, who lives in the same two-family house as my mom, started crying.

"Stop it, Michele," I said, smiling even as I felt tears popping into my own eyes. "No crying on Christmas."

"Oh, Jackie, I promised myself I wouldn't cry," she said. "I'm trying not to. But she's so beautiful."

I looked down at my little bundle and smiled. My brother's holiday tree twinkled in the corner, and suddenly, Christmas took on a new and unexpected meaning. In both religion and life, a new baby can be a savior, giving hope where there has been none.

Kasey, my personal savior. My beautiful baby.

A few days before New Year's, I left Kasey with a babysitter so I could spend some time at the cemetery. I felt bad that we had missed Christmas, but maybe it was best that I hadn't come and spoiled the day for Kasey and Warren.

Before Kasey, I had gone to visit the girls four or five times a week, but it was emotionally exhausting. The previous Mother's Day while I was pregnant, I brought a chair to the cemetery and sat for six hours, reading to the girls, decorating their headstones, and telling them stories. When I left, I got back in the car and wailed and screamed so loudly that the car rocked.

When I arrived now on this late December day, I picked up some of the gifts and flowers and trinkets people had left since my last visit. No snow had fallen and the season had been warmer than usual, but the ground still felt hard and brittle. The Christmas decorations could stay up a little longer, until it was time to redecorate for Valentine's Day.

Jeannine kept one bin in her garage with all the decorations that I used and reused, and another bin where I brought all the Barbies, charm bracelets, clothes, and magazines that people laid at their headstones. I no longer let the girls' things pile up at the cemetery for the grounds-keepers to handle, but I didn't want to be the one to throw anything away, either. What Jeanne did with the gift bin, I never asked.

This was the first year that I hadn't bought huge passels of Christmas gifts for the girls. Instead, I added up what I might have spent and made a contribution to the foundation.

In all my visits to the cemetery, I never went to Diane's side of the plot. I just glanced over in anger.

But now, for some reason, on this December afternoon, I walked slowly over to Diane's grave. Diane, my sister-in-law. Diane, the woman who killed my girls. I stared at the headstone for a while and rubbed the toe of my boot against the brittle earth. I thought about an inspirational guru I'd seen on *Oprah* that morning who said that hate is so powerful and destructive, it overwhelms any chance for love. Then I thought about Kasey, my baby at home, who deserved a mother who loved her with a full heart.

To do that, I suddenly understood that I needed to reconcile some of my emotions.

You can't love and hate at the same time, I thought. *You can't be happy and angry at the same time.*

If I continued to hate Diane, I risked depriving Kasey of the intense and pure love that I wanted to give her. And if I didn't let go of the unre-lenting fury I felt, I couldn't move forward in my own life with happiness and joy.

I knew better than anyone how little influence we have over the direction our lives take. Whether you call it destiny or fate or the ran-domness of the universe, some things happen for reasons that we can't begin to understand. Trying to exert control over the events of our lives is ultimately a fool's game. All we can truly master is our own responses.

Hating Diane no longer felt right. Diane was more than the de-praved person that everyone made her out to be. She loved me and

Warren and the girls. She had loved her own children. Until she drove the wrong way on the Taconic Parkway, everyone who knew her would have said she was a caring mother, aunt, sister, sister-in-law, and friend. Someone to be trusted. Did she have hidden demons that none of us saw? I don't know, but who doesn't have demons? Despite the intense scrutiny of her life and character after the accident, nothing diabolic had emerged to explain the horrors she had caused.

You can't love and hate at the same time.

I stepped a little closer to the headstone and, for the first time ever, reached out to touch it.

"I don't know why you did this, Diane," I said in a small voice.

I let my hand rest on the stone. I traced a pattern with my finger across the top. I thought about Kasey and wanting to love again. I thought about how sad it made Warren that I didn't hug him anymore. I thought of my own heart, which, instead of being a bright red valentine, had become encased in steel and ice.

This is so weird, I thought. But I suddenly knew what I needed to say.

"I'll never know what happened that day," I said, my voice louder. "But I always loved you, Diane. I still love you. And I forgive you."

No bolt of lightning came down from the sky and no crack opened up in the earth. If Diane, or God, or my angels in heaven heard me, they gave no sign.

Or maybe they did, because I felt an almost physical change once the words were out. The cold, clammy hand of hate that had been squeezing my chest suddenly seemed to loosen its grip.

"I forgive you," I said again.

I lingered at the headstone for another moment, then I walked slowly away, feeling an unexpected lightness. The weight of anger that I had been dragging around like so much concrete didn't seem to be pulling me down with quite the same force. Trying to build a future with love was more important than holding on to the past with hate.

When I got home, I didn't tell Warren about my experience at the cemetery, and though I usually shared every passing thought with my friends,

I avoided the topic with them, too. Forgiveness is a very private event. I hadn't done it for public consumption. And I wanted to see how I felt in the next few days.

Apparently, forgiveness works in mystical ways. A lot of people commented on how good I looked and how happy I seemed. Suddenly I was laughing and grinning much more, and my love for Kasey gushed forth. I told myself it could just be a coincidence of timing since Kasey had begun smiling all the time now, and at every toothless grin she gave, my heart melted more and more.

More likely, the two events played off each other. I think that by forgiving Diane, I opened myself up to accepting Kasey's smiley affection. I hadn't planned it or even expected it. And if I felt new compassion toward Diane, I had to extend the same benefit to Warren. Her actions weren't his responsibility. Warren always said that he and I both did everything we possibly could the day of the accident, and objectively, we knew that was true. We could say it aloud to convince anyone listening that we meant it. And we did. But late at night, when exhaustion and darkness blurred all rationality, the what-ifs attacked like well-armed invaders from another dimension.

I should have.

I could have.

If only.

Oddly enough, it may be easier to show mercy to others than to yourself. Personal forgiveness may be the hardest to give.

Twenty-nine

was feeling stronger in every way, and my health seemed good now, too. When I went to the usual follow-up visits with the obstetrician, she seemed pleased with how far I'd come. One day as I sat on her exam table after the checkup, my legs dangling, she reminded me that I was cleared to have sex again.

"Don't say that!" I told her, half laughing. "I'm terrified!"

"Why are you terrified?" she asked.

"It's been so long. I don't remember how. I feel like I'm sixteen again."

"Just close your eyes and do it," she said, half joking. "I think it will all come back to you."

Warren and I had a black-tie dinner coming up that we wanted to attend, and Melissa and Brad said they'd take the baby for an overnight. Warren and I could go to the dinner and relax, without having to rush back to a babysitter. Our first night alone since Kasey had been born, and I started to think about what was likely to happen.

"Can we talk?" I asked Warren one morning.

"You don't have to ask. Just talk to me," he said, hardly looking up.

"Okay." I took a deep breath. "The night of the dinner, I think we should have sex before we go out. Otherwise, I'll spend the whole evening worrying about it."

"We're having sex?" Warren asked, definitely looking up now.

"Isn't that what you thought?"

"I didn't think we'd have sex," he said.

"Why not? The baby won't be here."

"Jackie, I don't want to put any more pressure on you. I'm okay leading a celibate life."

My jaw dropped. "A celibate life? But that's so sad!"

"You've had so much to deal with. I don't want to add one more thing."

"You're not attracted to me anymore. That must be it," I said. I couldn't really blame him. I hadn't been that much fun to live with for the last couple of years. On the other hand, my mood had improved and even I could see that I had a certain sparkle back.

"Of course I'm attracted to you," Warren said.

"How would I know that?"

"I've always been attracted to you. That won't change. But you don't care about all that anymore."

"I work really hard to stay in shape, Warren. And it's not just for me, it's for you. I still want to look good for you. Don't you want to look good for me?"

Talk about feeling sixteen. We sounded like two teenagers struggling to regain our sexual confidence. But at least we had started the conversation. That afternoon, Warren called me from work.

"I just want you to know that I joined a gym. I want you to be as attracted to me as I am to you."

Ready for a night to reconnect, we dropped Kasey off at Melissa and Brad's. We didn't have time for my start-the-night-with-sex plan, but we had fun at the dinner, holding hands under the table and flirting. Warren let his hands linger on the back of my black one-shouldered dress as we danced. We had a baby, we had each other, we had a date. And, late that night, Warren made a convincing case that neither of us needed to lead a celibate life.

As Kasey got bigger and Warren and I wanted to go out more, my mom started coming over regularly to babysit. Emma, Alyson, and Katie had made her feel special and needed, especially after my dad died. I'd often call her and say "Hey, Mom, I need a babysitter tomorrow"—and she'd happily rush to Floral Park.

Warren liked having her around and so did I. She had a purpose. She felt useful. And now she doted on Kasey, just as she had on Emma, Alyson, and Katie.

"Why is she crying?" my mom asked one time when Kasey seemed unusually fussy.

"She's tired," I said without any hesitation. "She only cries if she's hungry or tired, and I can tell the difference."

"So what do I do?" she asked. Warren and I were heading out later and she wanted to know all the tricks.

"Put her in her baby seat, turn the TV to Nick Jr., give her her pacy, blanky, and her lamby," I said, reeling off the nicknames of her favorite blankets and stuffed animals. "I guarantee she'll fall asleep."

Mom followed the routine, and in a few minutes, Kasey was snoozing soundly.

"You know your baby," she said admiringly.

"I do," I said proudly.

"Katie is just beautiful," she said, looking into the crib. And then she gasped and gave a sharp intake of air. "I mean Kasey. Not Katie, Kasey. Oh, Jackie, I'm so sorry. Why did I say that?"

"It's okay," I said. "I've done it, too."

The first time I confused the names, I had gotten incredibly upset. Why had I given Kasey a name that sounded so similar to her sister's? But then I relaxed, and now I gave my mom the benefit of my wisdom.

"It's not such a bad thing to get the name confused. Remember you used to call Emma Alyson sometimes by mistake? It's just the same. They're sisters. And I love both of them."

My mom looked worried for a few minutes, but then she smiled.

"Kasey," she whispered, gently tucking the blanky around her. "Katie's sister Kasey."

In our circle, most of the women had two or three or even four kids by the time they reached their mid-thirties, and now here I was at forty, with a new baby. We had all been used to sharing parenting experiences, and I felt slightly out of step. While Isabelle and Jeannine cheered for their daughters doing flips at gymnastics competitions, I clapped when Kasey sat up on her own. Instead of buying Emma her first bra and getting her a dress for sixth-grade graduation, I was making bottles and pushing a baby carriage. I didn't expect to be watching *Sesame Street* or *Dora the Explorer* again at this point in my life, and I sometimes closed my eyes and pictured the conversations I should be having with Emma about boys and dates. But that part of my life had been derailed. I was on a new track, starting the ride again. Though the train was different, I might as well take advantage of the unexpected view.

When my friends' kids were at school, we could connect as grownups. But on school vacations, they went off bowling with their children or to museums in the city or to preteen movies, while I stayed home with Kasey. Thinking of our disparate positions reminded me that in the real-life version of Monopoly, I had been sent back to Go.

But at least I could still play the game. I had more chances to roll the dice, and for that I was grateful.

I also quickly realized that however homogenous our little group, women outside our circle maintained varied life plans. They did different things at different ages. Walking home from Isabelle's house one day, I noticed a woman on the street with a jogger stroller similar to mine. I waved and she stopped.

"Are you Jackie Hance?" she asked.

I nodded, not sure where this would be going.

"Oh, I'm so glad to meet you," she said, introducing herself. "I have a ten-month-old. Happy fortieth birthday to me."

I laughed. "Surprise baby?"

"Let's just say I also have a ten- and twelve-year-old. There aren't too many of us older moms with babies around here."

"I'm glad we met," I said, warmed by her good humor. "We'll make a plan to go to the park sometime."

When I got home, I immediately called Isabelle. "I made a friend!" I said.

I told her the story and she laughed.

"She seemed nice, but this is just the beginning," I said. "I can't believe that I'm starting all over again. Every place I take Kasey, I'll be with a new group of moms who'll mostly be twenty-six and have nothing in common with me."

"You don't always have to be best friends with your kids' friends' mothers," Isabelle reminded me. "It just happened that all of us fit together."

"Fit together perfectly," I said mournfully. Our children had overlapped so completely that Denine, whose youngest was a year younger than Katie, sometimes complained that she felt like something was off. And that was only a year.

But I already understood that my new phase of life wasn't going to be a repeat of the previous one. New mom at forty? You play the cards you're dealt. Emma and Alyson had been so close in age that they could always entertain each other, and when Katie came along, they loved to plop her in their laps and make her laugh. Now mine was the only lap for plopping.

With Emma, Alyson, and Katie, I dedicated myself to motherhood to such an extreme that I had no other identity. I cherished every minute, but when the role ended, the shock was beyond imagining. No wonder I continued to shop for them after the accident and celebrate birthdays and holidays and tell myself that I would always be their mother. I had nothing else to turn to, no other meaning or purpose. If I hadn't gotten pregnant again, would I have had any reason to exist on this earth at all?

With Kasey, Warren expected me to return to being a full-time, fully devoted mom. I agreed with "fully devoted," but I couldn't risk giving up the things that had pulled me through the worst times—from Tuesdays with Karen to the Thursday bowling league. Having activities scheduled and someplace to go had helped me get to the positive place I was in now, and I certainly wouldn't give them up.

I still got aggravated if Warren lay on the couch too much, and he could get overwhelmed by my energy and endless planning. We worried too much about each other. I wanted to make sure he had slept and he cared that I felt well. We stayed excessively sensitive to each other's moods. So many people marveled that we had remained together that we sometimes wondered about it, too.

One night we came home from therapy and Warren looked like he'd been through a war zone. The sessions always hit him harder than me because he felt less comfortable revealing his soul. Emotionally spent, he went upstairs and got into bed.

I still had plenty of energy and wanted to do something positive for myself. Figuring Warren had fallen asleep, I popped Kasey in the car and headed out to prayer group.

I had driven halfway there when my cell phone rang.

"Where are you?" Warren demanded.

"Going to prayer group," I said.

"Where's the baby?"

"She's with me."

Warren exploded. "Why didn't you leave her home? I panicked when I couldn't find her."

"I thought you were asleep. I was trying to be nice."

"No you weren't," he said angrily. "You were trying to make the point that you have to do everything. Or maybe you just don't trust me alone with Kasey."

I pulled over in the car, not wanting to argue while driving. Warren sounded sufficiently upset that after we hung up, I turned around to go home. I couldn't understand how my doing something positive—going to prayer group—had taken this negative turn.

"I'll do you a favor and leave," Warren said when I came back into the house.

"If that's what you want," I said coldly.

"I think that's what you want. You'd like me to finally leave for good."

For once, I took a deep breath and thought about what I wanted to say. "No, Warren. I've been through the wringer. I don't think I can do this on my own. Tonight was a stupid misunderstanding. We can get through these. We have to."

Warren sighed. "Thank you for that, Jackie."

We both felt the tension in the room—and in our bodies—melt away. Kasey had fallen asleep in my arms, and now I handed her to Warren.

"Of course I trust you with the baby," I said, my voice starting to quaver. "You're her father. She needs you."

Warren held Kasey in one strong arm and put his other arm around me. "We all need each other," he said simply.

Now that the idea of "leaving" had been said in the open, we both viscerally understood how much we wanted to stay together.

The next day I told Isabelle what had been going on.

"You two will never split," she said, as she often did. "You have all this drama and bickering, and then you're fine again. And as soon as the smallest thing happens, your first reaction is 'I've gotta call Warren and tell him.'"

True enough. Warren and I called each other at least five times during the day—sometimes to say hi or check in, sometimes with a funny story or question. Often he had barely left the house before he thought of something to tell me. Once we were talking on our cell phones and I realized we were still close enough to see each other. I had giggled and waved at him—but we still kept talking.

"Don't all couples do that?" I asked Isabelle.

From the funny look she gave me, I guessed not.

The next week, Dr. O'Brien cancelled our usual session because he was sick.

"I have a whole list I want to go over," I moaned to Warren when I called him at work—for the fourth time that day—to say he didn't need to rush home. Dr. O'Brien had urged me to start keeping a list all week of issues that bothered me so we could handle them calmly during a session, rather than my erupting over each one during the week.

"Okay, we'll go over the list ourselves tonight," he said.

He got home from work late and I said, "Are we still going to talk?"

"I thought we already talked," he joked.

"Very funny."

"Come on, sit down. Let's go over your list."

I pulled out the sheet of paper on which I'd written the little concerns that had cropped up all week, bugging me. I worried that without Dr. O'Brien, we wouldn't get anywhere, but we started at the top and talked about each one rationally. An hour later, we'd gotten through the list and Warren smiled.

"We just saved one hundred twenty dollars," he said.

"We can actually do this," I said, proudly tossing the finished list into the wastebasket. "We can talk to each other."

"Yup, we can do this," Warren said. He leaned over and kissed me. "We've done a lot of things these last couple of years we never thought we could. This one's easier than most."

Thirty

One day in late March, Bernadette drove me home after a morning run, and as she dropped me off, another car came whizzing by.

"Watch out!" she called as I stepped out of the car, unaware of the danger.

The car swerved around me and I turned back to Bernadette and grinned. "You don't have to worry about me," I said. "Apparently, I'll never die."

Bernadette threw her head back and gave a long, long laugh.

I make no serious claims for my own immortality, but I spent two years hoping to die and never did. Now I felt great relief in enjoying life again. The worst had already happened. It did not kill me. I learned that we are all stronger than we would have imagined.

When my dad died, at age fifty-six, he seemed so young, and I mourned his too-brief stay on this earth. Now, in comparison, it seems like he had a full life. Maybe in the face of death, time always seems fleeting and transient. Religions all try to help us come to terms with the uncertainty of death and to give us the hope that the sweetness—and pain—of this life will somehow pay off in an eternity yet to come. I don't know if that is true or not, but by the time Easter came, I was at peace with religion again and willing to take the comfort it offered.

Melissa and Brad had invited us to Easter dinner again, and we liked our new tradition with them. Throughout the winter, I hadn't bought anything new for Kasey. Friends had been generous and she already had more pretty clothes than one baby could wear. Odd as it was for me to admit, I didn't get a thrill anymore out of buying a cute new dress or sweet stuffed animal. Things no longer mattered very much. The years I had spent trying to convince Warren that we needed a bigger house seemed long, long ago. I liked where we lived. I could no longer remember why I had been so desperate for a new couch; as I sat relaxing on it with Kasey, I realized the one we had seemed just fine. I had a table in my living room covered with photographs of the girls, and that gave me a pleasure that no upholstery, house, or cute-as-a-button onesie could match.

On the other hand, I'd always taken pleasure in shopping, and letting myself feel that lift for my new baby was part of accepting her. When Kasey was five months old, I saw a monkey-in-a-box in a toy store—and bought my first gift for her. I felt the guilt I always did about being disloyal to her sisters.

How can you buy something for her and not for Emma, Alyson, and Katie?

But I had a new message for that shrill, guilt-inducing voice in my head.

Leave me alone!

Wanting to buy something for Kasey was an auspicious sign, not cause for contrition.

So, for Easter, I went all out and bought Kasey the cutest outfit I could find—a white dress with multicolored flowers in deep rose, pale pink, and yellow, and a pink sash with a big bow in the back. The matching hat had the same cheerful flowers and bow. Kasey gave a toothless smile when she was all dressed—even she knew how pretty she looked.

We drove over to the Katinases' house, and Melissa came outside as we pulled up.

"Oh my God," she said as I came around and took Kasey out of her car seat.

"I know, it's cute, isn't it?" I said, assuming she was exclaiming at Kasey's adorable outfit.

"Wait until you see," Melissa said.

We went into the house and she called Abby, who had been best friends with Katie, downstairs. Abby came bounding down the stairs—wearing the same sashed dress with pink and yellow flowers as Kasey.

"Oh my God!" I said, echoing Melissa's reaction.

But Abby just laughed delightedly. "Kasey is my heart," she said, kissing her real-life matching-dresses doll. "I love her so much."

I let Abby hold Kasey, and as usual, she didn't want to let her go. Ever since Kasey was born, Abby couldn't get enough of her. She had embraced her as passionately as if Kasey were Katie reincarnated. Melissa told me that one day when she was taking care of Kasey for me, she took her to the bus stop when she went to pick up Abby.

"My cousin's here!" Abby had exclaimed as she got off the school bus and raced toward her.

Now I looked at Abby holding Kasey and suddenly understood what it meant to be soul sisters. We could all feel the connection that ran from the beautiful little girl to the beautiful baby, their pretty matching dresses making a field of flowers that seemed to link them as one. I had worried about the fact that Kasey had no siblings with whom to share each day, but she would have other attachments, not the same, but equally meaningful. No, they wouldn't have the same friendship as Abby and Katie, but important bonds can come in many forms. The flowers on their matching dresses were bright harbingers of spring. And who knew what other blossoms would shoot up in the seasons ahead?

Yet, in the midst of all my determination to be positive and hopeful, I encountered some setbacks. A few weeks after Easter, I was driving home from the supermarket alone and pulled up to a stop sign. Not seeing anyone, I drove ahead. Just then, a car turned into the intersection, plowing right toward me. I swerved and jammed on my brakes, but too late. In an instant, I was reliving the absolute horror that the girls had experienced. The gut-wrenching crash and the car tumbling and smashing over on my head. Blood all over. Smoke. Fire. Sheer terror. I felt my ribs breaking, my face shattering against the glass. My body shook convulsively and blood squirted out everywhere.

I got out of the car screaming hysterically.

A woman ran over to me. "Are you okay? Let me call the police," she said.

I pictured the EMTs coming and not being able to save me, the ambulance, being rushed to the hospital. Then I looked over and saw my car, standing untouched in the intersection.

"Did you see what happened?" I asked the woman, my heart pounding.

"Close call," she said. "He just missed you. Very lucky. He drove on. Are you sure you're okay?"

We hadn't crashed. Nothing had actually happened.

I sat down on the curb and tried to catch my breath. The near miss had triggered a reaction so profound that I felt like I was reliving the girls' shock—a classic symptom of post-traumatic stress disorder. I felt the pain the girls must have suffered and envisioned their fear. I felt my body being tossed and turned. I was sick to my stomach thinking that was what the girls had experienced.

When I got back home, Warren was still at work and the baby was out for a walk with Mr. Hance. I had always avoided looking at any pictures of the crash, but now I went to my computer and typed "Taconic Car Accident" into Google. I had to know what the girls had been through.

But halfway through my search, I stopped myself. I sat back in my chair and pulled back. Why was I doing this to myself? My unconscious mind might suffer a PTSD response, and I couldn't do much about it. But I still had control over my conscious responses. If I wanted a positive life, I had to take every bit of energy and concentration and strength I possessed to focus on the good.

Still trembling, I turned off the computer and walked into the living room. Jake, my small fluffy white dog, had jumped up onto the windowsill. I went over and scratched him behind the ears, and the two of us stood there, looking out the window, waiting to see Kasey come home.

Since the accident, I had learned how incredibly kind people can be. But the depth of giving and caring continued to surprise me. One day I mentioned to a TV producer I met how inspired I felt hearing motivational speaker Tony Robbins on television. By complete coincidence, she encountered him the next day—and told him about me. That afternoon, Warren and I had a personal invitation to be his guest at a three-day seminar in New Jersey.

Excited at the prospect of hearing Tony's take on how to "Unleash the Power Within," Warren made plans to take some time off work and I arranged for my mom and some willing friends to babysit Kasey. Tony Robbins has reportedly coached everyone from President Bill Clinton to tennis star Serena Williams, and he's been heaped with praise from celebrities, sports stars, and politicians around the world. Now it was our turn.

We joined about three thousand people who had paid big bucks for the weekend, all seated in a huge auditorium. As Tony's guests we sat right near the front and leaned forward in our seats as he talked about the need to change your story and change your state of mind. He asked us to imagine that inside each of us were shelves with tapes—and we needed to take out the bad tapes and replace them with good ones.

So far I was with him.

We did various exercises, mental and physical, to teach ourselves how to change our state. At one point, Tony told us to close our eyes and go to the worst possible moment that ever happened to us.

"I want to leave," I said to Warren. "I'm not going to do this."

"Just skip this part," Warren whispered.

I didn't have to imagine the worst possible moment that ever happened—it was with me every day. But then Tony explained that we needed to be able to move on to the next chapter. He had us lie on the floor and go back to a favorite memory. I imagined being with the girls on a Friday night and watching *What Not to Wear*. I could feel them with me as we giggled at the show. And then I thought of my other favorite memory, playing the ha-ha game in the backseat of the car. However cranky anybody felt, we all had to laugh. I'd say "ha," then Emma "ha ha," followed by Alyson's "ha ha ha," and Katie's "ha ha ha ha." As we tried to keep the game going for another round, we all, of course, dissolved in giggles.

Lying there, in that huge hall, surrounded by so many other people, I started chuckling. Tony was right—change your story and you can change your state of mind. Instead of focusing on pain and the girls' last moments, I had to think about the happy times. Because they could still make me smile.

But the moment hadn't been as successful for Warren. Thinking about his happiest memory—a moment with the girls—only sent him spiraling back into despair. After the seminar, Warren sent a note to Tony, thanking him for his graciousness and asking what to do when your favorite memories are also your greatest source of pain. "How do you get beyond that?" Warren asked.

Since he is busy coaching tens of thousands of people each year, Tony could have taken the question as rhetorical and let it pass. But instead, Warren opened his email a few days later and found a personal voice message attached.

"Hey, Warren, it's Tony Robbins," the now-familiar voice said.

He offered some pleasant chatter and said he'd been traveling. He hoped Warren had gained strength from the event in New York. And then he got down to the business of answering Warren's questions.

"You have every right to continue to feel pain," he said. "But the problem with staying in that pain is that it isn't honoring your girls, it isn't making you more fulfilled, it isn't giving you more of the world. There's a time for everything, a time for sorrow and a time to grow, a time to feel sad and a time to figure out what your next choice to give is. For you to have a way to honor your daughters and honor your wife and honor yourself and feel alive again, you're going to have to put to bed what has been. It doesn't mean it didn't happen. You're not disrespecting the past to live in the here and now and think about building a future."

He talked about his own losses and said that while he had never experienced anything to compare with burying three daughters, "people's pain is people's pain." What had helped him cope during bad times was knowing that he wasn't alone, and others were going through similar situations. If we could find a way forward, Warren and I could help millions of people with our story.

My past with the girls was a part of me, and I had been clinging to it, afraid to let go. I worried that "moving on" meant abandoning the memories and moments that had been the core of my life. But now I understood that I didn't have to close one book to begin a new one. Warren and I would forever have the beautiful story we had begun with our girls, and what was written could last forever. But the book wasn't finished. We could begin a new chapter.

We scheduled Kasey's christening for early May, and I actually found myself looking forward to it. Sure, I still had some dread and guilt, especially when I realized that Katie's Communion would have been that same weekend. When I worried about giving a party for one and not the other, Bernadette quickly reminded me that Family Fun Day was just a few weeks away.

"You're doing something wonderful for Katie," she said with her usual high energy. "She's having a party with thousands of people at the Centennial Gardens. Everyone is there because of her. And six thousand girls already know Katie and her sisters because they've taken part in Beautiful Me."

It was hard to argue.

I bought Kasey the most beautiful christening gown I could find, white dupioni silk with crocheted flowers on the sleeves and a matching flowered headband. I even bought silk bloomers.

The morning of the christening, the church was packed with friends and family, and Warren and I brought Kasey to the altar. Her three sets of godparents—Melissa and Brad, Jeannine and Rob, and Isabelle and Mark—leaned lovingly over her, and the priest did his sacred rite with oil, then put water on her head. Kasey, our good little baby, never cried or fussed and she looked picture perfect as dozens of friends snapped photos like crazed paparazzi.

We had planned a party afterward at a Knights of Columbus hall, and while I worried that it might be too dreary, the room looked beautiful when we walked in, shining with flowers and balloons and more than two hundred people. The children raced around eating cakes and cupcakes, and a DJ got them playing games and dancing. Then Warren stood up to give a speech.

"We've come full circle," he said to everyone who gathered around, "and we're here because of you. Actually, I can't believe we're here. This is a time for moving on but not forgetting, and trying to have a good life. It's a happy occasion. Emma, Alyson, and Katie are with us and we miss them and love them, but this is Kasey's day."

Most of the people in the hall had been at the Communion party we'd had for Alyson after the accident more than two years earlier, when Warren had arranged for the Michael Bublé song "Hold On." I'd loved the song, but at the time, lyrics about how we were the lucky ones and things would be all right didn't seem to have anything to do with us.

Now I took the microphone from him. I reminded the crowd about the song.

"I thought Warren was crazy when he played that song at Aly's Communion," I said. "I didn't understand but I finally get it now. It takes time and hard work and a lot of love from family and friends to get through the toughest times. In any situation, you have to know everything will be okay. This time, it's a much happier moment than last."

The music started and Warren came over and wrapped me in his arms.

And we danced at our daughter's christening.

That night we got home and for once, instead of sinking into sadness and despair after a good time, our positive feelings lingered. I remembered a year earlier asking Warren if he thought we'd ever feel happiness again.

"We'll find moments of joy and contentment, but happiness is too much to ask," he had said. "Happiness is not what we'll ever feel."

"I just want to be happy again. I want to feel what other people do," I'd said.

"Your expectations are too high," he'd said.

Now, with Kasey, the feeling had changed. We were full of expectations and hope. Looking forward instead of looking back.

"I like what you said today about wanting to have a good life for Kasey," I said to Warren as I hung up Kasey's christening gown. "But good isn't enough. I want great."

We both went over to her crib, where she had easily fallen asleep after her long, exciting day. She seemed to have a little smile on her face. Who knew what dreams she might be having?

"I think we'll experience everything," Warren said, reaching down to move a stuffed animal closer to her. "Within one day we'll feel happiness, sadness, anger, love, sorrow, all of it. That's going to be our lives for the next twenty or thirty years."

"Even though Kasey's here, I can't bear to think that I won't see the girls for thirty years," I said with a sigh. "I wish I could take a quick trip to heaven to peek in on them and see that they're okay."

"They are okay," Warren said.

Instead of arguing, I nodded. How far I had come.

I gently picked Kasey up from her crib and gave her a kiss. I wanted to make sure she knew every single moment of her life that she was loved. There is no time in life to waste.

And then I turned and kissed Warren, too.

EPILOGUE

Will I see my girls in heaven? I have to believe that I will. But now I understand that I see them again every day of my life. Kasey is here because of them. And their souls live on in the goodness of people who were touched by them and care about making the world a better place for all our children. I see my girls when I look in the mirror, remember their smiling faces next to me, and know how their love and sweetness changed me. I see my girls every day in the friends working so hard to make the Hance Family Foundation a success so it can give happiness to the children still struggling on this earth.

We have a great need to find meaning in horrible events, and many people have said to me that perhaps Kasey is the meaning. She will do something great in life that will give a purpose to the loss that brought her here. I don't know that I believe anymore in that kind of grand design, and I wouldn't want my cherubic daughter to feel that her very existence requires that kind of cosmic success. On a much simpler level, Kasey is proof that we have only one direction to move in life—and that is forward. We have both fewer choices than we think—and more. I had no choice about what happened on July 26. And it took me a long time to understand that all I could control was how I lived every day after that.

People often tell me, "I couldn't have survived what you did." But they are wrong. I don't know how Warren and I got through. I am not stronger or more courageous than anyone else. I was just an ordinary woman when suddenly my world went haywire. When people going through their own tough times turn to me now for guidance, I have only the simplest advice. Make sure you take care of yourself. See the sun every day. Breathe fresh air and go outside. Do something that makes you happy—for me that means having coffee with my friends, going shopping, getting my hair blown dry. Exercise, because you need to be strong for the grief you're going through. It takes a lot out of you.

Three years after it happened, I have no explanation for the tragic accident that took my children. A happenstance, a misfortune, a twist of fate. I finally accept that there is a randomness to life and that God was not punishing me. My children were taken, but I was given all that I needed to survive—a husband who loves me, friends and family who surrounded me with care and protection. Dr. Rosenwaks appeared to give me another chance at life. And then I got Kasey.

A couple of weeks after Kasey's christening, some four hundred volunteers are preparing for Family Fun Day. Just three years in, Family Fun Day seems like a long-standing tradition in town. Warren spends three days straight working to make everything just right—he's at the Centennial Gardens almost around-the-clock overseeing crews and erecting new carnival games. On Saturday morning, fifteen hundred adults and children throng the starting lines for the races. People are running in teams, and we give awards for the most spirited team and biggest fund-raisers. I smile at some little girls from the local dance studio who are running in tutus and T-shirts that read "Emma, Alyson, and Katie." Another group wears shirts that say "The Beautiful Butterflies" and have wings attached to their backs. I watch everyone coming together to run through our town, showing their support, beautifully symbolic yet so very real.

That afternoon, 3,500 people return to the Centennial Gardens for our Family Fun Day activities, from a mud slide to face painting to carnival games. We have live music and Irish dancers, a DJ in the kids' corner, fabulous raffle prizes, and children swarming over to enjoy Katie's Dress-Up, Emma's Carnival Court, and Aly's Art Gallery.

"What a terrific day!" people keep saying to me as I wander from event to event. My mom brings Kasey to the park for a while, and I push her stroller across the grass.

As he does every year, Warren gives a short speech, and then he plays his favorite recording of the Judy Garland classic, "Somewhere Over the Rainbow."

The whole park grows quiet for a few moments as Garland's glorious voice fills the May afternoon. I look out at the families who have gathered and notice parents putting their arms around their children and a few people shedding tears. But mostly they are smiling at this beautiful day. Like Kasey, this day of families coming together in love and fun wouldn't exist if the tragedy hadn't happened. But we must take the good in life whatever its source.

Someday I'll wish upon a star
And wake up where the clouds are far
Behind me . . .

I look up into the sunny sky and think about Emma, Alyson, Katie, Kasey, Warren, and me, and how we will all be together again someday. Over the rainbow.

Acknowledgments

Warren, you are the strongest person I will ever know. Your pain is so deep, yet you never stopped being a father, a friend, and especially, a husband. You taught our girls wonderful values such as loyalty, honesty, and hard work. My greatest wish is for you to have peace and to be able to hug the girls again. How lucky we are to have Kasey, who has brought sunshine and love back into our lives. Your five ladies love you forever.

Mom, thank you for teaching me compassion and forgiveness. You truly are a rock star and always will be. I get my strength from you. Dad, I love you and miss you. You are the most generous person I know, and I learned what being a good friend is from you. You have a giant heart.

Stephen, my brother and friend, you have been holding my hand since we were kids and you will always be my rock. Mark, you have a heart as big as Dad's, and thank you for loving the girls as much as you do. I am happy you have the wonderful family you always deserved.

Mr. Hance, you are a wonderful example of selflessness, and you have been a wonderful role model for your children and grandchildren.

John and David, Warren is lucky to have you as his brothers. We are grateful for you both. David, the two years of weekends you spent at our house really made a difference.

Sheila and Mike, Dan and Sarah, Amy and Kristie, Jeff and Michele, Caroline, Emma, Maggie, Lori, and Melanie, thank you for being at our side at every birthday and foundation event. Cassie, you answered my calls and always came when I needed you, no matter what time of day.

Cortney, Kara, and Tiffany, my Jersey girls, you are my friends for life, my sisters. We have shared every moment, good and bad, together. Thank you for never letting a bridge get in the way of being by my side.

Isabelle, Jeannine, and Melissa, I love you, and feel blessed to have you as my friends. You are my family. I would not be where I am today without each one of you. Your love for my girls is beautiful. It brings me such peace to know how much love they have always had from you, and still do.

My running group—Bernadette, Carrie, Una, and Kerry—thank you for never taking no as an answer and for showing up on my doorstep before dawn. Running made me feel normal and gave me a reason to start my day. Without you, I may have stayed in bed forever, but you would never let me.

Karen, I am grateful for your dedication and friendship, and for making Tuesdays so important. Denine, thank you for coming to my house every Monday night and after Kasey was born, giving me peace and sleep and time to get my confidence back as a mom. Tara, you made me Charlotte's godmother when I didn't think I was ready, and it meant so much. To my many other Floral Park friends, including Heather, Maria, Liz, Stephanie, Tricia, Kathy, Jane, Jen, and so many more, you were incredibly kind to show up with food at my door and support and laughter always. You always knew what to do to make things better. Maria and Anthony, we are so happy for the Christmas Eve tradition you have given us.

Laura, Tia, Gina, Kathy, Libby, and Desi, having you as neighbors and friends gave Warren and me such comfort, and knowing the wonderful time my girls had living on this block gives my heart a little peace. Laura, we will never forget that you came running over too many times to count. Warren and I are so thankful for all you do. Denise, you are Warren's right arm, and in his professional and personal life you have never let him down.

My prayer group, thank you for helping me get back to the power of prayer. You always welcome me with open arms, and I leave each time with a sense of calm.

Dr. Rosenwaks, your generosity changed my life, or perhaps saved it.

Bernadette and Kate, thank you for your vision and extraordinary dedication to the foundation. To the board members, your devotion and love is truly amazing, and you have never faltered in your commitment to our mission. To the Beautiful Me board members, especially Liz and Peggy, your selflessness means so much. Thank you for making so many people feel beautiful inside and out.

I will forever be grateful to every person from our community and elsewhere who has volunteered for the foundation, attended events, and given their time. Time is a priceless gift; I know that for sure.

Jen Bergstrom, thank you for caring so deeply about my story and this book. Your sensitivity and dedication made it all possible. I am also grateful to Louise Burke, Carolyn Reidy, Michael Selleck, Jennifer Robinson, Alex Lewis, Kate Dresser, Kiele Raymond, and the whole amazing team at Gallery Books for all you have done.

Janice, you put my thoughts to paper, and helped me heal. Thank you for holding my hand through this entire journey of finding my way back to living again. Writing this book with you feels like a gift from the girls. You gave all of yourself to this project and kept me feeling safe and proud. Your warmth and commitment helped me let people know my beautiful girls.

And, above all, to Emma, Alyson, and Katie. You are the reason I was put on this earth and my purpose for being here. The love and laughter we shared gave me more joy than I could ever imagine in a lifetime. I would give anything to wrap my arms around you one more time. I am the proudest mommy in the entire world. Thank you for never leaving my side. I did not always realize it, but you never left me for a second.